Mastering Excel

Mastering Excel

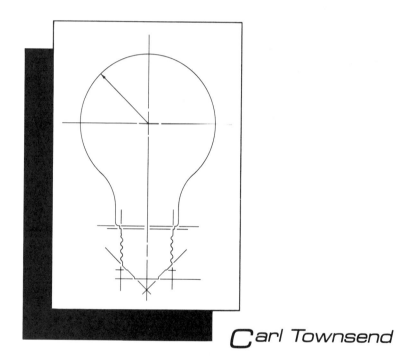

Carl Townsend

SYBEX®

San Francisco • Paris • Düsseldorf • London

Cover art by Mitch Anthony
Book design by Jeffrey James Giese

Library of Congress Card Number: 85-62540
ISBN 0-89588-306-6
Manufactured in the United States of America
10 9 8 7 6 5 4 3 2

To Sandy:

for helping to keep the ship on course as the book was written.

A cknowledgments

I would like to express my appreciation to the many people who helped to make this book possible.

At SYBEX, special thanks go to Bonnie Gruen for coordinating editorial and production work, Marilyn Smith for editing the book, Jeremy Elliott for giving the book a technical review, and Karl Ray and Carole Alden for helping during the early planning stages. I would also like to acknowledge Dave Clark for word processing the manuscript, Donna Scanlon for typesetting, Eileen Walsh for proofreading, and Jeff Giese for designing the book.

In Portland, Oregon, my Macintosh was supplied and supported by Third Wave Management. The Sears Business Centers at Clackamas Town Center and Beaverton also provided help and support. A special thanks to Max Lopez at the Sears Business Center in Clackamas. Nancy Morrice and Deborah Hastings with the Columbia Group helped as my agents, supplied some of the software that I needed, and supported my efforts in many other ways. A very special thanks to my wife Sandy. For more than a month, she had very little of my time, but constantly helped by managing my telephone calls, running errands, and typing dozens of shipping forms.

I also owe a thanks to Microsoft for not only providing a pre-release copy of Excel and its documentation, but also periodically sending updated versions and patiently answering many questions about the program as the book developed.

*T*able of Contents

Part Two: Advanced Excel

xv

Introduction

"There are corporate executives, wholesalers, retailers, and small-business owners who talk about their business lives in two time periods: before and after the electronic spreadsheet."

Steven Levy

Background

Before the invention of the personal-computer spreadsheet program, it was not unusual for a financial vice-president of a company to spend the night manually preparing the company's financial projections for an annual meeting, using nothing more than a hand calculator. If even a small error was made, it would ripple endlessly through all subsequent calculations on the entire spreadsheet. Spreadsheet programs did exist for large mainframe computers, but they were often cumbersome to use, and the computers were not very accessible to most employees.

VisiCalc, invented by Robert Frankston and Dan Bricklin in 1978 for the Apple II computer, suddenly changed all this. For the first time, a business manager could inexpensively set up an entire financial model and analyze any number of scenarios quickly and accurately.

The popularity and capabilities of personal-computer spreadsheet programs grew at a rapid rate. Sorcim's SuperCalc (1980), Microsoft's Multiplan (1982), and Lotus' 1-2-3 (1983) each added new features, capabilities, and integrated tools. These products represented important milestones in the evolution of the spreadsheet, but spreadsheet users still wanted more capabilities.

Users today need more cells in their spreadsheets to build larger models, and they want to be able to link spreadsheets to form hierarchical relationships. They also want to able to control the appearance of their output. The popularity of bit-mapped displays has encouraged users to explore the possibility of altering fonts and character attributes to make presentation-quality graphs, charts, and displays. Users have found macros to be the most powerful feature in spreadsheet programs, yet they have been cumbersome to use in the products that include them, and they have not been included at all in some spreadsheet programs marketed as late as 1985. Microsoft designed Excel to specifically address the needs of users who manage many types of data—those frustrated by the limitations of the numerical analysis products currently available.

The Philosophy of Excel

Before you begin using Excel, it is important to understand some of the philosophy in the design of the product. It is not, as many spreadsheet products, intended as integrated software that combines many applications, such as Jazz or Appleworks. Rather, Excel is limited to three applications—spreadsheet (or worksheet), database, and graphics—and it does each of these in a depth that is not available in competitive products.

Excel is an example of a *contextually integrated* product. That is, it combines the applications that are frequently used in the same context by users whose primary task is analyzing and processing numerical data. This contextual integration permits a user to quickly move from one application to another to see the results of an analysis.

Because Excel is specifically designed for users working with data in a large variety of numerical analysis contexts, it supports the data-processing application more thoroughly than any other personal-computer software product. However, Excel users are not restricted by the program's narrow range of applications. The Switcher, which comes with the Excel package, offers the user the capability to integrate Excel with many other software products, such as word processors and communication programs.

Book Organization

The first part of the book is a basic tutorial that covers all of the features that you will use in working with worksheets, on-screen databases, and charts. In Chapters 1 through 3, you will gain an introduction to the worksheet concept and work through one simple example. In Chapters 4 through 6, you will learn the basic principles for working with Excel worksheets. In Chapter 7, you will learn how to work with Excel's documents and windows, and in Chapter 8, you will learn about Excel's mathematical functions and how to use them. Chapter 9 will introduce you to database management, and Chapter 10 describes Excel's charting capabilities.

Part 2 of this book is for users who have already had some experience with Excel and wish to use the more advanced features. These features should be explored only after you are completely familiar with the information presented in Part 1.

In Chapters 11 through 13, you will learn about some of the special worksheet features that can help you be more productive. Chapters 14 through 16 take you another step further and introduce you to worksheet linking, advanced charting techniques, and arrays. In Chapters 17 through 19, you will learn how to use Excel's macro features. Chapter 20 explains how to interface Excel's data with other programs through the use of the Switcher.

The appendix section is extensive, and it is intended to be used as a reference manual. The appendices include a glossary, a summary of all the commands, and a summary of Excel functions.

Throughout this book, you will be given many tutorial examples showing how Excel can be used to meet a variety of needs. I encourage you to try these examples. Each of them will give you valuable insights about the special features of Excel.

Fundamentals of Excel

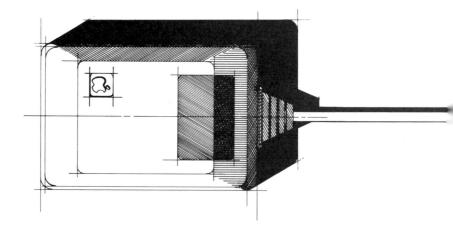

Part 1

There are certain features of Excel that you'll use with almost any worksheet or chart that you create. Part 1 of this book will introduce you to those basic features and guide you through the creation of a few simple worksheets and charts. The examples used in the exercises include an income sheet, a balance sheet, a cash-flow analysis, an amortization schedule, and a sales projections database. All of these are typical worksheet applications.

If you have never worked with a worksheet program before, the information in this part is essential, and you should take the time to work through each of the exercises in detail. Even if you are an experienced worksheet user, you should still plan to complete each exercise because many of the worksheets that you create in this part will be used later in the more advanced exercises of Part 2.

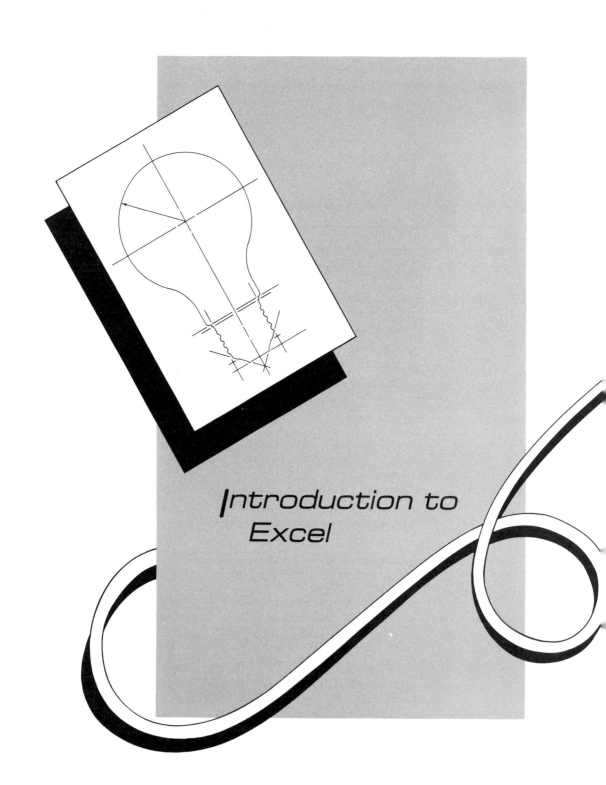

Introduction to Excel

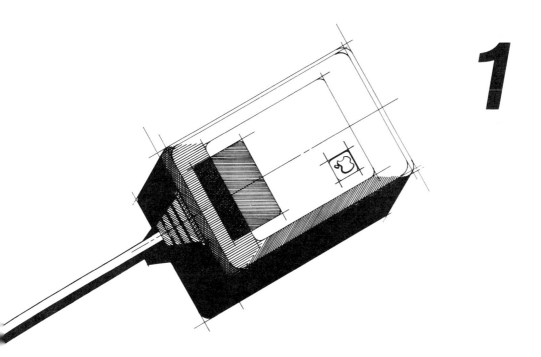

1

*W*hat Is Excel?

Excel is an advanced worksheet (or spreadsheet) product for the Macintosh that also provides database and graphic functions. It is not intended to be an integrated product. Excel is designed primarily for numerical processing applications, and it offers far more capabilities for this application than any other worksheet program that is currently available.

A worksheet program is essentially a replacement for the columnar pad, pencil, and calculator. The computer displays a two-dimensional worksheet, configuring the workspace into rows and columns. Each intersection of a row and a column is called a cell. An on-screen worksheet may look very similar to a paper one. However, the size of an electronic worksheet can be much, much larger than it's paper counterpart.

In fact, one of Excel's outstanding features is the amount of worksheet cells that it offers. Users are no longer limited to the approximately 500,000 cells provided by other worksheet programs. Excel has over 4 million cells available in 256 columns of 16,384 rows.

The features of Excel can be grouped into two classifications: analysis features and presentation features. The Excel package also comes with the Switcher, which makes it easy for users to integrate Excel with other programs, such as Microsoft Word, and to display windows for both data processing and word processing on the screen at the same time.

Analysis Features

Excel offers users the capability to link worksheets and develop hierarchical relationships among them. For example, marketing and production worksheets could be developed independently by department managers as components of a larger corporate worksheet, and these component worksheets could be linked hierarchically.

Excel's problem-solving capabilities are extensive. It can be used for array processing and to solve multiple-value problems. Excel also offers users the capability to simulate many, many possibilities, with only a few worksheet values changed in each simulation, through the use of a single table that controls input.

Users will also find that repetitive worksheet tasks can be automated with Excel's new and easy-to-use macros and user-definable functions.

Excel users can make extensive use of data already used with other worksheet software, even from other computers. Excel offers two-way file capability with Multiplan, Chart, Lotus 1-2-3, and any program using the Microsoft SYLK format.

Along with extensive worksheet capabilities, Excel includes integrated full-featured charting and on-screen databases with querying, extracting, and sorting functions.

Presentation Features

Excel can produce presentation-quality worksheet documentation, and it offers users a wide selection of fonts and formats. Its presentation features include the following:

- Variable fonts and font sizes

- Boldface and italics available at the cell level

- Five border styles

- Nineteen predefined number formats

- User-definable formatting

- Forty-two built-in chart formats

- Flexibility in adding legends, text, arrows, patterns, scaling, and symbols

- Capability to view multiple charts on the screen simultaneously

- Complete support of Apple-Talk network, LaserWriter, Image-writer, and other printers

The Switcher

The Excel data disk contains a program in the System Folder called the Switcher, which enables the Macintosh to run two or more programs at the same time. With the Switcher, users can work with Excel and a word processor or external database-management system, moving data quickly to and from the different programs.

When using the Switcher, all programs currently in use are in the Macintosh memory; that is, the memory is partitioned so that each application program has a slice of memory. The number of programs that you can run simultaneously is limited by the amount of memory in the Macintosh. Since Excel requires a minimum of almost 256K of memory, in a 512K Macintosh, the second application is limited to a little more than 128K, depending upon how the memory is partitioned. You can save about 22K of memory space for each application by not saving screens in the computer memory as you move between applications, but this will slow the Macintosh down. You should experiment with your partitioning until you find the best configuration to meet your needs. More information on the Switcher is included in Chapter 20 and in Appendix F.

What Can I Do With Excel?

Any type of application that involves numerical data processing can take advantage of Excel's extensive worksheet capabilities. For administration and record-keeping purposes, Excel can be used for check registers, expense reports, annual reports, and five-year forecasts. Excel's financial applications include amortization schedules, cash-flow projections, general ledgers, accounts receivable, accounts payable, comparative investment analysis, personal net worth statements, balance sheets, and tax planning. Some examples of sales and marketing applications are sales comparisons, marketing analyses, product line summaries, and sales-forecast and linear-regression analyses. For operations, Excel can be used for inventory-management systems, material-requirement planning, inventory-rate-of-turnover analyses, and last-in-first-out (LIFO) analyses.

Here are how some users might apply their Excel systems:

- Donald, a building contractor involved in competitive bidding, puts all his cost factors into an Excel worksheet, altering each factor to see how it affects his final proposed bid. Each factor that controls his cost can be studied and analyzed to produce a final bid that is as low as possible.

- Susan is trying to conserve energy in her home. She creates a "model" of her house on an Excel worksheet. This model includes factors that control heating and cooling costs, such as attic insulation, window caulking, and a high-efficiency furnace. She can also calculate the cost of installing each of these energy-saving features and analyze the results to see how long it would take her to recover the costs of each energy-saving idea.

- John invests in the stock market, commodities, and bonds. He uses Excel worksheets to create investment models and to perform "what-if" analyses to try to find the best investment opportunities.

- George is in charge of labor negotiations for his company. Every few years, the union contracts are renegotiated, and George has to be able quickly to study proposals from the unions and determine how they would affect the company earnings on both a short-term and a long-term basis. Using a worksheet, he can create a financial model of the company and quickly see how the union proposals will affect company earnings.

- Carol likes to do a little real-estate business from her home. She has several rental properties, and she needs to manage the rental costs as a factor of upkeep, taxes, and depreciation.

She also has to know when to buy and sell the properties that she manages. The Excel worksheet gives her instant information on her profits as these factors change.

- Widget Manufacturing has a large sales staff, and the Sales Department needs to keep tabs on sales productivity as it relates to specific target goals. It also needs to send monthly reports to the Administrative Department, which uses the numbers to create corporate reports that control planning factors for other departments, such as the status of the inventory and costs of advertising. The company uses an entire collection of Excel worksheets, all interlinked, and a company summary worksheet, which enables the company president to make quick decisions as the market changes.

All of these applications can be grouped into one of two broad classifications: reporting on what has happened or forecasting what could happen (called what-if analysis). In the first case, the user is taking data that describe something that has often happened in the past (such as the last three-months' sales of a product in three areas of the country) and putting these data into a form that can be analyzed (such as a pie chart), from which the user can make a decision (such as the marketing strategy for next month). In the second case, the user is changing one or more variables and seeing how these changes will affect a specific goal (such as changing various cost factors to see how this affects the bid on a project).

Now that you have some idea of what Excel is and what it can do, it's time to get started using this pioneer of a new generation of worksheet software.

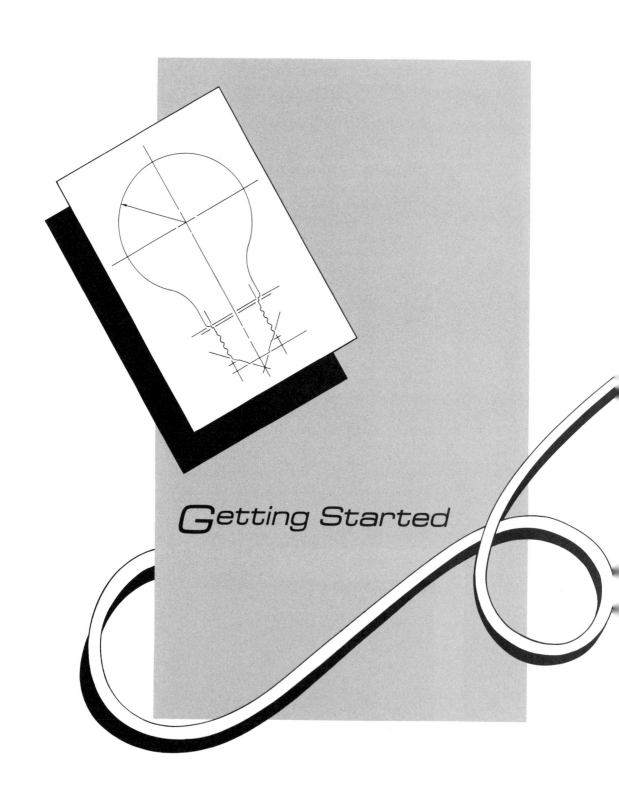

Getting Started

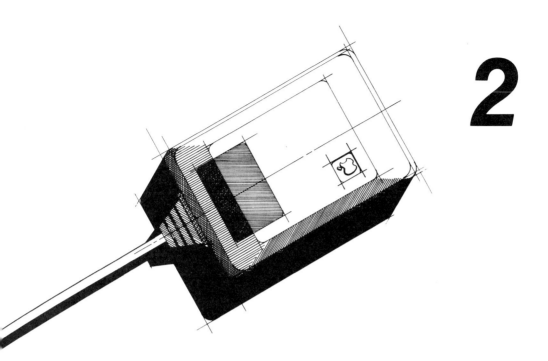

2

Beginning to use Excel is, without doubt, an exciting adventure. Before starting, however, you should be sure that you have everything that you will need. You should also take certain initial precautions, as you would when beginning to use any new computer program.

This chapter provides step-by-step instructions on how to make copies of the disks that come with your Excel package and how to start up Excel for the first and subsequent times. It also includes a brief review of Macintosh window techniques, such as scrolling and moving windows around on the screen.

Other important points covered in this chapter are how to set up a printer and how to get on-screen help if you need it.

What Do I Need?

Before starting Excel, be sure that you have the following hardware:

- A Macintosh computer with 512K of memory
- An external disk drive
- A printer

Although the printer and external disk drive are listed by Microsoft as optional, they are almost essential for using Excel effectively.

You also need the Excel program and data disks, extra disks, and the documentation that came with Excel. When you purchase Excel, you will receive one program disk, one data disk, and a backup copy of the program disk. Put the backup program disk in a safe place.

Both copies of the program disk are copy-protected. When you turn on your Macintosh, you must start Excel the first time by using one of the program disks that you received with the Excel package. As long as you have your computer turned on, you can quit and return to Excel again using any copy of the Excel program disk.

Creating Backup Copies

Before starting to use Excel, you should create copies of the program and data disks, following the steps listed below:

1. Start the Macintosh with a system disk in the internal drive.
2. Pull down the File menu and click Eject.
3. Put the Excel program disk in one drive and a blank disk in the second drive.
4. When the disk icons are displayed, use the mouse to move the icon for the program disk over the icon for your blank disk, then click.
5. When the dialog box asks for verification, check your disks and then click OK. The program disk will then be copied to the blank disk.

6. Be sure that the icon for the new program disk is selected, then type in the name of the new program disk from the keyboard (you can use the same name as the original disk).

7. Eject both disks by selecting the proper disk icon, pulling down the File menu, and then clicking Eject.

8. Place the new data disk in one drive and another blank disk in the other drive.

9. Use the mouse to move the data disk icon over the icon for the blank disk and click.

10. Check the dialog box message and click OK. The data disk will then be copied.

11. Be sure that the icon for the new data disk is selected, then type in the name of the new data disk from the keyboard.

12. Eject each of the data disks by selecting its disk icon, pulling down the File menu, and clicking Eject.

Starting Excel

Excel

Remember that you must use the Microsoft master program disk, not your copy, to start Excel for the first time after you turn on your computer. Turn your Macintosh on. Insert your copy of the data disk in the internal drive and the Microsoft master program disk in the external drive. Your screen should look like Figure 2.1. Be sure that the window for the Excel program disk is active, then double-click the Excel icon. The Excel program should start and display a worksheet, as shown in Figure 2.2. Now quit the program by pulling down the File menu and clicking Quit.

After you quit Excel, be sure that the program disk is selected. Pull down the File menu and click Eject. Insert your *copy* of the program disk in the external drive and wait for the window to appear. Double-click the Excel icon and wait for Excel to load. A blank worksheet will be displayed again.

As long as your Macintosh is not turned off, you can restart Excel as many times as you wish from your copy of the program disk. The program disk should always be in the *external drive,* and the data disk should be in the *internal drive.*

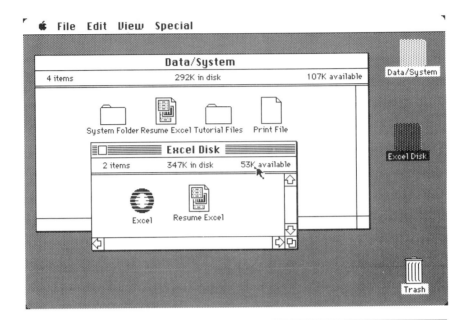

Figure 2.1: *Starting Excel.*

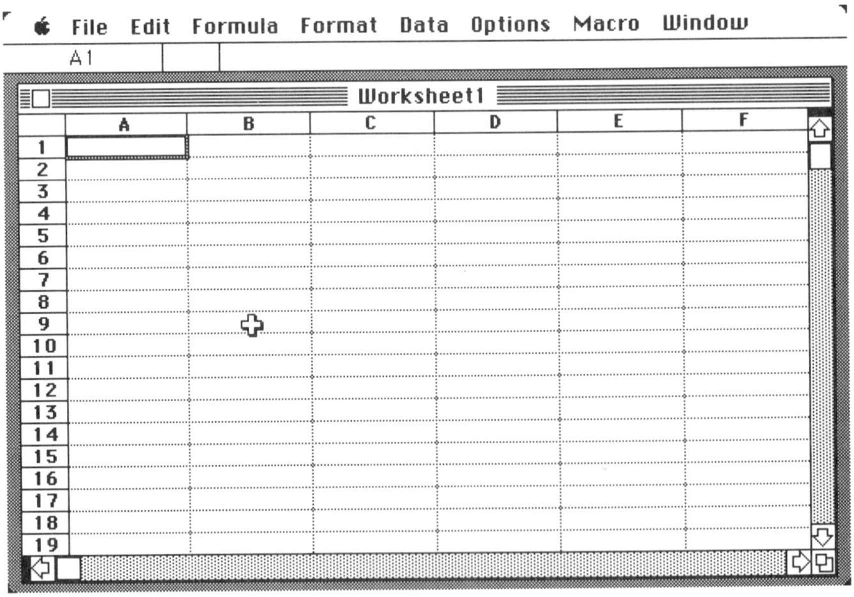

Figure 2.2: *The Excel menu bar and worksheet.*

Excel

Worksheet1

Resume Excel

Once you have used Excel to create worksheets, charts, and other files, you can start Excel in any one of three ways:

- Click the Excel icon twice, as you just did.

- Click the icon twice for any worksheet, chart, or macro file.

- Click the Resume Excel icon twice, which will start the program with the last document that was in use when you quit Excel.

You can also use Excel with a hard-disk system by copying the program disk contents onto the hard disk. Even with a hard-disk copy, you will still need to start Excel from your master program disk the first time that you turn your Macintosh on. Once you've started up using the master program disk, you can then start Excel from the hard disk as often as you like, providing that the Macintosh is not turned off.

The Worksheet Window

Excel's worksheet window is much like any other window that is displayed on the Macintosh screen. Try a few things now with the displayed window (refer to Figure 2.2).

1. You can change the size of the window by clicking the square in the lower right and dragging up or down, left or right.

2. You can move the window around on the screen by clicking its title bar and dragging.

3. You can scroll left or right in the worksheet using the arrows at the bottom of the window in the scroll bar.

4. You can move the window up or down in the worksheet using the arrows at the right of the window in the scroll bar.

5. You can use the small squares at the right or the bottom to quickly move the window to any place in the worksheet.

6. If more than one window is displayed, you can click any displayed window to make it active. Pull down the Window menu from the menu bar and click Show Clipboard. You will

now see the Clipboard window. The Clipboard windows will be active when it is opened.

7. You can close any window using the close box in the upper left of the window. Close the Clipboard window by clicking its close box.

Experiment with these Macintosh window features until you are comfortable with how they work in Excel.

Setting Up the Printer

Before using your printer to print any worksheets, you must set up the program interface to the printer. Pull down the Apple menu and click Choose Printer. The contents of the dialog box that appears depend on which type of printer you are using. Figure 2.3 shows a dialog box for an Imagewriter. Set up the system for your configuration, then click OK.

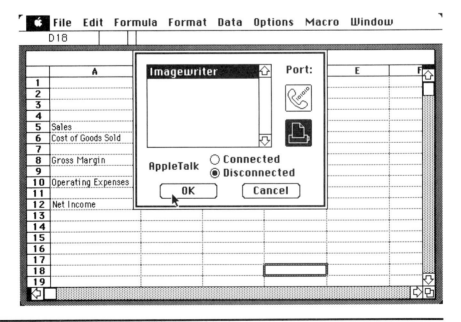

Figure 2.3: *Configuring the printer.*

Getting Help

Choose Printer
Scrapbook
Alarm Clock
Note Pad
Calculator
Key Caps
Control Panel
Puzzle

If you need help at any time while you're using Excel, pull down the Apple menu and click About Microsoft Excel. You will then see the Help dialog box. Click the topic about which you need help, then click Help. You will see a window that shows the information that you need. Click Next to see the next topic, Previous to see the last topic, Topics to return to the list of choices, or Cancel to return to your worksheet.

If you are working on a document, you can also get help by pressing the Command key and the question mark key at the same time. The cursor will change to a question mark. Move this question mark to the window area, dialog box query, or command about which you need help. Then click or choose the command to get help. To return to your work, click Cancel.

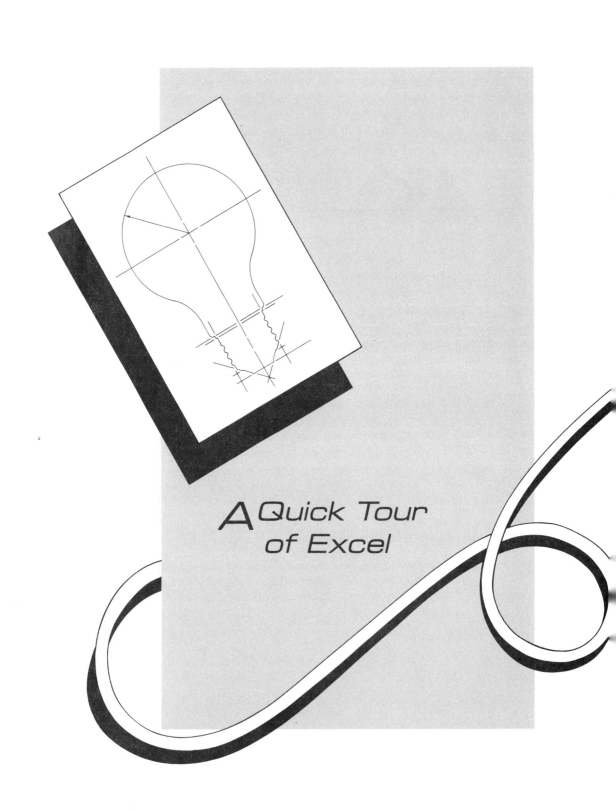

A Quick Tour
of Excel

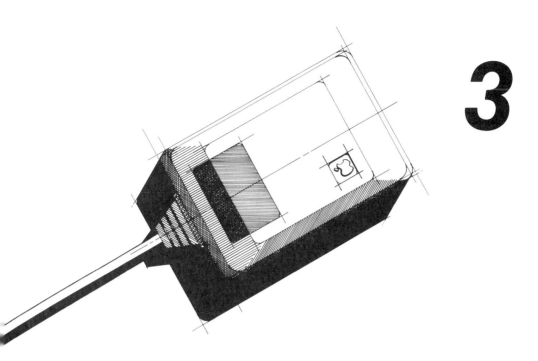

3

Although Excel can solve very complicated problems, it is actually quite easy to use. You'll discover this for yourself right now if you follow along with the quick exercise in this chapter. You will use Excel to create a worksheet, complete with formulas; format it; save it; and print the finished product. Then you will create a chart using some of the values on your worksheet.

This exercise will give you a feel for Excel and let you know what it can do. Don't worry too much about how or why you did things—I'll explain all the steps in detail in later chapters.

Creating an Excel Worksheet

Bring up the Excel program by selecting the Excel icon from the display. Double-click the icon to start the program. Excel creates an empty window, as shown in Figure 3.1.

Window Features

Notice several things about this window before you do anything:

- Columns are defined by letters and rows by numbers. Each cell is shown as a box. Cells are designated by the column letter and row number. For example, cell B4 refers to the intersection of the fourth row with the second column.

- A cursor (in the shape of a cross) is on one cell.

- The first cell, A1, is highlighted with bold lines. This is the *active cell*.

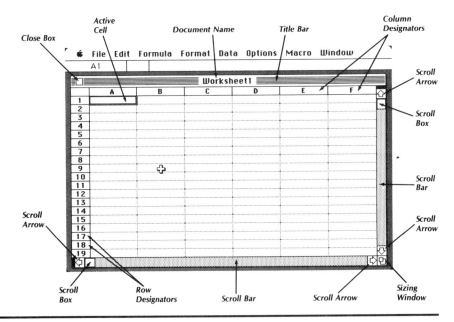

Figure 3.1: *The worksheet window.*

- The window has a title: Worksheet1.

- Now refer to Figure 3.2. There is a display line under the menu bar that contains the name of the active cell (C1). There is also a second entry area, call the *formula bar,* which displays any text entered from the keyboard into the active cell.

Move the mouse about, and you will see the cursor move around the worksheet. The highlighted cell does not change, and neither does the active-cell designator on the display line under the menu bar.

Scrolling

Place the cursor on the scroll box in the scrolling bar at the right of the window. The cursor is now in the shape of an arrow. Click and drag the box downward. Notice that the small box in the upper left changes, always showing the current row number as you drag the scroll box. When you release the mouse button, the last row number displayed will be at the top of the worksheet.

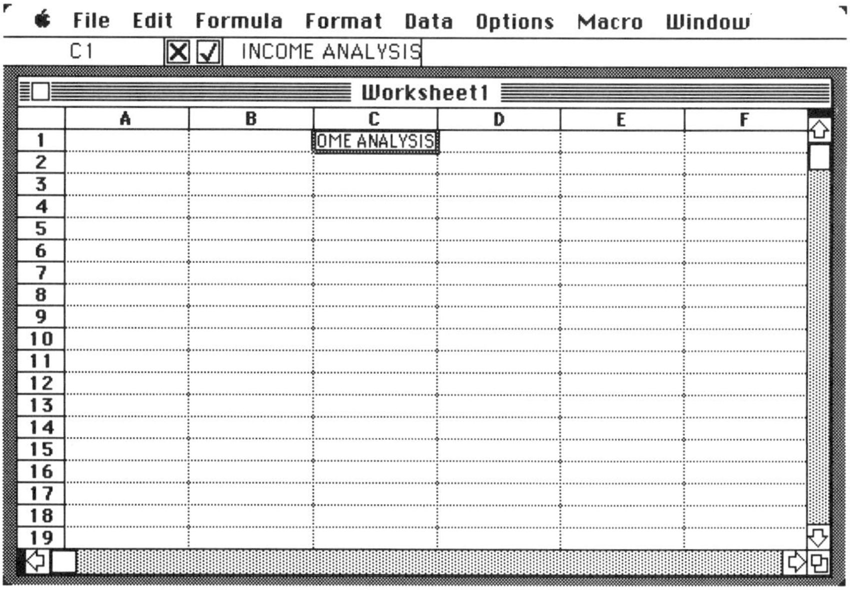

Figure 3.2: *Entering the worksheet title.*

Click the scroll box again and drag it to the top of the scroll bar so that row 1 is at the top of the worksheet. Now, click the scroll box in the scroll bar at the bottom of the window and drag it to the right. Watch the designator under the menu bar change to indicate the current column number. Release the mouse button and see where the last displayed column is now located. Finally, click the scroll box again and move it all the way to the left so that column A is the first column.

Entering Titles

Move the cursor back to the worksheet, and it becomes cross-shaped again. Use the mouse to move the cursor to cell C1, then click. Cell C1 is now highlighted, and the active-cell designator on the display line changes to C1. Use the keyboard to enter the title for your worksheet as **INCOME ANALYSIS.**

Notice that, as you enter your data, two new boxes appear near the formula bar: the enter box with a check (✔) and a cancel box with an X, as shown in Figure 3.2. The entire title appears in the formula bar, and the portion that will fit appears in cell C1. After you enter the title, press the Enter key or click the enter box to complete the entry. You will now see the entire title on the worksheet.

Enter the titles for the rows next:

1. Click cell A5 and drag to cell A12 (see Figure 3.3).

2. Type **Sales** and press Enter.

3. Type **Cost of Goods Sold** and press Enter twice (to skip one row).

4. Type **Gross Margin** and press Enter twice.

5. Type **Operating Expenses** and press Enter twice.

6. Type **Net Income** and press Enter.

If you make a mistake in typing any title before you press Enter, you can use the Backspace key to backspace and correct the entry. If you notice a mistake after you've pressed Enter, go ahead and finish entering the row titles, then click the cell to be corrected and reenter the title.

```
  ⬤  File  Edit  Formula  Format  Data  Options  Macro  Window
     A5              Sales
```

	A	B	C	D	E	F
1			INCOME ANALYSIS			
2						
3						
4						
5	Sales					
6	Cost of Goods Sold					
7						
8	Gross Margin					
9						
10	Operating Expenses					
11						
12	Net Income					
13						
14						
15						
16						
17						
18						
19						

Worksheet1

Figure 3.3: *Entering the row headings.*

After you have entered the row headings, you will notice that column A is not wide enough for two of the row titles. To widen the column:

1. Click once on cell A1.

2. Pull down the Format menu and select Column Width.

3. You will now see the Column Width dialog box shown in Figure 3.4. Enter **15** as the new width, then click OK.

You will see column A widen to accommodate your titles, as shown in Figure 3.5.

Now enter the column titles shown in Figure 3.6:

1. Click cell B4 and drag to cell D4.

2. Type **1982** and press Enter.

3. Type **1983** and press Enter.

4. Type **1984** and press Enter.

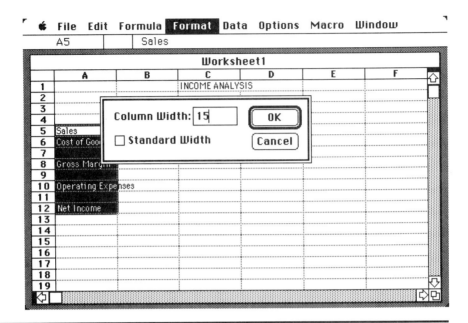

Figure 3.4: *Setting the column width.*

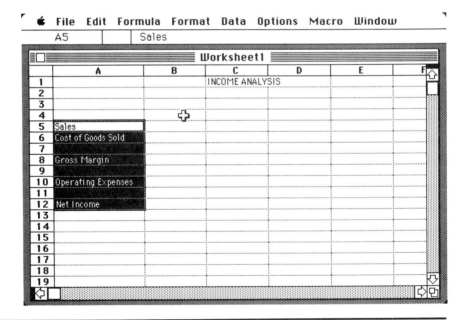

Figure 3.5: *Column widths adjusted.*

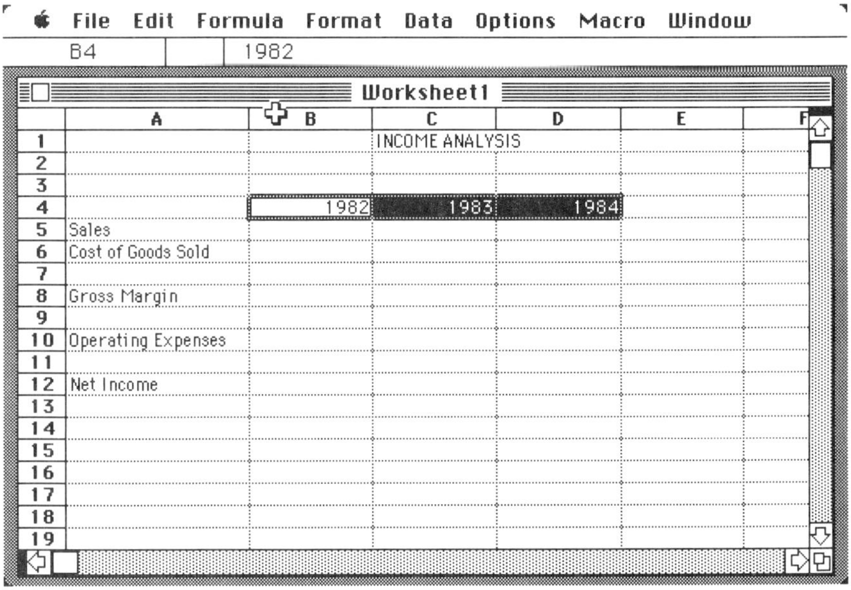

```
  *  File  Edit  Formula  Format  Data  Options  Macro  Window
      B4              1982
```

	A	B	C	D	E	F
1			INCOME ANALYSIS			
2						
3						
4		1982	1983	1984		
5	Sales					
6	Cost of Goods Sold					
7						
8	Gross Margin					
9						
10	Operating Expenses					
11						
12	Net Income					
13						
14						
15						
16						
17						
18						
19						

Figure 3.6: *Entering the column headings.*

Entering Data

Now click cell B5 and enter the numbers shown in Figure 3.7 into rows 5, 6, and 10. (Do **not** enter data into rows 8 or 12.) You can include commas in the numbers if you wish, but they will disappear each time that you press Enter.

Entering Formulas

Enter the first formula by clicking cell B8 and typing **= B5 – B6.** Remember to type the equal sign first. After you enter the formula, press Enter. The gross margin, 240000, will appear in cell B8. If you make a mistake, click cell B8 and try entering the formula again.

Now you can try a slightly different approach for entering the formula into cell B12:

1. Click cell B12 and enter an equal sign (=).

2. Click cell B8 and enter a minus sign (–).

3. Click cell B10 and press Enter.

 File   Edit   Formula   Format   Data   Options   Macro   Window

E12

	A	B	C	D	E	F
1			INCOME ANALYSIS			
2						
3						
4		1982	1983	1984		
5	Sales	800000	850000	830000		
6	Cost of Goods Sold	560000	590000	580000		
7						
8	Gross Margin					
9						
10	Operating Expenses	170000	190000	184000		
11						
12	Net Income					
13						
14						
15						
16						
17						
18						
19						

Figure 3.7: *Entering the data.*

The net income, 70000, will appear in cell B12.

To enter the formulas in rows C and D, you can use a faster method. Click cell B8 and drag to cell D8. Pull down the Edit menu and click Fill Right. The correct totals are now in row 8. Click cell B12 and drag to cell D12. Pull down the Edit menu and click Fill Right. The correct totals are now in row 12. In both cases, as the formula is copied, the cells referenced are automatically changed to reflect the new columns. Select cell C8 and examine the formula in the formula bar. Compare this with the formula shown when you select cell B8.

After you've entered all the formulas, your worksheet should look like Figure 3.8.

Formatting the Worksheet

Now you can format the worksheet. Excel stores two things for each cell in the worksheet: the value (constant or formula) and information about how the value is to be displayed. Data are now displayed

 File   Edit   Formula   Format   Data   Options   Macro   Window

D19

	A	B	C	D	E	F
1			INCOME ANALYSIS			
2						
3						
4		1982	1983	1984		
5	Sales	800000	850000	830000		
6	Cost of Goods Sold	560000	590000	580000		
7						
8	Gross Margin	240000	260000	250000		
9						
10	Operating Expenses	170000	190000	184000		
11						
12	Net Income	70000	70000	66000		
13						
14						
15						
16						
17						
18						
19						

Figure 3.8: *Worksheet after the formulas are entered.*

with text left-justified and numbers right-justified. Place the cursor on cell B5 and drag to cell D12. All the numeric cells should be highlighted. Pull down the Format menu and select Number. The Format Number dialog box shown in Figure 3.9 appears. Click the first currency format (without cents), then click OK.

You can do a few more things to make the worksheet more readable. First, put the title in bold print:

1. Click cell C1.

2. Pull down the Format menu and click Style.

3. The Style dialog box shown in Figure 3.10 appears. Click Bold, then OK.

Next, center the column titles:

1. Click cell B4 and drag to cell D4.

2. Pull down the Format menu and click Alignment.

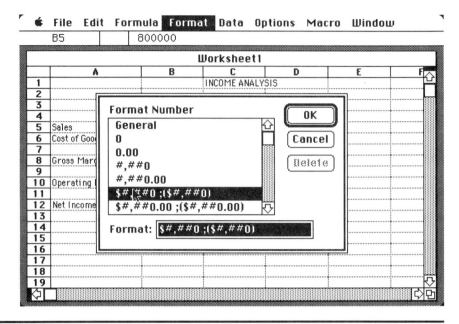

Figure 3.9: *Formatting the numbers.*

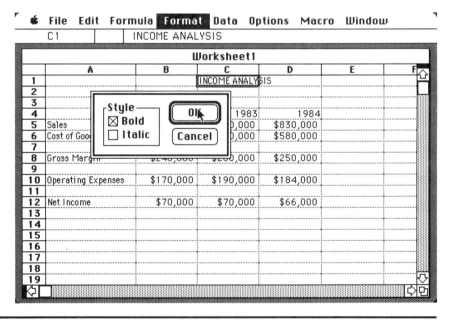

Figure 3.10: *Putting the title in boldface print.*

3. The Alignment dialog box shown in Figure 3.11 appears. Click Center, then OK.

Finally, you can add some hyphens to separate the totals from the other numbers:

1. Click cell B7 and enter ten hyphens to fill the cell.

2. Click cell B7 and drag to cell D7.

3. Pull down the Edit menu and click Fill Right.

4. Repeat steps 1 through 3 for row 11 (cells B11 through D11).

Your final worksheet should look like the one shown in Figure 3.12. You can now experiment by changing the values in rows 5, 6, and 10. You'll see that the numbers in rows 8 and 12 automatically change to reflect the new values.

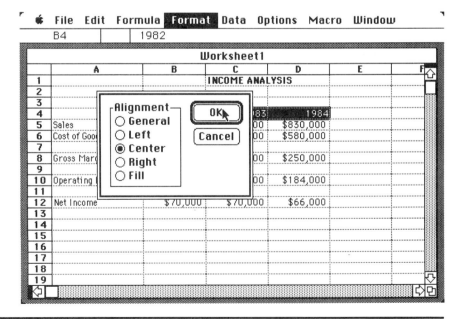

Figure 3.11: *Aligning the column titles.*

```
 ┌                                                                  ┐
   🍎  File  Edit  Formula  Format  Data  Options  Macro  Window
      D18  │    │    │
```

	A	B	C	D	E	F
1			INCOME ANALYSIS			
2						
3						
4		1982	1983	1984		
5	Sales	$800,000	$850,000	$830,000		
6	Cost of Goods Sold	$560,000	$590,000	$580,000		
7						
8	Gross Margin	$240,000	$260,000	$250,000		
9						
10	Operating Expenses	$170,000	$190,000	$184,000		
11						
12	Net Income	$70,000	$70,000	$66,000		
13						
14						
15						
16						
17						
18						
19						

Figure 3.12: *The final worksheet.*

Printing the Worksheet

To print the worksheet, you should first turn off the row and column designators on the printout. Pull down the File menu and click Page Setup. The dialog box shown in Figure 3.13 appears. Click both Print Row & Column Headings and Print Gridlines to turn these options off, then Click OK.

Now print the worksheet. Pull down the File menu and click Print. Be sure that the printer is on and selected. When the Print dialog box shown in Figure 3.14 is displayed, click OK. The final output is shown in Figure 3.15.

Saving the Worksheet

Before quitting Excel, you should save the worksheet. Be sure that the data in rows 5, 6, and 10 are correct. Pull down the File menu and click Save As. When the Save dialog box shown in Figure 3.16

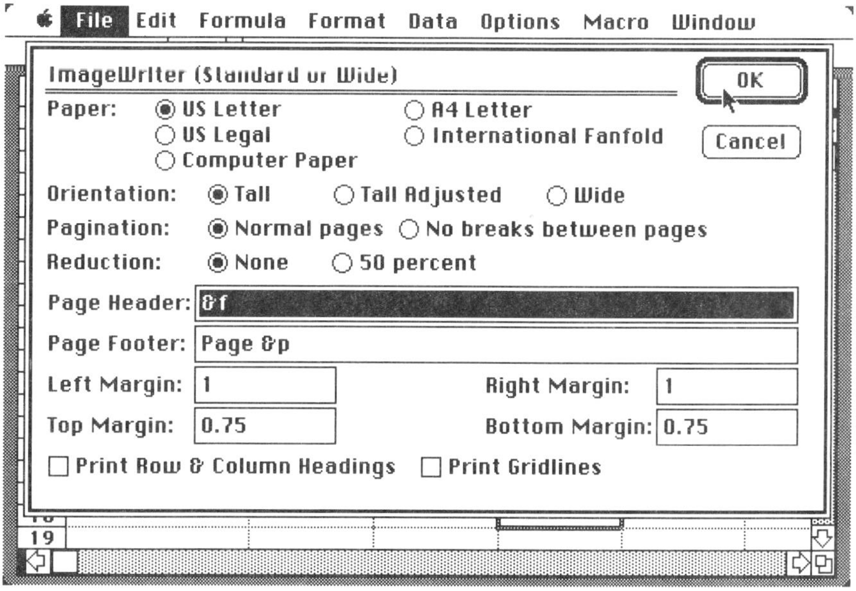

• File Edit Formula Format Data Options Macro Window

ImageWriter (Standard or Wide)   (**OK**)

Paper: ◉ US Letter   ○ A4 Letter
          ○ US Legal   ○ International Fanfold   (Cancel)
          ○ Computer Paper

Orientation: ◉ Tall   ○ Tall Adjusted   ○ Wide

Pagination: ◉ Normal pages   ○ No breaks between pages

Reduction: ◉ None   ○ 50 percent

Page Header: &f

Page Footer: Page &p

Left Margin: 1   Right Margin: 1

Top Margin: 0.75   Bottom Margin: 0.75

☐ Print Row & Column Headings   ☐ Print Gridlines

Figure 3.13: *Turning off the grid lines and designators.*

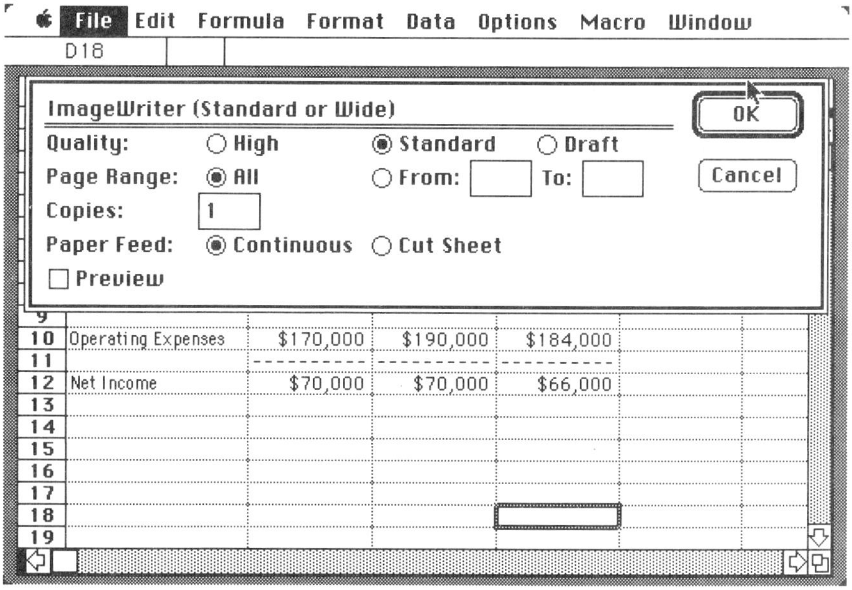

• File Edit Formula Format Data Options Macro Window

D18

ImageWriter (Standard or Wide)   (**OK**)

Quality: ○ High   ◉ Standard   ○ Draft

Page Range: ◉ All   ○ From: [ ] To: [ ]   (Cancel)

Copies: 1

Paper Feed: ◉ Continuous   ○ Cut Sheet

☐ Preview

9				
10	Operating Expenses	$170,000	$190,000	$184,000
11		---------	---------	---------
12	Net Income	$70,000	$70,000	$66,000
13				
14				
15				
16				
17				
18				
19				

Figure 3.14: *The Print dialog box.*

INCOME ANALYSIS

	1982	1983	1984
Sales	$800,000	$850,000	$830,000
Cost of Goods Sold	$560,000	$590,000	$580,000
Gross Margin	$240,000	$260,000	$250,000
Operating Expenses	$170,000	$190,000	$184,000
Net Income	$70,000	$70,000	$66,000

Figure 3.15: *The printout.*

is displayed, be sure that the data disk is active. If not, click Drive. Now enter the title **Income** and click Save.

Note: If you wish to make changes and save the document again, clicking Save will save it under the same name, and you will not see the dialog box. Clicking Save As permits you to enter a new name for the document or to change the disk drive.

Creating a Graph

Now you can create a graph from the sales figures on your Income worksheet. You will find that it takes only a few clicks of the mouse. Follow these steps:

1. Click the designator for row 4 and drag to row 5 to designate the data to use for the graph, as shown in Figure 3.17.

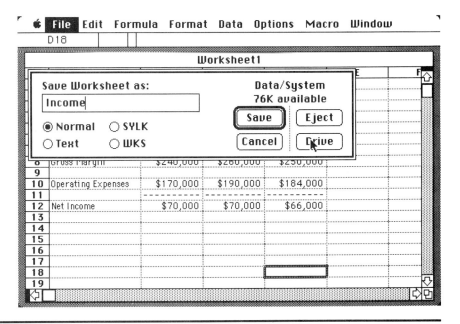

Figure 3.16: *Saving the document.*

	A	B	C	D	E	F
1			INCOME ANALYSIS			
2						
3						
4		1982	1983	1984		
5	Sales	$800,000	$850,000	$830,000		
6	Cost of Goods Sold	$560,000	$590,000	$580,000		
7						
8	Gross Margin	$240,000	$260,000	$250,000		
9						
10	Operating Expenses	$170,000	$190,000	$184,000		
11						
12	Net Income	$70,000	$70,000	$66,000		
13						
14						
15						
16						
17						
18						
19						

Figure 3.17: *Selecting the data for the chart.*

2. Pull down the File name and click New.

3. When the dialog box shown in Figure 3.18 is displayed, click Chart, then click OK.

Excel will draw the chart shown in Figure 3.19 in a new window on the screen. Notice that a different menu bar for charts is now displayed.

   🍎 **File** Edit Formula Format Data Options Macro Window

A1

You can improve the chart by selecting another graph type:

1. Pull down the Gallery menu and click Column.

2. When the chart selection is displayed, as shown in Figure 3.20, double-click the third chart.

Excel will redraw the chart, as shown in Figure 3.21. You can print this chart following the steps that you used to print the worksheet.

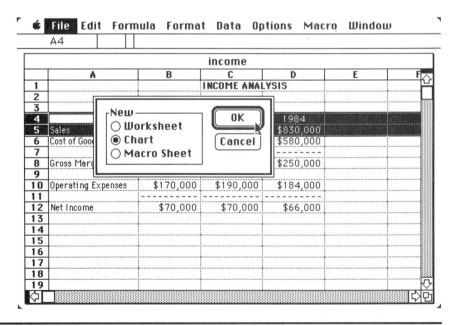

Figure 3.18: *Opening a new chart document.*

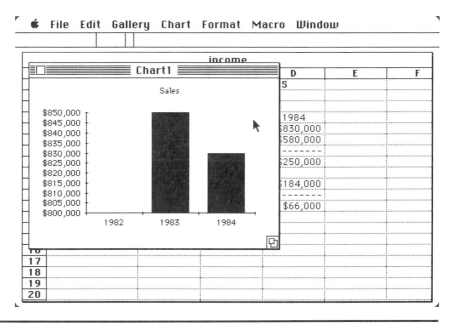

Figure 3.19: *The first chart draft.*

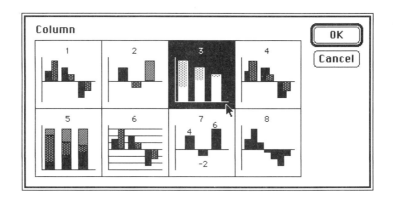

Figure 3.20: *The column chart selection.*

When you are finished with the chart, click the close box in the chart window. When the dialog box shown in Figure 3.22 appears, click No to indicate that you do not want to save the chart.

Quitting Excel

When you wish to leave Excel, there are only two simple steps: save your work and then exit. After using Save or Save As to save the document, pull down the File menu and click Quit.

Note:

If you forget to save your document before quitting, Excel will catch this and prompt you with a dialog box, giving you another chance. Your best insurance, however, is to always save your document before quitting Excel.

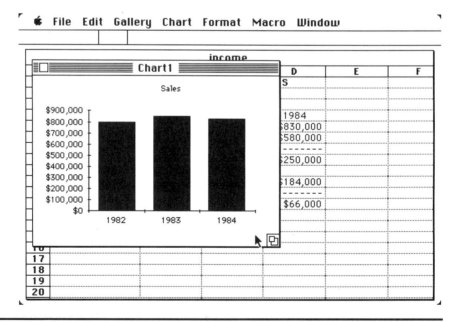

Figure 3.21: *The final chart.*

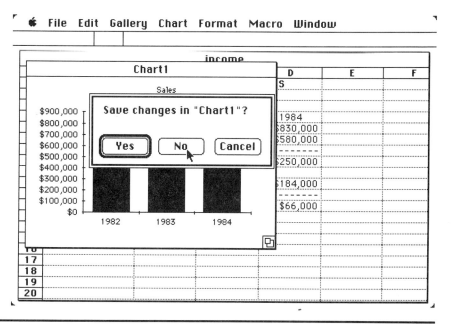

Figure 3.22: *Closing the chart document.*

Summary

You have now created a simple worksheet that includes formulas and a chart using some of the data on that worksheet. You also learned how to do some formatting, how to print the worksheet, and how to save it to disk. In the next chapter, you will learn how to use additional worksheet features.

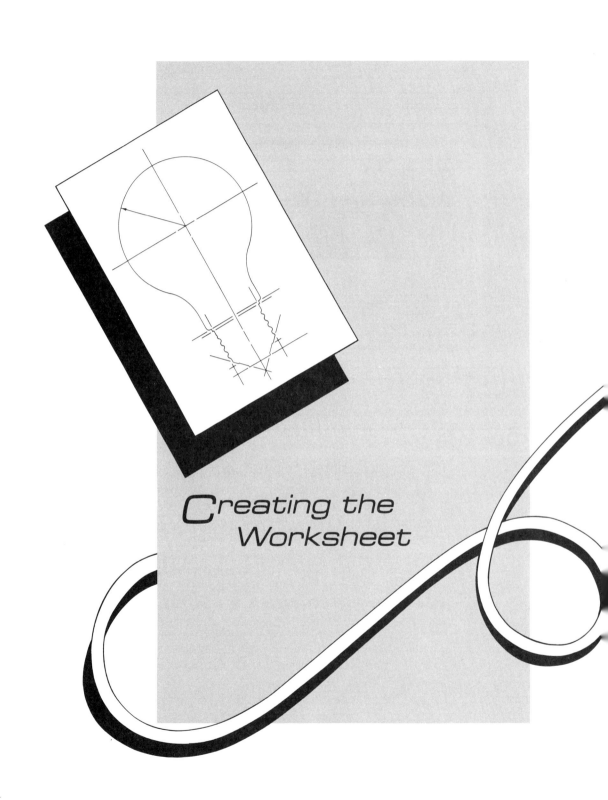

Creating the
Worksheet

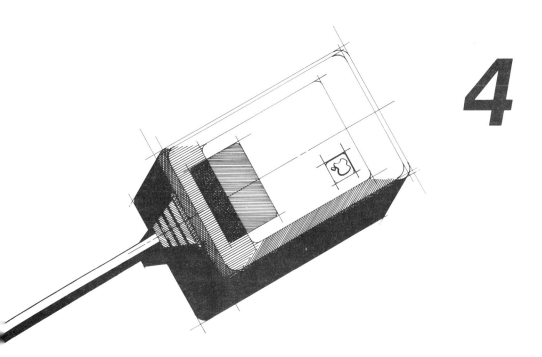

4

There are four basic steps in making a worksheet: creating, editing, formatting, and printing. In each of these steps, there are a few basic rules that are essential for working with any type of worksheet. In Chapters 4 through 6, you will learn these basic rules by creating, editing, and printing a simple balance sheet. Even if you have created worksheets before, take the time to work through these exercises. You will be surprised at how much easier it is to do them with Excel than with any other spreadsheet program that you may have used.

In this chapter, you will take the first step: the creation of the worksheet. Do not be too concerned about any errors that you make when entering data. In the next chapter, you will learn how to correct those errors.

First, I'll review the basic parts of a worksheet and the techniques to use in creating one.

The Worksheet

The basic parts of the worksheet are shown in Figure 4.1. Excel provides 16,384 rows with 256 columns in each row. Thus, Excel makes 256 times 16,384, or 4,194,304, cells available to the user. The columns are designated by the letters of the alphabet (A through Z, then AA through IV), and rows are designated by numbers.

You can select a single cell or a range of cells for any operation. If a single cell is selected, it is the active cell, and its cell designator is displayed in the upper left under the menu bar.

The formula bar also appears under the menu bar. Anything typed on the keyboard is entered into the active cell and displayed in the formula bar. Once anything is typed, the enter box and cancel box appear on the formula bar. Clicking the enter box or pressing the Enter key completes the entry.

The worksheet display is a window, and you can move this window to view or work with any area of the worksheet. To view various parts of the worksheet, you can scroll the window to that area. When you scroll around in the worksheet, the hidden parts of the worksheet are not erased; they are kept in the computer

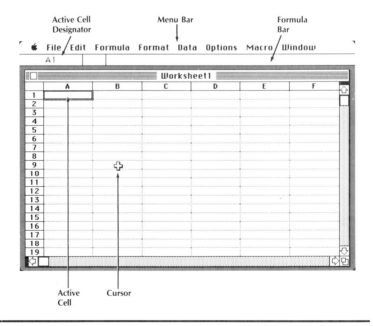

Figure 4.1: *The Excel worksheet.*

memory. When you're printing or saving a worksheet, all the worksheet (not just the visible part) is available.

You can enter text, numbers, or formulas into any cell of the worksheet. A *formula* is used to define the cell contents as a function of other cells on the worksheet. The contents of a cell with a formula will change automatically to reflect any changes in the cells on which the formula cell is dependent. For example, you could define cell B6 as the sum of cells B2 and B3. If you alter the contents of cell B2 or B3, the value in cell B6 will automatically change to the new total.

Worksheet Techniques

Generally, you enter data into worksheet cells by selecting a cell or range of cells (using one of the methods described below) and then entering the cell contents, pressing Enter after you complete each entry. You can enter up to 255 characters into a single cell.

The basic techniques for entering data into a worksheet are described below. You will then use these techniques to begin to create a more complex worksheet than the simple one that you set up in Chapter 3.

Selecting Cells and Ranges

When you want to enter data or perform an operation on a cell or cell range, you must first select the cell or range. Each time that you select a new cell or range, the previous selection is canceled. You can tell which cell, or cell range, is selected at any given time because it is highlighted.

Selecting a cell or range of cells does not change the contents of the cell. The cell contents will only be changed if you enter data from the keyboard after the cell is selected.

There are a number of ways to select cells:

- You can select a single cell by placing the cursor on the cell and clicking once.

- You can select a cell range by placing the cursor on the first cell in the range, clicking the mouse button, and dragging the cursor to the last cell in the range. To select cells in more than one column or row, start the selection in the upper left and drag to the lower right.

- You can select an entire row by placing the cursor on the row designator at the left of the window and clicking once.

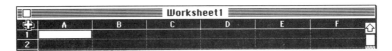

- You can select an entire column by placing the cursor on the column designator and clicking once.

	A	B	C	D	E	F	
1							
2							

- You can select the entire worksheet by placing the cursor on the small box to the left of the column headings and above the row headings and clicking once.

Worksheet1

	A	B	C	D	E	F	
1							
2							

- You can select a range of rows by clicking a row designator and dragging to another row. In the same way, you can select a range of columns by selecting a column designator and dragging to another column.

- You can make multiple selections by clicking your first selection and then holding down the Command key while you click to select additional cells or cell ranges.

- Another way that you can select multiple rows or columns is by clicking on the cell in one diagonal, then holding down the Shift key and clicking the cell at the opposite diagonal.

Before continuing, you should practice making each type of selection listed above.

Note: | You can also enter data into a selected cell or cell range by using the mouse to point to other cells or names that you have defined. You will learn more about this technique later in this chapter and in Chapter 11.

Clearing the Worksheet

If you made any data entries to cells in practicing cell selection, clear the worksheet:

1. Select the entire worksheet, as described above.

2. Pull down the Edit menu and click Clear.

Correcting Errors

If you make a mistake before you press the Enter key, use the Backspace key to back up and correct the error. If you have already pressed the Enter key, use one of the following methods to make the correction:

- Press the Shift and Enter keys or the Shift and Tab keys to back up to the cell that contains the error and reenter the value.

- Continue entering data until you've completed the entries for the entire range, then click the cell with the mistake and reenter that cell's data.

Finding the Active Cell

If you are working with a large worksheet, the active cell may not be visible on the screen. To find the active cell, the quickest method is to pull down the Formula menu and click Show Active Cell. To find the last cell in the worksheet, pull down the Formula menu and click Select Last Cell.

Entering Text

Any characters that Excel cannot interpret as a number, date, time, logical value, or formula are considered text. Unless you select otherwise, text data are always left-justified in a cell.

You can enter numbers as text by enclosing them in quotation marks. You can enter text in formulas by enclosing the text in quotation marks.

Entering Numbers

You can enter numbers in one of three formats:

Format	Examples
Integer	1, 45, −45
Decimal fraction	43.5, −56.75
Scientific notation	25E23, 4E−3

You can use a minus sign or parentheses to enter negative numbers. Dollar signs, percent signs, and commas can also be used as a part of numeric entry. Unless you select otherwise, numbers are right-justified in a cell. If a number has too many characters to fit in a specific cell, Excel will either display ###### in that cell to indicate the overflow, or use scientific notation.

Regardless of how numbers are displayed, they are stored with 14 digits of accuracy, unless you change this by using the Precision As Displayed command on the Options menu.

Entering Dates and Times

Excel stores both dates and times as serial numbers. The serial number that is stored for the date represents the number of days since January 1, 1904. This makes it possible for Excel to calculate the number of days between two dates by subtracting the earlier date from the later one. When you type in a date or select any cell in which a date is already stored, the formula bar displays the serial number. However, in the cell, the date is displayed in the same form that you entered it.

You can enter dates in mm/dd/yy format using slashes or hyphens. You can also enter dates in any of three other formats: dd/mm/yy (e.g., 25/May/85), dd/mm (e.g., 25/May), or mm/yy (e.g., May/86). If you enter a date in any other format, Excel will not display an error message; it will simply store it as text rather than as a serial number.

You can enter times in either standard (e.g., 3:30:30 PM) or military (e.g., 13:15:45) format. The seconds entry is optional, and you can use A or P instead of AM or PM. You can enter both a date and time into a single cell.

Dates and times can only be used as constants. They cannot be entered into formulas. If you need to use a date or time in a formula, enter it as text (inside quotation marks). Excel will convert any date in a valid date format into a serial number when it evaluates the formula.

Entering Logical Values

You can enter logical values either as TRUE or FALSE (in all capital letters, as shown). The use of logical values is discussed in Chapter 8.

Entering Formulas

You use formulas to tell Excel how to calculate values.

Creating Formulas   To create a formula, first select the cell or cell range that you want to contain the value calculated by the formula. Then you can enter the formula in one of three ways:

- By typing in the formula from the keyboard. First, type an equal sign, then type the formula. Complete the entry by clicking the enter box on the formula bar or by pressing the Enter key.

- By clicking the cells that are referenced in the formula. For example, to enter cell B5 minus cell B7, you would type an equal sign, place the cursor on cell B5 and click, type a minus sign, and then place the cursor on cell B7 and click. To complete the formula, click the enter box or press the Enter key. You can only use this method with relative cell referencing (see Chapter 8).

- By typing in or pasting the name that you assigned to a cell or range of cells. Once you've defined names for cells (see Chapter 11), you can use the Paste Name command on the Formula menu to enter the formula (Excel will automatically begin the formula with an equal sign), or you can type an equal sign and then type in the formula using the names. Again, click the enter box or press the Enter key to complete the formula.

Remember to begin each formula with an equal sign and to complete the entry by clicking the enter box on the formula bar or by pressing the Enter key. If you don't type in an operator (described below), Excel will automatically insert a plus sign. If you make a mistake while you're entering a formula, click the cancel box on the formula bar or backspace to the error. Methods for building and using formulas are discussed in detail in Chapters 8 and 11.

Formula Operators   In creating formulas, you use operators to indicate how Excel is to produce new values from other cell values. The mathematical operators are:

Operator	Function
+	Addition
−	Subtraction
*	Multiplication
/	Division
^	Exponentiation

You can also use an ampersand (&) as an operator with text fields to join two text values to create a new text value. For example *"Mr." &* *" Smith"* becomes *Mr. Smith*.

You can also use a formula to compare cell values. The result of using comparison operators is always a logical value—TRUE or FALSE. The following comparison operators are available:

Operator	Function
=	Equal to
<	Less than
<=	Less than or equal to
>	Greater than
>=	Greater than or equal to
<>	Not equal to

Reference operators are used to refer to two or more cells in formulas and in function arguments. There are three reference operators available:

Operator	Function
:	Range: references all cells in the given range
,	Union: includes two references
space	Intersection: includes cells common to two references

For example, to indicate the range from cell A1 to cell A10, you could use A1:A10. With reference operators, you can combine relative and absolute referencing (see Chapter 8), and you can use the names that you assigned to a cell or range of cells (see Chapter 11).

Filling

If you enter a value or formula into a cell, you can enter the same value into all the cells in a horizontal or vertical range by using the Fill commands. To use a Fill command:

1. Select the range, including the cell that already contains the value.

2. Pull down the Edit menu and click Fill Right or Fill Down, as appropriate.

Excel moves the value into each cell selected and automatically adjusts formulas that contain relative addressing.

Note: | There is a shorthand way of filling right and down (using the Option key), as described in the tip in the next section.

Moving and Copying

When you use the Fill Right or Fill Down command, you are copying. When you copy, you take a value or a formula in one cell and copy it into a cell or range of cells. Moving is similar, except that the original cells are cleared. You move data by using the Cut and Paste commands on the Edit menu. You copy data from any cells to other cells by using the Copy and Paste commands. You can do a fill right or fill down by using the Copy command—an operation that is far more versatile than using a Fill command and only requires a few more clicks.

When formulas are moved or copied into other cells, they are automatically adjusted to reflect their new cell position. This is called relative addressing. It is also possible to prevent this adjustment to formulas by using absolute addressing. You will learn more about relative and absolute addressing in Chapter 8.

Tip:

In creating a worksheet, there is a quick way to copy or fill formulas or data. Before entering the original formula (or data) select the entire range to which the formula will be applied (such as cells B13 to D13). Enter the formula into the formula bar, hold down the Option key, then press the Enter key to complete the entry. Excel will move the formula (or data) into each cell of the range.

Changing Column Widths

In creating worksheets, you will often need to change the width of a column to display the entire cell contents or to improve the appearance of the worksheet. You can change column widths either by using the Column Width command on the Format menu or by dragging the column.

Changing the Column Width Using a Command   To change the width by using the Column Width command, pull down the Format menu and click Column Width. When the Column Width dialog box appears, type in the new width from the keyboard, and then click OK. The column width will change to reflect the value entered. The contents of the cells in that column will not be changed.

Changing the Column Width By Dragging   To change the width by dragging, move the cursor to the line between the column heading designators. The shape of the cursor will change to a vertical line. Click and drag the cursor to the right. The width of the column on the left will follow the cursor. Release the mouse button at the desired width.

Note:

You can use both methods to enter fractional column widths (e.g., 20.5 characters).

Saving the Worksheet

After you have created the worksheet, you will need to save it on your disk. Although the worksheet is displayed on the screen, it is

Tip:

only stored in the computer memory, and if you turn the computer off or close the worksheet, the current worksheet will be lost. To save the worksheet on disk, pull down the File menu and click Save As. Enter the name of the worksheet in the dialog box, be sure that the disk designator is correct (click Drive if necessary), and then click OK. You can load another worksheet without losing the current worksheet.

As a general rule, while you're creating a worksheet, you should save it approximately every 20 minutes. This will protect your work against power failures, hardware failures, or inadvertent user mistakes. Use Save As on the File menu only the first time that you save your file. On subsequent saves, pull down the File menu and click Save. Excel won't display the dialog box; it saves the worksheet under the same name that you used previously.

The Balance Worksheet

During this and the next two chapters, you will create the worksheet shown in Figure 4.2. Now you will use the techniques described in this chapter to enter the worksheet data and formulas. When you're done, the worksheet should look like Figure 4.3. In comparing the two figures, notice the difference in the quality of presentation that is achieved by formatting. Formatting is described in Chapter 6.

Creating the Worksheet

Excel

To get started, begin with the Excel disks in your Macintosh and double-click the Excel icon. You will see Excel load with a blank worksheet called Worksheet1.

Now start creating the worksheet by selecting cells A8 through A43. Enter the row titles shown in Figure 4.4. Press the Enter key after you've typed each title. Press the Enter key twice to skip a line.

Expand the width of column A by pulling down the Format menu and clicking Column Width. The dialog box shown in Figure 4.5 appears. Enter **25,** and then click OK.

ACME MANUFACTURING COMPANY

Balance Sheet for 1984
(Figures in Thousands of Dollars)

	Qtr 1	Qtr 2	Qtr 3	Qtr 4
Current Assets				
Cash	$28,653	$42,894	$64,882	$91,053
Accounts Receivable	$35,700	$44,150	$48,450	$55,230
Inventory	$11,400	$12,930	$14,500	$16,490
Total Current Assets	*$75,753*	*$99,974*	*$127,832*	*$162,773*
Fixed Assets				
P,P, and E				
Furniture, Fixtures	$12,100	$12,100	$12,100	$12,100
Equipment	$6,500	$16,600	$21,100	$42,300
Office Equipment	$4,100	$4,100	$4,100	$4,100
Gross P, P, and E	$22,700	$32,800	$37,300	$58,500
Accumulated Depreciation	$6,600	$8,700	$11,400	$13,400
Total Fixed Assets	*$16,100*	*$24,100*	*$25,900*	*$45,100*
Total Assets	*$91,853*	*$124,074*	*$153,732*	*$207,873*
Current Liabilities				
Accounts Payable	$17,340	$41,000	$42,300	$75,200
Income Taxes Payable	$4,043	$6,132	$7,301	$9,245
Total Current Liabilities	$21,383	$47,132	$49,601	$84,445
Non-current Liabilities				
Long-term debt	$22,000	$20,000	$18,000	$16,000
Total Liabilities	*$43,383*	*$67,132*	*$67,601*	*$100,445*
Common Stock, $1 per var	$40,000	$40,000	$40,000	$40,000
Retained Earnings	$8,470	$16,942	$46,131	$67,428
Total Liabilities & Equity	*$91,853*	*$124,074*	*$153,732*	*$207,873*

Figure 4.2: *The final Balance worksheet.*

                              ACME MANUFACTURING COMPANY

                              Balance Sheet for 1984
                              (Figures in Thousands of Dollars)

	Qtr 1	Qtr 2	Qtr 3	Qtr 4
Current Assets				
Cash	28653	42894	64882	91053
Accounts Receivable	35700	44150	48450	55230
Inventory	11400	12930	14500	16490
Total Current Assets	75753	99974	127832	162773
Fixed Assets				
P,P, and E				
Furniture, Fixtures	12100	12100	12100	12100
Equipment	6500	16600	21100	42300
Office Equipment	4100	4100	4100	4100
Gross P, P, and E	22700	32800	37300	58500
Accumulated Depreciation	6600	8700	11400	13400
Total Fixed Assets	16100	24100	25900	45100
Total Assets	91853	124074	153732	207873
Current Liabilities				
Accounts Payable	17340	41000	42300	75200
Income Taxes Payable	4043	6132	7301	9245
Total Current Liabilities	21383	47132	49601	84445
Non-current Liabilities				
Long-term debt	22000	20000	18000	16000
Total Liabilities	43383	67132	67601	100445
Common Stock, $1 per var	40000	40000	40000	40000
Retained Earnings	8470	16942	46131	67428
Total Liabilities & Equity	91853	124074	153732	207873

Figure 4.3: *The Balance worksheet before formatting.*

	A	B	C	D	E
1			ACME MANUFACTURING COMPANY		
2					
3			Balance Sheet for 1984		
4			(Figures in Thousands of Dollars)		
5					
6		Qtr 1	Qtr 2	Qtr 3	Qtr 4
7					
8	Current Assets				
9	Cash	28653	42894	64882	91053
10	Accounts Receivable	35700	44150	48450	55230
11	Inventory	11400	12930	14500	16490
12		---------	---------	---------	---------
13	Total Current Assets				
14					
15	Fixed Assets				
16	P,P, and E				
17	Furniture, Fixtures	12100	12100	12100	12100
18	Equipment	6500	16600	21100	42300
19	Office Equipment	4100	4100	4100	4100
20		---------	---------	---------	---------
21	Gross P, P, and E				
22	Accumulated Depreciation	6600	8700	11400	13400
23		---------	---------	---------	---------
24	Total Fixed Assets				
25					
26	Total Assets				
27					
28	Current Liabilities				
29	Accounts Payable	17340	41000	42300	75200
30	Income Taxes Payable	4043	6132	7301	9245
31		---------	---------	---------	---------
32	Total Current Liabilities				
33					
34	Non-current Liabilities				
35	Long-term debt	22000	20000	18000	16000
36		---------	---------	---------	---------
37	Total Liabilities				
38					
39	Common Stock, $1 per var	40000	40000	40000	40000
40					
41	Retained Earnings	8470	16942	46131	67428
42		---------	---------	---------	---------
43	Total Liabilities & Equity				

Figure 4.4: *Entering text and numbers.*

Note: In this and the following data entries, do not be too concerned about mistakes. If you make a mistake, continue to create your worksheet working around it. In the next chapter, I will show you how to edit the worksheet and correct your mistakes.

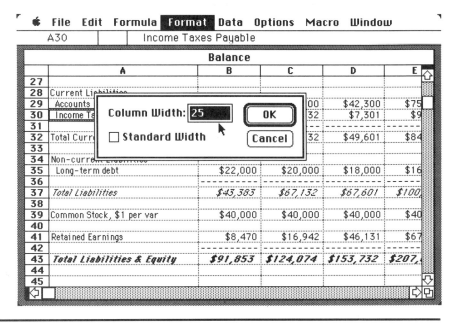

Figure 4.5: *Changing the column width.*

Next, drag from cell B6 to cell E6 and enter the column headings shown in Figure 4.4. Press Enter after each entry. Add a title to the worksheet by selecting cell C1 and entering **ACME MANUFACTUR-ING COMPANY** from the keyboard. Select cell C3 and enter **Balance Sheet for 1984.** Select cell C4 and enter **(Figures in Thousands of Dollars).**

Now enter the numbers shown in Figure 4.4 into the worksheet. Do **not** enter the values for rows 13, 21, 24, 26, 32, 37, and 43. You'll use formulas to fill these in, as described below.

Enter the following formulas for column B:

Select	Type
B13	= B9 + B10 + B11
B21	= B17 + B18 + B19
B24	= B21 − B22
B26	= B13 + B24
B32	= B29 + B30
B37	= B32 + B35
B43	= B37 + B39 + B41

In Figure 4.6, column B shows the values that should appear on your worksheet after you've entered these formulas.

Now you need to fill in the formulas. Click cell B13 and drag to cell E13. Pull down the Edit menu and click Fill Right. Repeat this procedure for all the rows with formulas.

Before you continue, save the worksheet. Pull down the File menu and click Save As. Enter the name **Balance** into the dialog box that appears (see Figure 4.7). Be sure that the disk designator shows the data disk (otherwise, click Drive), then click OK.

Experimenting with the Worksheet

Now you can try some different techniques. First, try copying a formula. Instead of entering the formulas for cells C13, D13, and E13 using the Fill Right command as you did, you could copy the formula from cell B13 into the rest of the row. First, click cell B13. Pull down the Edit menu and click Copy. Notice that the highlighting on cell B13 changes. Now, click cell C13 and drag to cell E13. Although cells C13, D13, and E13 are now selected, cell B13 is still

     File   Edit   Formula   Format   Data   Options   Macro   Window

| B13 | | =B9+B10+B11 |

Balance

	A	B	C	D	E
1		ACME MANUFACTURING COMPANY			
2					
3		Balance Sheet for 1984			
4		(Figures in Thousands of Dollars)			
5					
6		Qtr 1	Qtr 2	Qtr 3	Qtr
7					
8	Current Assets				
9	Cash	$28,653	$42,894	$64,882	$91
10	Accounts Receivable	$35,700	$44,150	$48,450	$55
11	Inventory	$11,400	$12,930	$14,500	$16
12					
13	*Total Current Assets*	*$75,753*	*$99,974*	*$127,832*	*$152*
14					
15	Fixed Assets				
16	P,P, and E				
17	Furniture, Fixtures	$12,100	$12,100	$12,100	$12
18	Equipment	$6,500	$16,600	$21,100	$42
19	Office Equipment	$4,100	$4,100	$4,100	$4

Figure 4.6: *The worksheet after entering a formula.*

marked to indicate the "from" cell range for the copy. Now pull down the Edit menu again and click Paste. The correct totals will immediately show in the rest of the row.

Notice that the totals in cells C13, D13, and E13 are correct. The formula in cell B13 was automatically adjusted for the new columns when it was moved. To check this, click cell C13 and look at the formula in the formula bar at the top of the page (see Figure 4.8).

Now, just for practice, move row 43 to row 44. First, select row 43 by placing the cursor on the row designator and clicking once. Pull down the Edit menu and click Cut. Notice that the entire range is marked. Place the cursor on the designator for row 44 and click once. Pull down the Edit menu again and select Paste. Row 43 will move to row 44 (row 43 will be cleared). Notice that the formulas are automatically adjusted. Recover the former worksheet by pulling down the Edit menu and clicking Undo Paste.

Both cutting and copying use the Clipboard. You can watch the Clipboard change during a cut and paste operation. First, make the worksheet window a little smaller by clicking the box in the lower right and moving it up and to the left slightly. Then, pull down

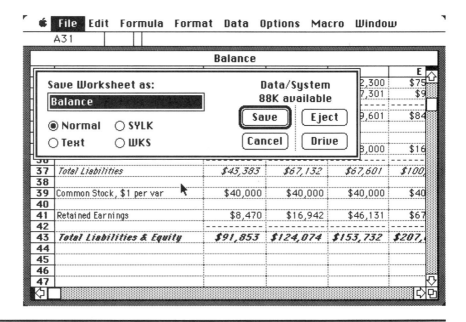

Figure 4.7: *Saving the document.*

```
‹   É   File   Edit   Formula   Format   Data   Options   Macro   Window   ›
    C13              =C9+C10+C11
```

	A	B	C	D	E
1		ACME MANUFACTURING COMPANY			
2					
3		Balance Sheet for 1984			
4		(Figures in Thousands of Dollars)			
5					
6		Qtr 1	Qtr 2	Qtr 3	Qtr
7					
8	Current Assets				
9	Cash	$28,653	$42,894	$64,882	$91
10	Accounts Receivable	$35,700	$44,150	$48,450	$55
11	Inventory	$11,400	$12,930	$14,500	$16
12		---------	---------	---------	------
13	*Total Current Assets*	*$75,753*	*$974*	*$127,832*	*$162*
14					
15	Fixed Assets				
16	P,P, and E				
17	Furniture, Fixtures	$12,100	$12,100	$12,100	$12
18	Equipment	$6,500	$16,600	$21,100	$42
19	Office Equipment	$4,100	$4,100	$4,100	$4

Figure 4.8: *Examining a formula created by a copy command.*

the Window menu and click Show Clipboard. The Clipboard window opens and is the active window, as shown in Figure 4.9.

The Clipboard can be moved, scrolled, and closed, like any other active window. Again, repeat the cut exercise described above. Watch the active window switch back to the worksheet and the Clipboard contents change as you cut and paste. Notice that the pasting operating does not clear the contents of the Clipboard—you can do two pastes from one Copy command. Once you have completed pasting, make the Clipboard window active, click its close box, and then adjust the worksheet window again to fill the entire display. Be sure that the total appears on row 43.

As a last experiment, change the width of column A by dragging. Move the cursor to the line between column A and column B. Click and drag the cursor, which now appears as a vertical line, as shown in Figure 4.10. Release the mouse button when the column is wider.

Before going on, be sure that the column width of column A is 25 characters.

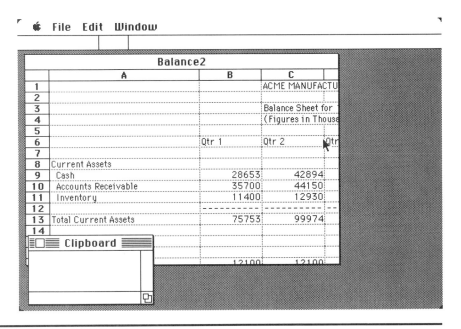

Figure 4.9: *The Clipboard window.*

	File	Edit	Formula	Format	Data	Options	Macro	Window	

B37   =B32+B35

Balance

	A	⊹⊹	B	C	D	E
29	Accounts Payable		$17,340	$41,000	$42,300	$75
30	Income Taxes Payable		$4,043	$6,132	$7,301	$9
31			---------	---------	---------	----
32	Total Current Liabilities		$21,383	$47,132	$49,601	$84
33						
34	Non-current Liabilities					
35	Long-term debt		$22,000	$20,000	$18,000	$16
36			---------	---------	---------	----
37	*Total Liabilities*		*$45,383*	*$67,132*	*$67,601*	*$100*
38						
39	Common Stock, $1 per var		$40,000	$40,000	$40,000	$40
40						
41	Retained Earnings		$8,470	$16,942	$46,131	$67
42			---------	---------	---------	----
43	*Total Liabilities & Equity*		*$91,853*	*$124,074*	*$153,732*	*$207,*
44						
45						
46						
47						

Figure 4.10: *Changing the column width by dragging.*

Note: During this chapter and the next two chapters, you will be changing this document in exercises. When you leave Excel (pull down the File menu and click Quit), you will see a dialog box that indicates that the document has been changed and asks if you wish to save the new document. If you do not wish to save the altered document, click No.

Worksheet Design Strategies

The following are some general guidelines for creating useful worksheets:

1. Work out the general worksheet idea on paper first before using Excel.

2. Always use a heading. It should contain, as a minimum, a descriptive title and version number. Generally, you will also want to include the date of the last modification (see Chapter 8 for more information about how to add a date).

3. Use more formulas to link cells and avoid using absolute values unless necessary. For example, the worksheet may have a price that affects several cells and changes periodically. Put the price in a separate parameter block on the page and use a formula to move it to other cells in the worksheet.

4. Avoid large worksheets. Instead, try to use a series of small worksheets and, if necessary, link them together (see Chapter 14).

5. Use blank rows, columns, and cells liberally to improve worksheet readability.

6. Add special documentation and notes at the end of the page as text if you need to explain any special features of the worksheet.

7. Use the Fill and Copy commands to enter new columns and rows when possible. Use the Option key to enter the same value or formula into many cells.

8. Check the worksheet over carefully before printing it. People have used electronic worksheets to make major decisions based on incorrect data. If the input data are wrong or if a formula is wrong, the results will be wrong. The computer can only do what you tell it to do.

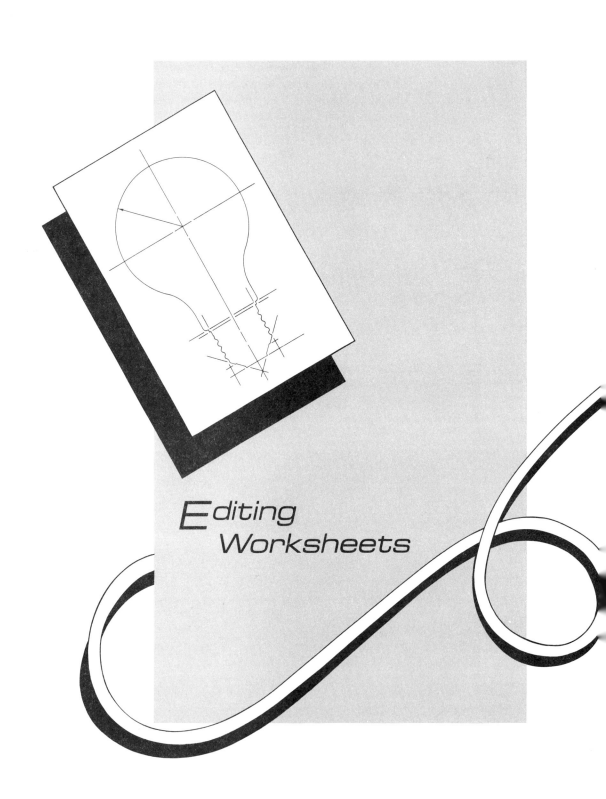

*E*diting
    Worksheets

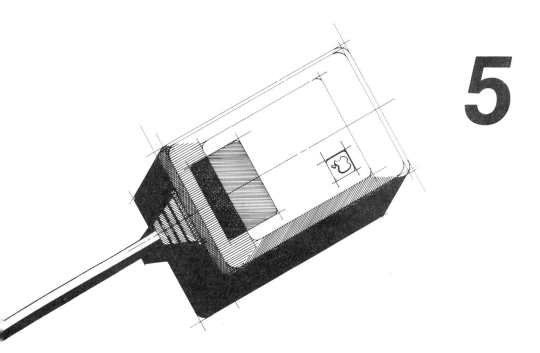

5

Excel has many editing features that can make your work easier. You can clear a cell or cell range, recover from an accidental cut, delete or clear, and insert or delete rows and columns. You can also use standard Macintosh editing techniques to edit any data in the formula bar.

In this chapter, you will learn the basic editing skills techniques to use with Excel worksheets. These will enable you to correct any mistakes that you made in the last chapter. Even if your worksheet does not have any mistakes, take the time to try some of the editing described here.

This chapter also includes information about adding comments to worksheets, using other commands for editing, and saving your edited worksheet. More advanced editing techniques are discussed in Chapter 13.

Editing Techniques

A variety of worksheet editing techniques are available to the Excel user. They make it easy for you to keep your worksheets up-to-date and accurate, as well as to use one basic worksheet structure for many purposes. The techniques discussed in this section include:

- Clearing cells
- Undoing various operations
- Editing cells
- Editing formulas
- Inserting and deleting rows and columns

Loading the Worksheet

Balance

To begin editing, start up your Macintosh with your Excel disks and double-click the Balance icon on the data disk. In a few minutes, you will see the Balance worksheet that you created in the last chapter.

Clearing a Cell or Cell Range

Sometimes, when you've entered data into the wrong range of cells, the easiest way to correct the error is to clear the entire range.

To clear an area, first select the cell or cell range that you want to clear. Pull down the Edit menu and click Clear. The Clear dialog box shown in Figure 5.1 appears (the dot in the circle next to All indicates that everything in the selected area will be cleared). Click OK in the dialog box, and the cell or cell range will be cleared.

Note:

Another way to delete the contents of a cell is described under Editing a Cell Value, later in this chapter.

You can try this now with your Balance worksheet. Select cells C13, D13, and E13. Pull down the Edit menu, click Clear, and then click OK. The cells will clear. You will also notice that two totals in row 26 change, as you have just changed data that are used to compute these totals. Before going on to anything else, pull down the Edit menu and click Undo Clear (undoing is discussed below).

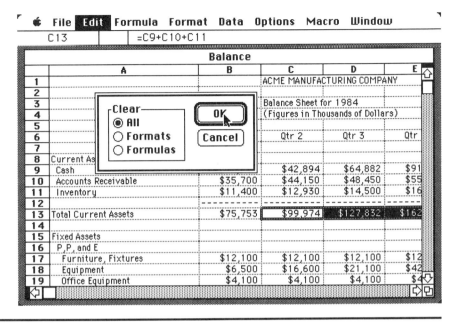

Figure 5.1: *Clearing a cell or cell range.*

Tip:

To clear an entire worksheet, it is faster to pull down the File menu, click New, and create a new worksheet. Another way to clear the whole worksheet is to: (1) select the entire worksheet by clicking the empty square above the row 1 designator, (2) pull down the Edit menu, and (3) click Clear.

The Clear dialog box also has options for clearing formulas only and Format only. Clearing a format puts the range in the default General template. These other options are discussed in Chapter 13.

Undoing

If you make a mistake while you're changing a worksheet, you can recover the previous version by using the Undo command. The Undo command applies to almost any type of operation: inserting, deleting, moving, copying, and pasting. However, only the last

operation can be undone—once you have gone on to something else, the undo capability is lost. For example, it you did a cut and paste operation with the Clipboard window open (as you did in the last section), closing the Clipboard would cause you to lose the capability to undo the cut and paste. Each time that you select the Edit menu, if the Undo command is available, it will be shown in boldface, and the function that you can undo will be the second word, such as **Undo Cut** or **Undo Paste.**

You can see how this works by moving row 13 to row 14 and then undoing the operation:

1. Select row 13.

2. Pull down the Edit menu and click Cut.

3. Select row 14.

4. Pull down the Edit menu and click Paste. Row 13 has now moved to row 14.

5. Pull down the Edit menu and click Undo Paste. Row 14 is now moved back to row 13.

Notice that the window is still marked for another paste operation. As shown in Figure 5.2, row 13 is marked as a *from,* range and row 14 is marked as a *to* range. You can select another paste range and paste again (without cutting), or you can select another cell or cell range and start a new operation (enter cell contents, cut, copy, etc.).

Before leaving this section, be sure that the Total Current Assets row is row 13 on the Balance worksheet.

Editing a Cell Value

Once you have entered a value or formula into a cell, you can edit or delete the cell contents at any time. Simply click the cell that you wish to edit or clear and enter the new information into the formula bar. The new data will replace the old.

Try this now with cell B10 of your Balance worksheet. Click the cell. The current value (35700) is displayed in the formula bar. Now, reenter the same value. When you enter the first number, the formula bar clears, and you will see a *3.*

A cancel and enter box also appear in the formula bar. You can use the enter box like the Enter key—if you click it, the value in the formula bar will become the cell's value. You can use the cancel box

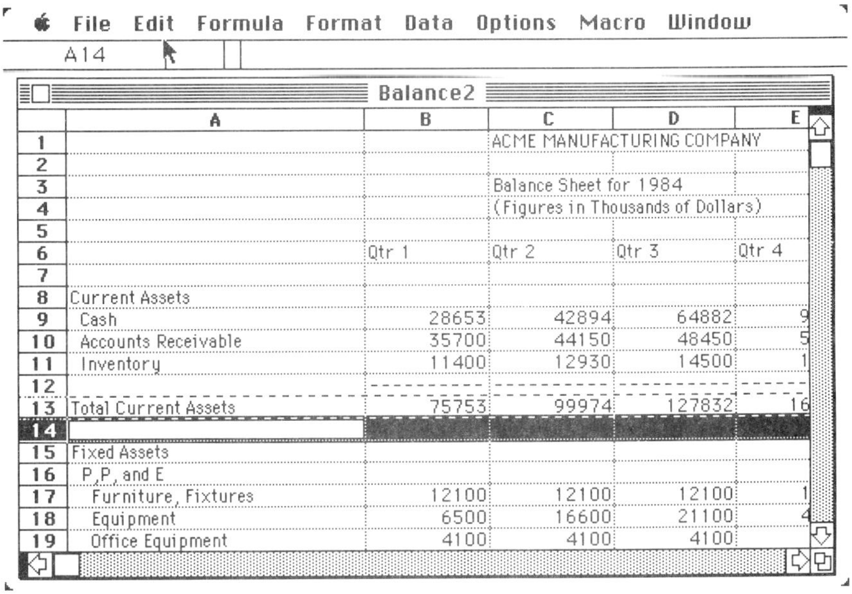

Figure 5.2: *The worksheet after undoing a paste.*

to cancel the entry. If you click the cancel box, the cell will revert to its former value.

You can move the cursor into the formula bar and click at any point on the value. Notice that the cursor changes to an I-beam form when it is in the formula bar. You can then enter characters from the keyboard, and they will be inserted at the cursor position. The remaining characters will be moved over. You can also use the Backspace key to remove characters in the formula bar. Another way to delete characters in the formula bar (and thus in the active cell) is to click anywhere in the formula bar and drag the cursor over the characters that you wish to delete. Then, pull down the Edit menu and click Cut. The Cut, Copy, and Paste commands work with characters in the formula bar in the same way that they work with those in cells.

Editing Formulas

You can edit formulas that appear in the formula bar in the same way that you edit cell values. Select the cell that contains the formula that you want to edit, then reenter the entire formula, insert or delete characters, or use the Cut or Copy and Paste commands.

Whenever the formula bar is active, you can click the cell that you want to reference in the formula instead of typing it in from the keyboard. To use this technique, first click the cursor in the formula bar where you want the reference to be inserted, then click that cell in the worksheet. If you insert the new cell reference immediately after an existing reference, without including an operator, Excel will automatically insert a plus sign between the two. (If you insert immediately after an existing operator, a plus sign will not be added.)

Any time that you click the formula bar, the cancel and enter boxes are displayed, along with the contents of the active cell. Click the enter box to enter the edited formula or click the cancel box to revert to the original formula. You can undo any editing if you make a mistake.

On your Balance worksheet, try editing the equation in cell B21:

1. Select the cell.

2. Enter the equal sign into the formula bar.

3. Click cells B17 and B18, then click cell B19.

4. Click the enter box.

The equation in cell B21 now contains the correct total.

Inserting and Deleting Rows and Columns

When you're creating a worksheet, you may find that you need to add or delete rows and columns. With Excel, this is as easy as two clicks. For example, you can add a new blank row just after the Total Current Assets row (row 13). New rows are always inserted *before* the selected row. Therefore, you need to select row 14. Click the row 14 designator, pull down the Edit menu, and click Insert. Excel will create a new row just before the previous row 14, as shown in Figure 5.3.

Notice that the row numbers below the added row have been increased by one. Excel also automatically adjusts the formulas to compensate for the new row.

To delete a row, use the Delete command on the Edit menu. Now you can delete the row that you just added. Select row 14, pull down the Edit menu, and click Delete. The rows will move up, and the worksheet will be as it was before.

Try this again with a row that contains data and see what happens. Select row 13, which contains the Total Current Assets. Pull down the Edit menu and click Delete. Row 13 vanishes, and the rows below move up and assume new numbers. Recover the deleted row before doing anything else by pulling down the Edit menu and clicking Undo Delete.

You can insert or delete columns by using the same method: Click the column designator, then click Insert or Delete on the Edit menu.

You can also insert or delete portions of columns or rows. To do this, select a cell or cell range rather than a row or column designator. Then click Insert or Delete on the Edit menu. The dialog box shown in Figure 5.4 appears. It asks if other cells or rows should be moved to adjust for the insertion or deletion. Click the appropriate response, then click OK.

Try this with your Balance worksheet:

1. Select cells B17 through B19.

2. Pull down the Edit menu and click Delete.

🍎 File Edit Formula Format Data Options Macro Window

A14

	A	B	C	D	E
1			ACME MANUFACTURING COMPANY		
2					
3			Balance Sheet for 1984		
4			(Figures in Thousands of Dollars)		
5					
6		Qtr 1	Qtr 2	Qtr 3	Qtr 4
7					
8	Current Assets				
9	Cash	28653	42894	64882	9
10	Accounts Receivable	35700	44150	48450	5
11	Inventory	11400	12930	14500	1
12					
13	Total Current Assets	75753	99974	127832	16
14					
15					
16	Fixed Assets				
17	P,P, and E				
18	Furniture, Fixtures	12100	12100	12100	1
19	Equipment	6500	16600	21100	4

Figure 5.3: *Adding a row.*

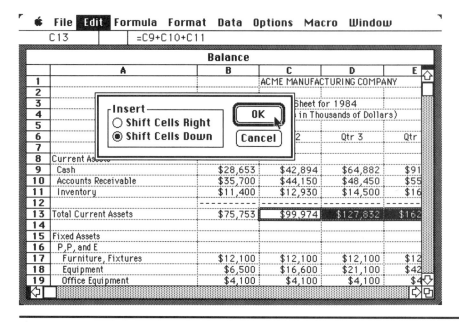

Figure 5.4: *The Insert/Delete dialog box.*

3. When the dialog box appears, click Shift Cells Up, then click OK.

4. The cells will be shifted, and several error messages will appear on your worksheet.

5. To recover the deleted cells, pull down the Edit menu and click Undo Delete.

If you delete a cell or range of cells on which the values of other cells depend (because they are based on a formula that uses the deleted cell), Excel will beep, and the dependent cells will display *REF!* after the deletion. You will then need to correct the formula that used the deleted cell. You can see how this works by deleting row 21 from the Balance worksheet. Because the values in what will be rows 23 and 25 after the deletion depend on the values that were in row 21, you will see REF! in rows 23 and 25, as shown in Figure 5.5. Now restore row 21 by pulling down the Edit menu and selecting Undo Delete.

Commenting Cells

Sometimes you may wish to add a comment about a cell that will be useful to someone entering data into the worksheet, but you don't want the comment to appear on the worksheet. Here is one way to add such a comment with Excel:

1. Add a new column immediately after the column that contains the cell or cells about which you wish to comment. You will comment on cell B11, so select column C, pull down the Edit menu, and click Insert.

2. Change the width of this column to a single character. Pull down the Format menu, click Column Width, enter **1** in the dialog box, and click OK.

3. Select the single-character cell immediately to the right of the cell about which you're commenting on (cell C11).

4. Press the spacebar three times and then enter your comment.

		File Edit Formula Format Data Options Macro Window				
	A21		Accumulated Depreciation			

Balance

	A	B	C	D	E
8	Current Assets				
9	Cash	28653	42894	64882	9
10	Accounts Receivable	35700	44150	48450	5
11	Inventory	11400	12930	14500	1
12					
13	Total Current Assets	75753	99974	127832	16
14					
15	Fixed Assets				
16	P,P, and E				
17	Furniture, Fixtures	12100	12100	12100	1
18	Equipment	6500	16600	21100	4
19	Office Equipment	4100	4100	4100	
20					
21	Accumulated Depreciation	6600	8700	11400	1
22					
23	Total Fixed Assets	#REF!	#REF!	#REF!	#RE
24					
25	Total Assets	#REF!	#REF!	#REF!	#RE
26					

Figure 5.5: *Deleting cells on which other cells depend.*

(You can use the comment shown in Figure 5.6 or make up your own.) Click the enter box. The comment will not show on the worksheet.

You will be able to see the entire comment in the formula bar whenever you select the single-character cell, as shown in Figure 5.6. If you wish, you can enter a column width of 0.5 and enter only two spaces before the comment.

If you try this little experiment, you will see that you can actually enter rather large comments into the tiny cell. The size of the formula bar will adjust automatically to accommodate large comments. The maximum comment size is 255 characters.

Other Operations

Many of the commands on the Edit menu that you used in creating the worksheet are also available for editing it. You can move data from one cell to another using the Cut and Paste commands. You

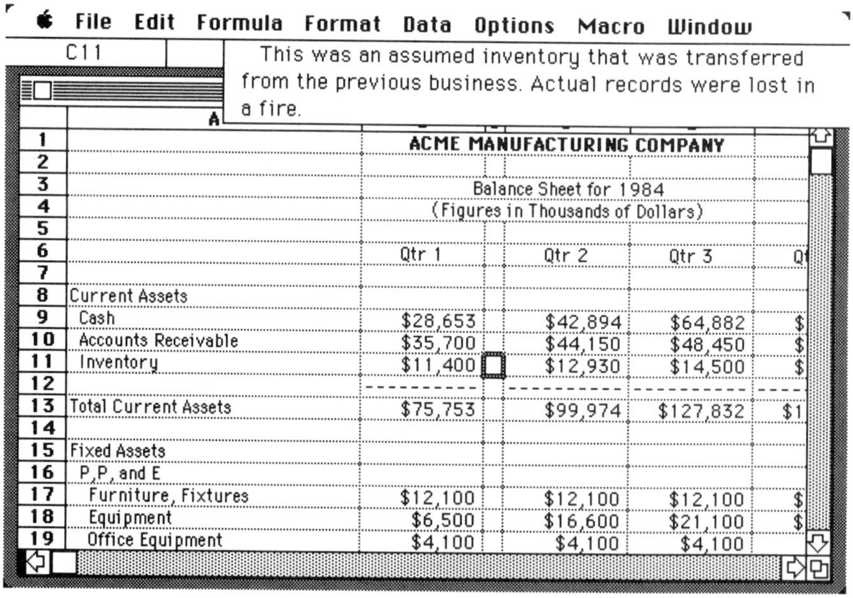

Figure 5.6: *Adding comments.*

can copy data from one cell to another using the Copy and Paste commands or the Fill Right or Fill Down commands. Refer to Chapter 4 if you need to learn how to use these commands. You will learn about the more advanced editing commands in Chapter 13.

Saving Your Edits

Whenever you are editing, remember to save your worksheet when you have finished making changes. The first time that you save your worksheet after it is created, you need to pull down the File menu and select Save As. Enter the document name in the dialog box, be sure that the disk designator is the data disk (click Drive if necessary), and then click OK. On subsequent saves, you can simply use the Save command on the File menu. You won't see a dialog box, and Excel will save the document under the name that you gave it previously.

Tip:

When you're editing a worksheet, save your work approximately every 20 minutes.

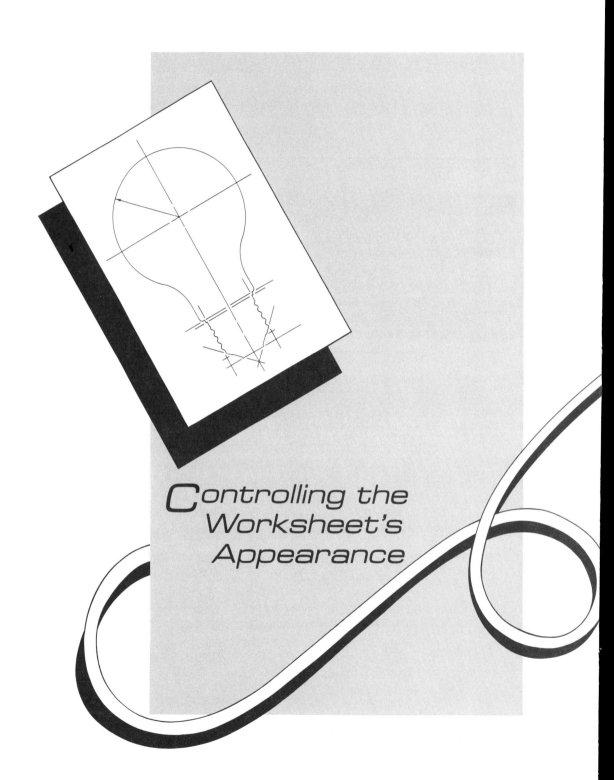

Controlling the Worksheet's Appearance

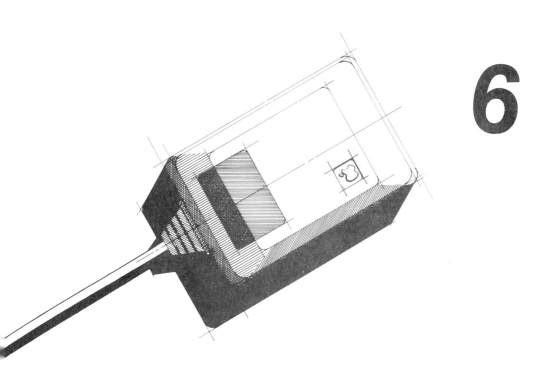

6

In this chapter, you will learn how to control the appearance of your worksheets. There are two things that Excel stores for each cell in a worksheet: the cell's value (constant or formula) and the cell's formatting information. The formatting information, which controls the appearance of the cell's display, includes the following:

- How numbers are to be displayed

- The alignment of the cell's display (left, center, or right)

- The style of the cell's display (regular, boldface, or italics)

- The font used in the cell's display (Chicago, New York, Geneva, or Monaco)

In addition, you can control the display of the worksheet's grid lines, add borders around cells or cell ranges, and alter the worksheet's font type and size.

Formatting is important for creating presentation-quality documents. It makes the worksheet easy to read and understand and emphasizes the conclusions that you wish to portray so that they stand out from the rest of the worksheet. Excel offers you extensive formatting control, so you can exercise your creativity in setting up your worksheets.

Templating

The term *templating* is used here to refer to how a number, date, or time is displayed. The term *formatting* refers to the cell's template as well as its alignment, style, and font.

Excel includes 19 predefined templates for cell display: 10 for numeric displays and 9 for dates and times. In addition, you can define new templates, which are useful for worksheets that involve special values, such as foreign currency.

Predefined Templates

Excel's predefined templates give you the following choices:

- How many digits appear to the right of the decimal

- Whether commas are used in numbers

- Whether a dollar sign appears with currency

- Whether a percent sign is used with percentages

- Whether dates and times appear with hyphens, dashes, or colons

In the default mode (when Excel is first started up), Excel displays all cells using the General template, which shows all numbers as precisely as possible. In other words, if you enter 123, the cell will display 123; if you enter 123.23, the cell will display 123.23. If a General template number is too large for the current column width, Excel will attempt to display the number in scientific notation. For example, if you entered the value 10 billion (a one followed by ten zeros) into a blank cell of standard width (10 characters), Excel would display **1E + 10** in that cell. It would use scientific notation because the 11-digit number would not fit in a 10-character cell.

To choose another predefined template for a cell or range of cells:

1. Select the cell or range of cells that you want to reformat.

2. Pull down the Format menu and click Number.

3. The Format Number dialog box shown in Figure 6.1 appears. Click the format that you wish to use. If you need to, you can click the scroll arrows or drag the scroll box to scroll to other templates listed in the box.

4. Click OK, and the cell or cell range will be formatted according to the template that you selected.

Here are some examples of how the predefined templates can be used to format a particular display:

Entry	Template	Display
123	0.00	123.00
123.67	0	124
123	$#,##0.00	$123.00

Defining New Templates

Instead of using a predefined template, you can create your own. For example, if you need to enter social-security numbers, you can define a template that automatically puts in the dashes. Other uses for new templates include telephone numbers and foreign currencies. You can even create a template that uses text (such as "lbs").

As an example, you can set up a template that puts *No.* in front of any number entered into a cell. First, start up Excel with your

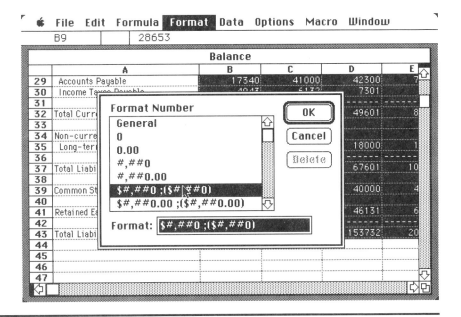

Figure 6.1: *Selecting a template.*

Balance worksheet by double-clicking the Balance icon. Then, follow the steps below:

Balance

1. Select a blank cell or cell range on the screen.

2. Pull down the Format menu and click Number.

3. In the entry bar at the bottom of the Format Number dialog box, enter **"No."** ###. Then click OK.

Now, enter a few numbers and see what happens. Remember that only the cells or cell range that you selected will use the new template.

Now that you have defined this new template for the Balance worksheet, it will appear as one of your choices in the Format Number dialog box that is displayed when this worksheet is active. So, you can easily format other cells using the new template by simply selecting it from the dialog box. However, the new template that you define for a particular worksheet will not be available to other worksheets unless you enter it into the Format Number dialog box when you're formatting that worksheet.

Table 6.1 lists the symbols that you can use for creating your own templates. You can delete templates from the Format Number dialog box by selecting the format that you want to remove and then clicking Delete (see Figure 6.1).

Symbol	Meaning
0	Template for a single numeric digit. If the number has less digits on either side of the decimal point than there are zeros in the template on either side of the decimal point, Excel displays the extra zeros. If the number has more zeros to the right of the decimal than zeros in the template to the right of the decimal, Excel rounds the number to the number of zeros to the right of the decimal. If the number

Table 6.1: *Symbols Used for Creating New Templates.*

Symbol	Meaning
	has more digits to the left of the decimal than zeros in the template to the left, the extra digits are displayed. Example: Template: 0.0; Entry: .8; Displayed: 0.8.
#	Template for a single numeric digit. Follows the rules for 0 above, except extra zeros are not displayed to the right and left of the decimal. Example: Template #.#; Entry: .8; Displayed: .8.
.	Decimal point. Will display as in the template.
%	Multiply by 100 and add a percent sign.
,	Thousands separator. Thousands are separated by commas if this is included in the template surrounded by zeros.
E-, E+, e-, e+	Scientific format notation.
:, $, -, +, ( )	Display the character.
space	Display the character.
*	Repeat next character to fill cell width.
"XXXX"	Display characters within quotation marks as text.
m, mm, mmm, mmmm	Display month in number format without leading zeros.
d, dd, ddd, dddd	Display the day without leading zeros.
yy, yyyy	Display the year.

Table 6.1: *Symbols Used for Creating New Templates [continued].*

Symbol	Meaning
h, hh	Display the hour without leading zeros.
m, mm	Display minutes without leading zeros (must be after hours).
s, ss	Display seconds without leading zeros (must be after minutes).
AM, PM, A, P	Display hour using 12-hour clock with AM or PM.

Notes:

1. Two templates can be entered for a cell separated by a colon(s). With one colon, the first applies to positive numbers and the second to negative. If you use two colons, the third template will be applied to numbers equal to zero.

2. If you do not want negative numbers displayed, enter the format for positive numbers followed by a semicolon. If you do not want any numbers displayed, use two semicolons.

Table 6.1: *Symbols Used for Creating New Templates [continued].*

Now you can template the numeric cells in your Balance worksheet:

1. Select cell B9.

2. Pull down the Format menu and click GOTO. When the Reference box is displayed, enter **E43.** Hold down the Shift key and click OK. You have selected cells B9 through E43.

3. Pull down the Format menu and click Number.

4. Click the first currency format (highlighted in Figure 6.1) in the Format Number dialog box, then click OK.

All the numbers are now displayed as currency, with dollar signs but without decimals and cents.

A *lignment*

Excel offers you a choice of five alignments within a cell:

- General, which left-justifies text and right-justifies numbers
- Left, which left-justifies all entries (numbers, dates, and text)
- Right, which right-justifies all entries
- Center, which centers each entry
- Fill, which repeats the entry until the cell is filled

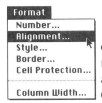

When you first start up Excel, all entries use General alignment. To change the alignment of text or numbers, first select the cell or cell range that you want to realign. Then, pull down the Format menu and click Alignment. The dialog box shown in Figure 6.2 appears. Click the alignment that you want, then click OK.

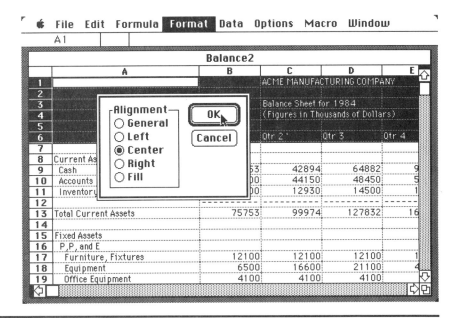

Figure 6.2: *Selecting the alignment.*

Now you can center the information at the top of your Balance worksheet:

1. Select cells A1 through E6 by dragging.

2. Pull down the Format menu and click Alignment.

3. Click Center (shown with a dot in the circle next to it in Figure 6.2) in the Alignment dialog box, then click OK.

All the text in the selected cell range is now centered.

S*tyle*

Format
Number...
Alignment...
Style...
Border...
Cell Protection...
Column Width...

You can display your worksheet entries in boldface, italics, or both, as well as in regular style. Different styles can be selected for the individual cells or for a range of cells. To change the style, select the cell or cell range that you want to display in the different style. Pull down the Format menu and click Style. The Style dialog box shown in Figure 6.3 appears. Click Bold, Italic, or both. These options are *toggles,* which you use to turn each of these styles on and off by successive clicking. When you've made your selection, click OK.

The X next to Bold or Italic in the Style dialog box marks the current style of the selected cell or cell range. If the cells in the selected range are in more than one style, the box next to the style of the active cell will be filled with dots (as shown in Figure 6.4) to indicate the mixed styles of the range.

Now you can change the styles on parts of your Balance worksheet. The title will be in boldface; the Total Current Assets, Total Fixed Assets, and Total Liabilities rows will be in italics; and the Total Assets and Total Liabilities & Equity rows will be in both boldface and italics. Follow these steps:

1. Click cell C3 to select the title.

2. Pull down the Format menu and click Style.

3. Click Bold, then click OK.

4. Click the designator for row 13. Hold down the Command key and click the designators for rows 24 and 37. All three rows are now selected.

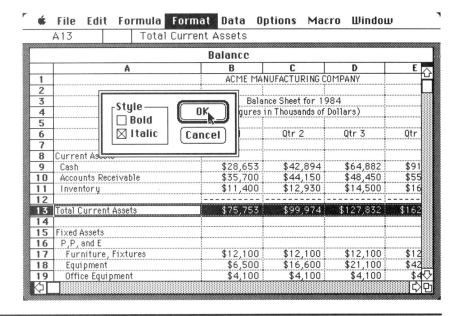

Figure 6.3: *Changing the style.*

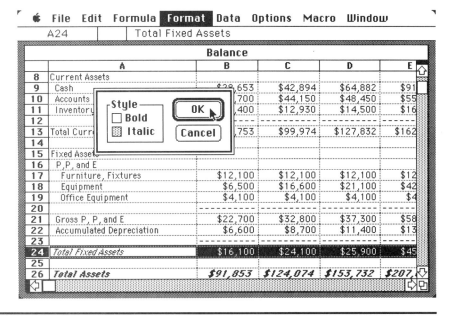

Figure 6.4: *Showing mixed styles in a cell range.*

5. Pull down the Format menu and click Style.

6. Click Italic, then click OK.

7. Click the designator for row 26. Hold down the Command key and click the designator for row 43. Both rows are selected.

8. Pull down the Format menu and click Style.

9. Click both Bold and Italic, then click OK.

The totals on your Balance worksheet now stand out from the rest of the entries.

Changing the Font

You can also change the font and font size of the worksheet entries, but you cannot do it by individual cells or cell ranges. Whatever font and font size you select will be applied to the entire worksheet.

Excel offers a choice of the Chicago, New York, Geneva, or Monaco fonts. The default font is 10-point Geneva. You can add other fonts using the Font Mover program in the Macintosh System Folder.

CHICAGO   NEW YORK   GENEVA   MONACO   VENICE   LONDON   ATHENS

To change the worksheet font:

1. Pull down the Options menu and click Font.

2. When the Font dialog box shown in Figure 6.5 appears, click the font that you want. Excel then displays the available sizes for that particular font. You can use the scroll arrows to scroll through the list of font sizes.

3. Select the font size that you want, click it, and then click OK.

The entire worksheet will be displayed on the screen, as well as printed out, in the new font. Whatever styles that you selected from the Style dialog box will remain in effect.

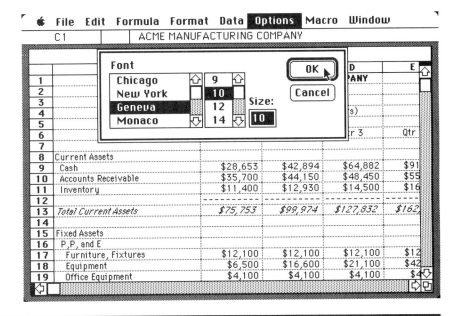

Figure 6.5: *Changing the font and font size.*

Note:	Each of the fonts is displayed best at a certain size. If you use another size for a particular font, you will lose some of the image quality. If the display looks ragged or otherwise of poor quality, select another font size.

Hiding a Column

There may be times when you want to hide a column on a worksheet so that it is not displayed or printed. For example, you may not want to print some constants that you put in one area of a worksheet to use as a part of formulas in other areas of that worksheet.

To hide columns, you change the column width to zero. This can be done in one of two ways:

- Pull down the Format menu, click Column Width, and type in a zero for the width.

• Place the cursor on the right edge of the designator of the column to be hidden (the cursor will change to the shape of a line) and drag it left until it overlaps the left edge of the column.

To recover a column, do just the opposite: enter a new nonzero column width or drag the column designator edge back to the right.

Note: If you use dragging to restore a hidden column, be sure to drag from the *right* side of the column designator. If you drag from the left side, instead of restoring the hidden column, you will widen the column to the left of it.

Controlling Grid Lines

On the worksheet screen display, cells are separated by vertical and horizontal grid lines. You may want to turn the grid lines off to see how a worksheet looks without them.

To turn off the grid lines, pull down the Options menu and click Display. The Display dialog box shown in Figure 6.6 appears. Click Gridlines to remove the X in the box next to it, then click OK. The Gridlines option is a toggle that switches the grid-line display on and off. If an X is displayed, the option is on; if not, it is off. By clicking the option, you can switch between the two conditions. However, no matter what you select in this dialog box, the grid lines will still be printed. You can only control the *screen display* of the grid lines this way.

You use the Page Setup command on the File menu to turn off the grid lines on the printed worksheet.

You can do this now to prepare for printing your Balance worksheet without grid lines:

1. Pull down the File menu and click Page Setup.

2. The Page Setup dialog box shown in Figure 6.7 appears. Click Print Gridlines to remove the X in the box next to that option (this is a toggle like the options in the Display dialog box), then click OK.

The grid lines will still appear on the screen display while you work with the worksheet, but they will not show on the printed version.

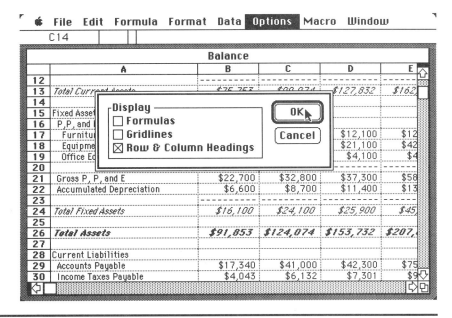

Figure 6.6: *The Display dialog box.*

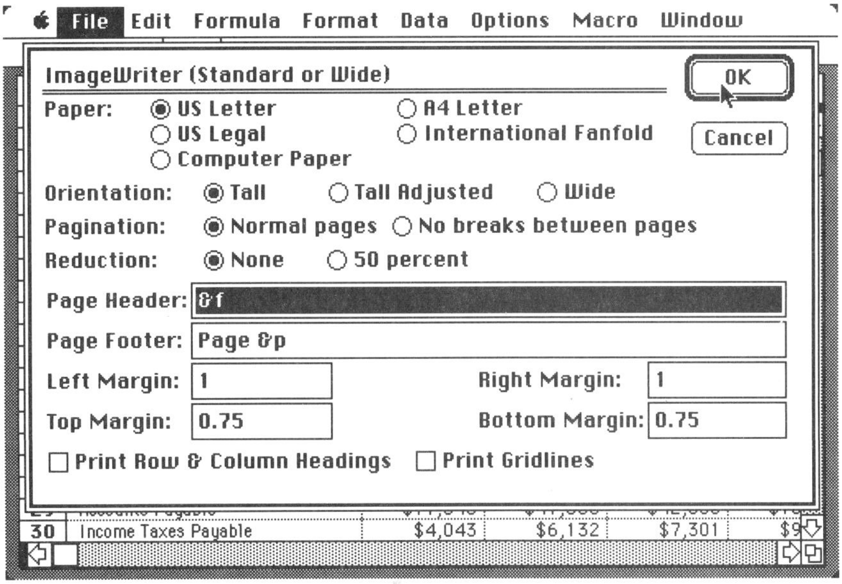

Figure 6.7: *The Page Setup dialog box.*

Controlling Designators

At the top of each column is a column designator—A, B, C, and so on to IV. At the left edge are the row designators, numbered from 1 to 16,384. Like the grid lines, you can turn these off so that they don't appear on the worksheet screen display. To turn off the display of designators, pull down the Options menu and click Display. When the Display dialog box shown in Figure 6.6 appears, click Row & Column Headings (another toggle) to remove the X in the box next to that option, then click OK. Remember, the Display dialog box options only control the screen display, not the printed output.

To eliminate the designators on the printed worksheet, you use the Page Setup command on the File menu.

Follow the steps below to eliminate the row and column designators from your printed Balance worksheet:

1. Pull down the File menu and click Page Setup.

2. When the Page Setup dialog box (shown in Figure 6.7) appears, click Print Row & Column Designators to remove the X in the box next to that option (another toggle). Then click OK.

The row and column designators will still be displayed on the screen, but you won't see them on the printed worksheet.

Displaying Formulas

There may be times when you need to see the formulas associated with a particular worksheet. To display the formulas, pull down the Options menu and click Display. When the Display dialog box (see Figure 6.6) appears, click Formulas and then click OK. The screen display will then show the formulas. Each column will now be twice as wide as it was in your normal display to permit room for the formulas. You can switch the display back by repeating this operation.

Tip: If you need a printout of the formulas, use the Display command to display the Formulas, then print the worksheet as usual (using the Print command on the File menu).

A dding Borders

You may wish to add a border to parts of the worksheet display or printout to make it easier to read. To add a border, first turn off the grid lines using the procedure described earlier (if the grid lines are not turned off, you will have a hard time seeing the borders on the display). Select the cell or range of cells that you want to put the border around. Now pull down the Format menu and select Border. When the Border dialog box shown in Figure 6.8 appears, click one or more options, then click OK.

Excel offers these choices for borders:

- Outline, which outlines the entire range with a border.

- Left, which draws a horizontal line at the left of each cell.

- Right, which draws a horizontal line at the right of each cell.

- Top, which draws a horizontal line at the top of each cell.

- Bottom, which draws a horizontal line at the bottom of each cell.

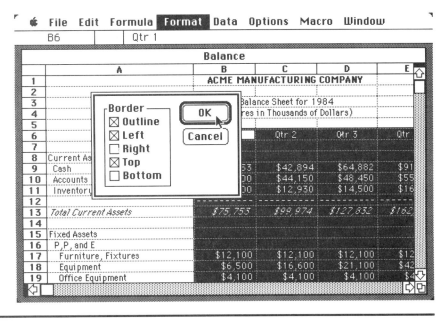

Figure 6.8: *Selecting borders.*

You can choose one or more of these border options for the selected cells. The added borders appear on both the screen display and the printed worksheet. By using a combination of styles and borders, you can emphasize any values on your worksheets. Figure 4.2 in Chapter 4 shows how bordering can be used effectively.

Now you can put the borders shown in Figure 4.2 on your Balance worksheet:

1. Select cell B9.

2. Pull down the Formula menu, click Goto, enter E24 into the Reference box, hold down the Shift key, and click OK. You have selected cells B9 through E24.

3. Pull down the Format menu. Click Border, then click Outline, and then click OK.

4. Select the range of cells B29 to E41 by using the method described in step 2.

5. Pull down the Format menu. Click Border, then click Outline, and then click OK.

6. Clear row 42 by selecting the row designator, pulling down the Edit menu, clicking Clear, and then clicking OK.

Your worksheet should now have borders defining two separate parts of the sheet.

Note: | Be sure that the grid lines are turned off, or you will not be able to see the borders.

*P*rinting the Worksheet

To print an entire document, pull down the File menu and click Print. When the Print dialog box shown in Figure 6.9 appears, click OK.

Many of the features already discussed affect the printed worksheet. Remember that grid lines and column and row designators are turned off and on using the Page Setup command on the File menu. If you add borders, they will also be printed. Your selection

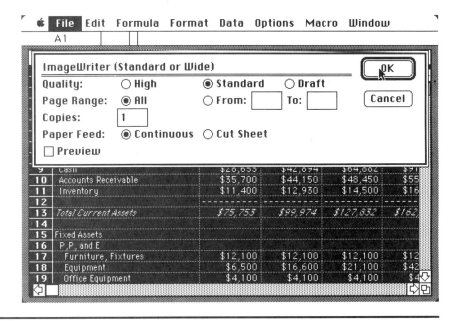

Figure 6.9: *The Print dialog box.*

of fonts and styles also applies to both the screen display and the printout of the worksheet. Here are some other features that apply to only the printed worksheet.

Note: The contents of the Page Setup and Print dialog boxes (Figures 6.7 and 6.9) will vary with the type of printer that you are using. The figures in this book apply to the ImageWriter printer.

Headers and Footers

A header is a line of text that prints on the top of every page. A footer is a line of text that prints at the bottom of every page. By default, Excel will print the file name of the document as a header and the page number as a footer.

To set a header or footer, pull down the File menu and click Page Setup. When the Page Setup dialog box (Figure 6.7) appears, enter the text for the header or footer in the Page Header or Page Footer box. Then click OK.

You can justify headers and footers and include a date, time, and page number. You can also control the style of headers and footers. The control codes that you can use in creating headers and footers are listed in Table 6.2.

Now, turn off the default headers and footers on your Balance worksheet. Pull down the File menu and click Page Setup. When the Page Setup dialog box appears, the cursor will be on the Page Header entry. Press the Backspace key, and the Page Header box will clear. Drag the cursor over the Page Footer box until it turns dark, then press the Backspace key again to clear the current footer entry. Click OK, and your worksheet will be printed without a file name or page number.

Printing a Range

You can also print just part of a worksheet. This is particularly useful when you're working with only a portion of a very large worksheet.

Symbol	Function
&L	Left-justify following characters.
&C	Center following characters.
&R	Right-justify following characters.
&P	Print page number.
&D	Print current date.
&T	Print current time.
&F	Print the name of the document.
&B	Print in boldface.
&I	Print in italics.
&&	Print an ampersand.

Note: You can combine two or more of these in a header or footer.

Table 6.2: *Header and Footer Control Codes*

To print part of a worksheet, first select the range to be printed. Pull down the Options menu and click Set Print Area. Then, pull down the File menu and click Print. Excel names the area that you selected Print_Area. You can refer to this area in other commands by using this name (see Chapter 11).

Setting a Page Break

If you wish to force a page break at any point in the worksheet, first select any cell in the row that you want the page break to come *before*. Pull down the Options menu and click Set Page Break. The row with the selected cell will be the first row of the next page.

To remove a page break, select a cell in the row below the page break, pull down the Options menu, and click Remove Page Break.

Printing Page Titles

You can select certain rows or columns to be printed on each page. This is particularly useful for printing column or row titles on each page of a worksheet.

To print a particular row at the top of each page: select the row, pull down the Options menu, and click Set Print Titles. When you print the worksheet, the selected row will be at the top of each page. If you want to print a column at the left edge of each page, first select the column, then follow the same procedure. Excel names the area that you selected Print_Titles. You can refer to this area in other commands by using this name (see Chapter 11).

Previewing a Print

You may want to see a screen display showing what a particular worksheet will look like when it's printed. To do this, pull down the File menu and select Print. When the Print dialog box (Figure 6.9) appears, click Preview. Then click OK. The display that appears shows how the entire printed page will look.

Miscellaneous Options

There are various other normal Macintosh printing options available to Excel users. For example, with the ImageWriter printer, you can use the Page Setup command on the File menu to print a worksheet vertically or horizontally.

Note:

The type of Page Setup dialog box displayed depends on the type of printer that you are using. To select the printer type, use the File menu and click Printer Setup. If a worksheet is very wide, you can elect to print it horizontally, and you may still be able to get it on a standard sheet of paper. Using the same dialog box, you can also elect to reduce a worksheet by 50%.

The Final Balance Worksheet

If you followed along with the examples in this chapter, you have done the following with your Balance worksheet:

- Put the title in boldface print

- Centered all column headings

- Put rows 13, 24, and 37 in italics

- Put rows 26 and 43 in boldface and italics

- Turned off all the headers and footers

- Turned off the grid lines and row and column designators in the printout

- Added borders

Now you can print the worksheet by pulling down the File menu and clicking Print. Then, click OK when the Print dialog box appears. Your final printout should look like Figure 4.2.

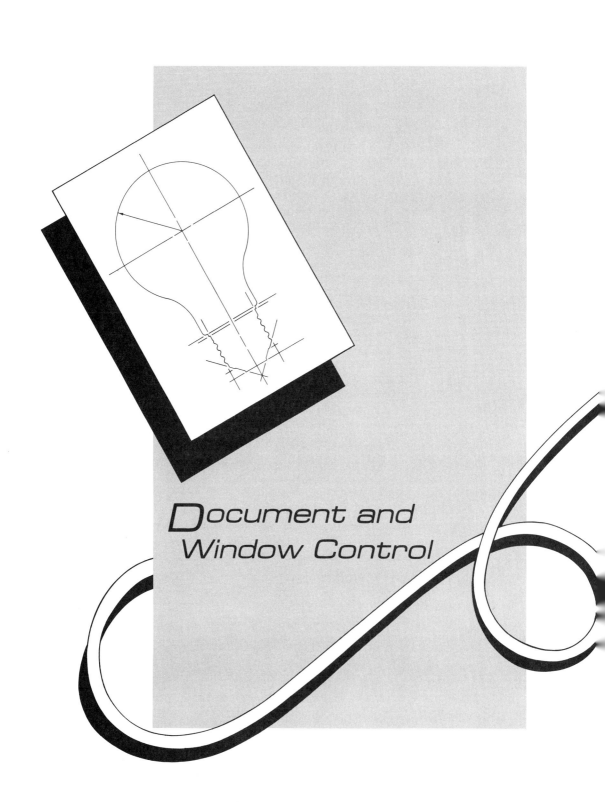

Document and
Window Control

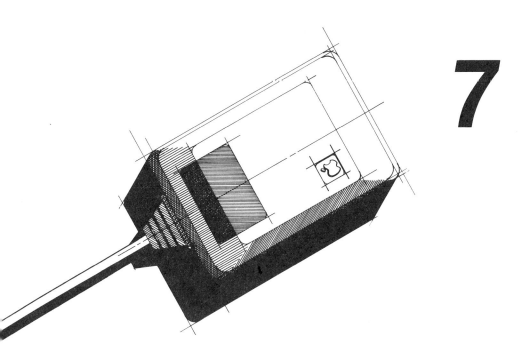

7

The worksheet document is always displayed as a window. With Excel, you can have several windows (worksheets) displayed simultaneously. Although only one window can be active at a time, other windows can be partially active.

Since all documents are created and edited using windows, learning how to control windows is important in managing your worksheets. In this chapter, you will learn some of the special window-management techniques that are a part of Excel. You will learn more about opening and closing windows, how to switch windows, and how to open additional windows into the same document. Finally, you will learn how to create panes in a window to make it easier to enter data into large worksheets.

*W*indow Overview

The worksheet document is always displayed as a window. You also use windows to display almost any type of Excel data: charts, databases, and even macros. The basic Macintosh window-management commands apply to any type of Excel document. You can scroll a window by using the scroll bars, move a window by dragging its title bar, and resize a window by dragging the small box in the lower right.

*C*ontrolling Documents

As you are working with Excel, you will need to open, close, and delete documents.

Opening Documents

To create a new document, pull down the File menu and click New. The New dialog box shown in Figure 7.1 appears. As this figure shows, Worksheet is already selected as the type of document. To create a new worksheet, click OK. Excels displays a blank worksheet titled Worksheet1 (if a worksheet with this title already exists on the disk, the new document will be Worksheet2).

To open a document that you have already created and stored on the disk, pull down the File menu and click Open. The dialog box shown in Figure 7.2 appears. It lists the names of the documents currently on the disk. You can use the scroll bar to see additional documents on the same disk. The name of the currently active disk drive is in the upper right of the dialog box. The active drive should always be the one with a data disk. If it is not, click Drive. The dialog box will then list the names of the documents on the data disk. You can complete the command either by double-clicking the document name or by clicking the name and then clicking OK.

Excel allows you to have more than one window open. If you are working on a worksheet and need to open another document, pull down the File menu and click New or Open again. You will then see the windows for both documents on the screen.

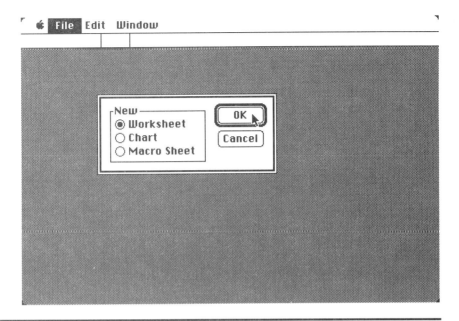

Figure 7.1: *Creating a new worksheet.*

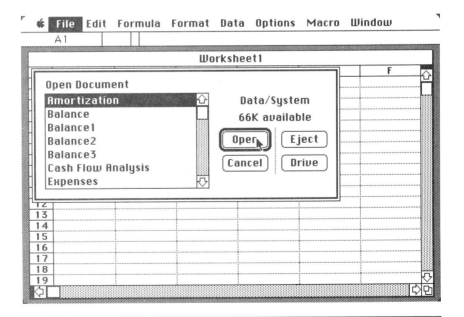

Figure 7.2: *Opening an existing worksheet.*

Closing Documents

When you are done working with an Excel document, you should close the document. The document, as displayed, is only in the computer memory. It has not, as yet, been written to the disk where it can be stored when the computer power is off. There are five ways to store a document to disk:

- Click the close box in the upper left of the window's title bar. This will save the document under the name currently displayed on the worksheet (for example, Worksheet1). If the document has already been saved under this name, Excel will ask if you wish to save any changes. When you close a document this way, you do not automatically exit Excel. After the window is closed, a short menu bar is displayed. You can use the commands on the File menu to open or create another document. This method is useful if you have finished working with one document and you wish to work on another.

- Pull down the File menu and click Quit. This will write all documents to the disk and then exit Excel. This method is a quick way to exit Excel and save changes.

- Pull down the File menu and click Save. This will save the current worksheet under the name displayed on the worksheet. The window remains active. This method is useful for saving the worksheet periodically as you work on it.

- Pull down the File menu and click Close All. This will work the same as closing a window, except that all windows that were displayed will be closed.

- Pull down the File menu and click Save As. You will then see a dialog box with the current worksheet name, as shown in Figure 7.3. Enter the name that you wish to assign to the document. Be sure that the disk assignment is correct; click Drive if necessary to select the drive with the data disk. Then click OK. This is the only method that permits you to save a document under a name that you assign.

You cannot change the name of a document that you previously stored using any of the commands on the File menu. To rename a document, you must exit Excel using the Quit command on the File menu. Then, click the icon representing the document that you want to rename and enter the new name from the keyboard. Then press Enter.

Tip:

> If you inadvertently save a document under a wrong or mis-spelled name, there is another way to correct it that is quicker than exiting Excel. Use the Save As command on the File menu to save it under the correct name. Then use the Delete command on the File menu to delete the old document with the incorrect name.

Deleting Documents

To delete a document from the disk, pull down the File menu and click Delete. You will then see the Delete Document dialog box shown in Figure 7.4. If necessary, scroll to the document that you wish to delete. Click Disk if you need to switch to another disk. Click the name of the document that you want to delete, then click OK.

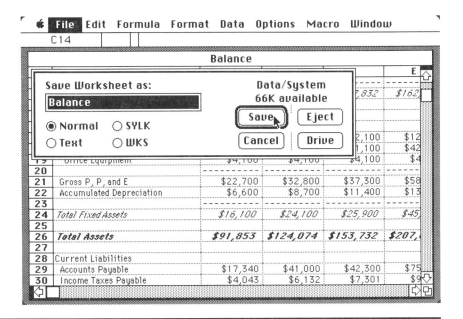

Figure 7.3: *Saving the document.*

*U*sing *Additional Windows*

There may be times when you need to open additional windows. This permits you to view two or more documents at once and to move data from one document to another. The other windows may be into other documents or into the same document, as described later in this section.

The commands on the Edit menu are still available when you have more than one window open, so you can easily move data and formulas between windows. Use the Copy and Paste or Cut and Paste commands, just as if you were working with a single window.

Linking worksheets in different windows is discussed in Chapter 14.

Opening Windows into Other Documents

At any time that you are using one window and then want to open a second window into another document, pull down the File menu and click Open, just as you did to open the first document. You can

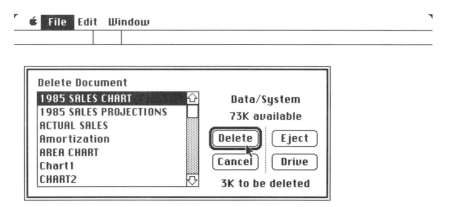

Figure 7.4: *Deleting a document.*

switch active windows by clicking anywhere on the window that you wish to make active.

Another way to switch between windows is to pull down the Window menu and click the name of the window that you want to make active. The Window menu always lists all the open documents.

Opening Additional Windows onto the Same Document

There may be times when you need to open a second window into the same worksheet. Multiple windows are primarily useful with large worksheets in which one part of the worksheet is dependent upon another part of the same worksheet. You can edit or change values in one part of the worksheet and immediately see the effect in the other window. Each window can be controlled independently by using the scroll bars on that window.

You can try this now with your Balance worksheet:

1. Open the worksheet by double-clicking the Balance icon.

2. Make the window smaller (see Figure 7.5) by dragging the size box in the lower right.

3. Pull down the Window menu and click New Window.

4. When the new window opens, make it smaller, too, as shown in Figure 7.5.

Notice that the new window is titled Balance:2, and your original window has become Balance:1.

If you already have more than one window open and you click New Window, Excel will create a new window into the worksheet that is currently active. To close either window, click the close box in its title bar. You cannot close a document unless all windows on a particular worksheet are closed.

Splitting Windows

In the next few sections, you will learn some strategies for working with windows when you have large worksheets. In most applications, you can simplify your work by using *panes.*

Creating the Cash-Flow Analysis Worksheet

To understand how to work with panes, you need a large work-sheet. You should create the worksheet shown in Figure 7.6. This is a Cash-Flow Analysis worksheet for a six-month cycle—a very common type of worksheet application. The formulas for the first three columns are shown in Figure 7.7. You can use a Fill Right command from column B to complete the other columns. When printed, the worksheet should look like Figure 7.8. To get it on a single page, you will need to use a size 12 font, print horizontally, and use a 50% reduction.

Notice that the key parameters for the analysis (interest rate, cost and sale of goods, and advertising and sales) are stored at the top of column L. These are then used as absolute references in the various columns. If these assumptions are changed, the entire worksheet will change to reflect the new assumptions. This allows you to do a what-if analysis to see how changing a factor influences the year's cash flow.

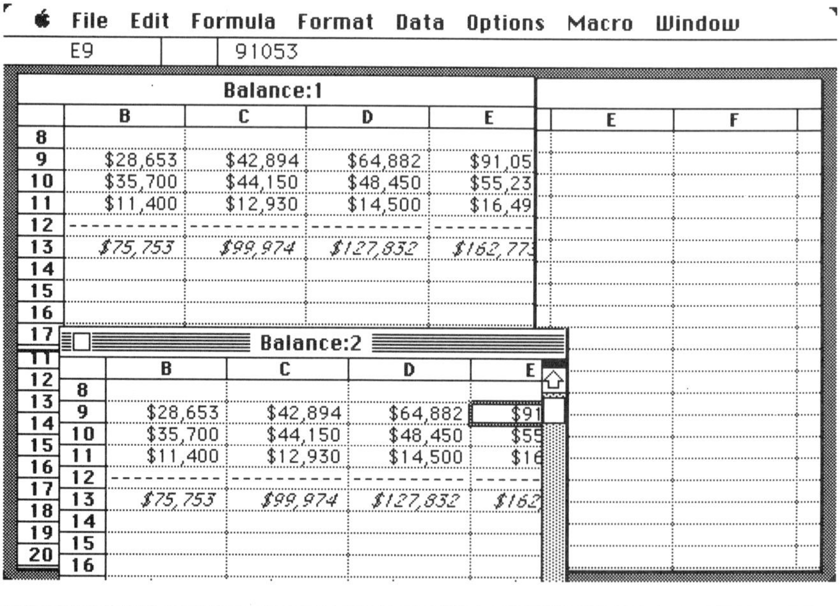

Figure 7.5: *Opening another window into the same document.*

Cash Flow Analysis

WIDGET MANUFACTURING
CASH FLOW ANALYSIS – 1985

Assumptions:
Interest Rate .95
Cost of Goods/Sale of Goods 0.55
Advertising/Sales 0.1

	Jan-85	Feb-85	Mar-85	Apr-85	May-85	Jun-85	Jul-85	Aug-85	Sep-85	Oct-85	Nov-85	Dec-85
CASH ON HAND	$43,000	$34,079	$64,151	$81,409	$162,935	$176,866	$179,810	$180,421	$224,747	$255,956	$272,039	$286,751
INCOME												
Sale of Goods	$63,394	$110,237	$114,563	$117,239	$123,291	$108,345	$98,234	$132,074	$143,619	$132,764	$123,127	$31,872
Sale of Services	$6,432	$10,234	$11,784	$78,123	$10,523	$11,239	$9,272	$11,555	$10,234	$12,812	$13,916	$14,123
Total Sales	$89,826	$120,471	$126,347	$195,362	$133,814	$119,584	$107,506	$144,429	$154,053	$145,576	$137,043	$45,995
Internet Income	$323	$323	$262	$461	$611	$1,222	$1,327	$1,349	$1,353	$1,666	$1,920	$2,040
Total Income	*$90,149*	*$120,794*	*$126,609*	*$195,843*	*$134,425*	*$120,806*	*$108,833*	*$145,778*	*$155,406*	*$147,242*	*$138,963*	*$48,035*
EXPENSES												
Cost of Goods	$45,067	$45,667	$60,630	$63,010	$64,481	$67,010	$59,590	$54,029	$73,081	$79,100	$73,020	$31,072
Rent	$11,543	$8,923	$8,923	$8,923	$8,923	$8,923	$8,923	$8,923	$8,923	$8,923	$8,923	$8,923
Salaries	$19,094	$15,234	$15,234	$15,234	$15,234	$15,234	$15,234	$15,234	$15,234	$15,234	$15,234	$15,234
Taxes	$1,204	$1,094	$1,094	$1,094	$1,094	$1,094	$1,094	$1,094	$1,094	$1,094	$1,094	$1,094
Supplies	$2,050	$2,050	$2,050	$2,050	$2,050	$2,050	$2,050	$2,050	$2,050	$2,050	$2,050	$2,050
Repairs	$2,073	$2,073	$2,073	$2,073	$2,073	$2,073	$2,073	$2,073	$2,073	$2,073	$2,073	$2,073
Advertising	$6,339	$8,905	$12,047	$12,635	$19,536	$13,361	$11,958	$10,751	$14,443	$15,405	$14,350	$13,704
Insurance	$734	$734	$734	$734	$734	$734	$734	$734	$734	$734	$734	$734
Utilities	$2,345	$2,345	$2,345	$2,345	$2,345	$2,345	$2,345	$2,345	$2,345	$2,345	$2,345	$2,345
Emp. Benefits	$1,234	$1,234	$1,234	$1,234	$1,234	$1,234	$1,234	$1,234	$1,234	$1,234	$1,234	$1,234
Dues, Subscription	$254	$254	$254	$254	$254	$254	$254	$254	$254	$254	$254	$254
Travel	$1,432	$1,432	$1,432	$1,432	$1,432	$1,432	$1,432	$1,432	$1,432	$1,432	$1,432	$1,432
Miscellaneous	$500	$500	$500	$500	$500	$500	$500	$500	$500	$500	$500	$500
Total Expenses	*$98,269*	*$91,522*	*$109,350*	*$112,317*	*$120,491*	*$117,064*	*$108,221*	*$101,452*	*$124,197*	*$151,179*	*$124,251*	*$118,097*
Net Income	($5,121)	$29,271	$17,258	$81,526	$13,934	$2,942	$611	$44,325	$31,210	$16,063	$14,712	$29,938
Net Cash on Hand	$34,079	$64,151	$101,409	$162,935	$176,866	$179,810	$180,421	$224,747	$255,956	$272,039	$286,751	$316,689

Figure 7.6: *Cash-Flow Analysis worksheet.*

Cash Flow Analysis

	A	B	C
1			
2			
3			
4			
5			
6			
7		29586	29617
8			
9	CASH ON HAND	43000	=B37
10			
11	INCOME		
12	Sale of Goods	83394	110237
13	Sale of Services	6432	10234
14	Total Sales	=B12+B13	=C12+C13
15	Interest Income	=($L$3/12)*B9	=($L$3/12)*B9
16		----------	----------
17	*Total Income*	=B14+B15	=C14+C15
18			
19	EXPENSES		
20	Cost of Goods	=$L$4*B12	=$L$4*B12
21	Rent	11543	8923
22	Salaries	19894	15234
23	Taxes	1204	1094
24	Supplies	2050	2050
25	Repairs	2873	2873
26	Advertising	=$L$5*B12	=0.1*B14
27	Insurance	734	734
28	Utilties	2345	2345
29	Emp. Benefits	1234	1234
30	Dues, Subscriptions	254	254
31	Travel	1432	1432
32	Miscellaneous	500	500
33		----------	----------
34	*Total Expenses*	=SUM(B20:B32)	=SUM(C20:C32)
35			
36	Net Income	=B17-B34	=C17-C34
37	Net Cash on Hand	=B9+B36	=C9+C36
38			

Figure 7.7: *Formulas and data for the Cash-Flow Analysis worksheet.*

WIDGET MANUFACTURING
CASH-FLOW ANALYSIS - 1985

Assumptions: Interest Rate 9%
Cost of Goods/Sale of Goods 0.35
Advertising/Sales 0.1

	Jan-85	Feb-85	Mar-85	Apr-85	May-85	Jun-85	Jul-85	Aug-85	Sep-85	Oct-85	Nov-85	Dec-85	Totals
CASH ON HAND	$43,000	$34,879	$64,151	$81,409	$162,935	$176,868	$179,810	$180,421	$224,747	$255,956	$272,039	$286,751	
INCOME													
Sale of Goods	$83,394	$110,237	$114,563	$117,239	$123,291	$108,345	$98,234	$132,874	$145,819	$132,764	$123,127	$131,872	$1,419,759
Sale of Services	$6,432	$10,234	$11,704	$76,123	$10,523	$11,239	$9,272	$11,555	$10,234	$12,812	$13,916	$14,123	$198,247
Total Sales	$89,826	$120,471	$126,347	$193,362	$133,814	$119,584	$107,506	$144,429	$154,053	$145,576	$137,043	$145,995	$1,618,006
Interest Income	$323	$323	$262	$481	$611	$1,222	$1,327	$1,349	$1,353	$1,666	$1,920	$2,040	$12,894
Total Income	$90,149	$120,794	$126,609	$193,843	$134,425	$120,806	$108,833	$145,778	$155,406	$147,242	$138,963	$148,035	$1,630,900
EXPENSES													
Cost of Goods	$45,867	$45,867	$60,630	$63,010	$64,481	$67,810	$59,590	$54,020	$73,061	$79,100	$73,020	$67,720	$754,205
Rent	$11,543	$8,923	$8,923	$8,923	$8,923	$8,923	$8,923	$8,923	$8,923	$8,923	$8,923	$8,923	$109,696
Salaries	$19,694	$15,234	$15,234	$15,234	$15,234	$15,234	$15,234	$15,234	$15,234	$15,234	$15,234	$15,234	$187,468
Taxes	$1,204	$1,094	$1,094	$1,094	$1,094	$1,094	$1,094	$1,094	$1,094	$1,094	$1,094	$1,094	$13,238
Supplies	$2,050	$2,050	$2,050	$2,050	$2,050	$2,050	$2,050	$2,050	$2,050	$2,050	$2,050	$2,050	$24,600
Repairs	$2,873	$2,873	$2,873	$2,873	$2,873	$2,873	$2,873	$2,873	$2,873	$2,873	$2,873	$2,873	$34,476
Advertising	$8,339	$8,983	$12,047	$12,635	$19,336	$13,381	$11,958	$10,751	$14,443	$15,405	$14,558	$13,704	$155,541
Insurance	$734	$734	$734	$734	$734	$734	$734	$734	$734	$734	$734	$734	$8,808
Utilities	$2,345	$2,345	$2,345	$2,345	$2,345	$2,345	$2,345	$2,345	$2,345	$2,345	$2,345	$2,345	$28,140
Emp. Benefits	$1,234	$1,234	$1,234	$1,234	$1,234	$1,234	$1,234	$1,234	$1,234	$1,234	$1,234	$1,234	$14,808
Dues, Subscription	$254	$254	$254	$254	$254	$254	$254	$254	$254	$254	$254	$254	$3,048
Travel	$1,432	$1,432	$1,432	$1,432	$1,432	$1,432	$1,432	$1,432	$1,432	$1,432	$1,432	$1,432	$17,184
Miscellaneous	$500	$500	$500	$500	$500	$500	$500	$500	$500	$500	$500	$500	$6,000
Total Expenses	$98,269	$91,522	$109,350	$112,317	$120,491	$117,864	$108,221	$101,452	$124,197	$131,179	$124,251	$118,097	$1,357,211
Net Income	($8,121)	$29,271	$17,259	$81,526	$13,934	$2,942	$611	$44,325	$31,210	$16,083	$14,712	$29,938	$273,689
Net Cash on Hand	$34,879	$64,151	$81,409	$162,935	$176,868	$179,810	$180,421	$224,747	$255,956	$272,039	$286,751	$316,689	

Figure 7.8: *Final printout of the Cash-Flow Analysis worksheet.*

Note: | The concept of absolute and relative cell addressing is discussed in Chapter 8. This example will be used again in that chapter. For the moment, it is only necessary to enter the equations as indicated.

Creating Panes

When you try to enter the data and formulas for this worksheet, you will quickly discover a difficulty. Entering the data for the first few months is easy, but what happens when you try to enter the data for a later part of the year? As Figure 7.9 shows, you no longer see the row headings. What happens when you enter the last part of the data for any particular month? You will not be able to see the column headings. With Excel, you can solve this problem by splitting the window into panes. Panes let you view two parts of the same worksheet and scroll them together.

You can experiment with your Balance worksheet. After you open that worksheet, place the cursor on the small black box in the lower left (the cursor will change into the shape of two vertical bars) and

 File   Edit   Formula   Format   .Data   Options   Macro   Window

| B7 | | 29586 | | | | |

Cash Flow Analysis

	B	C	D	E	F	G
14	$89,826	$120,471	$126,347	$193,362	$133,814	$119,584
15	$323	$323	$262	$481	$611	$1,222
16	--------	---------	---------	---------	---------	---------
17	*$90,149*	*$120,794*	*$126,609*	*$193,843*	*$134,425*	*$120,806*
18						
19						
20	$45,867	$45,867	$60,630	$63,010	$64,481	$67,810
21	$11,543	$8,923	$8,923	$8,923	$8,923	$8,923
22	$19,894	$15,234	$15,234	$15,234	$15,234	$15,234
23	$1,204	$1,094	$1,094	$1,094	$1,094	$1,094
24	$2,050	$2,050	$2,050	$2,050	$2,050	$2,050
25	$2,873	$2,873	$2,873	$2,873	$2,873	$2,873
26	$8,339	$8,983	$12,047	$12,635	$19,336	$13,381
27	$734	$734	$734	$734	$734	$734
28	$2,345	$2,345	$2,345	$2,345	$2,345	$2,345
29	$1,234	$1,234	$1,234	$1,234	$1,234	$1,234
30	$254	$254	$254	$254	$254	$254
31	$1,432	$1,432	$1,432	$1,432	$1,432	$1,432
32	$500	$500	$500	$500	$500	$500
33	--------	---------	---------	---------	---------	---------

Figure 7.9: *The Cash-Flow Analysis worksheet without panes.*

drag it to the right until this split bar is between columns A and B. Release the mouse button.

You now have two panes in a single window. Each pane has its own horizontal scroll bar, but there is only one vertical scroll bar. Leave the left pane as it is, and scroll the right pane so that only the four columns for each of the four quarters are visible, as shown in Figure 7.10. Now scroll vertically until the row with the column headings is at the top of the window.

Now you can create four panes. Split the window again by placing the cursor on the small black box at the top of the vertical scroll bar and dragging it down so that the new horizontal pane separation is just under the top row that displays the column headings. Release the mouse button. Scroll the lower right pane one row so that the columns are shown only once, as shown in Figure 7.11.

Now there are four panes. The only pane that you will have to scroll for data entry is in the lower right. Scroll this vertically and horizontally, and you will see that the headings for both the rows and columns are always displayed in the adjacent panes as you enter data into the pane in the lower right.

** File   Edit   Formula   Format   Data   Options   Macro   Window**

C14

Balance

	A	B	C	D	E
12		- - - - - - - - -	- - - - - - - - -	- - - - - - - - -	- - - -
13	*Total Current Assets*	*$75,753*	*$99,974*	*$127,832*	*$152*
14					
15	Fixed Assets				
16	P,P, and E				
17	Furniture, Fixtures	$12,100	$12,100	$12,100	$1
18	Equipment	$6,500	$16,600	$21,100	$4
19	Office Equipment	$4,100	$4,100	$4,100	$
20		- - - - - - - - -	- - - - - - - - -	- - - - - - - - -	- - - -
21	Gross P, P, and E	$22,700	$32,800	$37,300	$5
22	Accumulated Depreciation	$6,600	$8,700	$11,400	$1
23		- - - - - - - - -	- - - - - - - - -	- - - - - - - - -	- - - -
24	*Total Fixed Assets*	*$16,100*	*$24,100*	*$25,900*	*$45*
25					
26	*Total Assets*	*$91,853*	*$124,074*	*$153,732*	*$207,*
27					
28	Current Liabilities				
29	Accounts Payable	$17,340	$41,000	$42,300	$7
30	Income Taxes Payable	$4,043	$6,132	$7,301	$

Figure 7.10: *The Balance worksheet with two panes.*

Now look at Figure 7.12. This shows how the use of panes can help you to work with the Cash-Flow Analysis worksheet. By using panes, you can "lock" column and row headings, which permits you to scroll around the rest of the worksheet while the row and column headings remain displayed.

You can select a cell in any pane and enter new data. The corresponding cells in the other panes will also show the new data. Remember that you are looking at only a single window.

The black bars in the scroll boxes that separate the panes are called *split bars*. You can close any pane by dragging the split bar. In our Balance worksheet example, dragging the lower split bar all the way back to the left closes both of the left panes. Dragging the split bar in the right scroll bar back to the top closes the top panes.

Quitting Excel

When you wish to exit Excel, pull down the File menu and click Quit. You will see the dialog box shown in Figure 7.13, asking whether you want to save your changes. Click Yes if you wish to

⬛ File Edit Formula Format Data Options Macro Window				
C14				

	A	B	C	D	E
		Qtr 1	Qtr 2	Qtr 3	Qtr
6					
7					
8	Current Assets				
9	Cash	$28,653	$42,894	$64,882	$9
10	Accounts Receivable	$35,700	$44,150	$48,450	$5!
11	Inventory	$11,400	$12,930	$14,500	$1(
12					
13	*Total Current Assets*	*$75,753*	*$99,974*	*$127,832*	*$16.*
14					
15	Fixed Assets				
16	P,P, and E				
17	Furniture, Fixtures	$12,100	$12,100	$12,100	$1.
18	Equipment	$6,500	$16,600	$21,100	$4.
19	Office Equipment	$4,100	$4,100	$4,100	$.
20					
21	Gross P, P, and E	$22,700	$32,800	$37,300	$5!
22	Accumulated Depreciation	$6,600	$8,700	$11,400	$1.
23					
24	*Total Fixed Assets*	*$16,100*	*$24,100*	*$25,900*	*$4!*

Figure 7.11: *The Balance worksheet with four panes.*

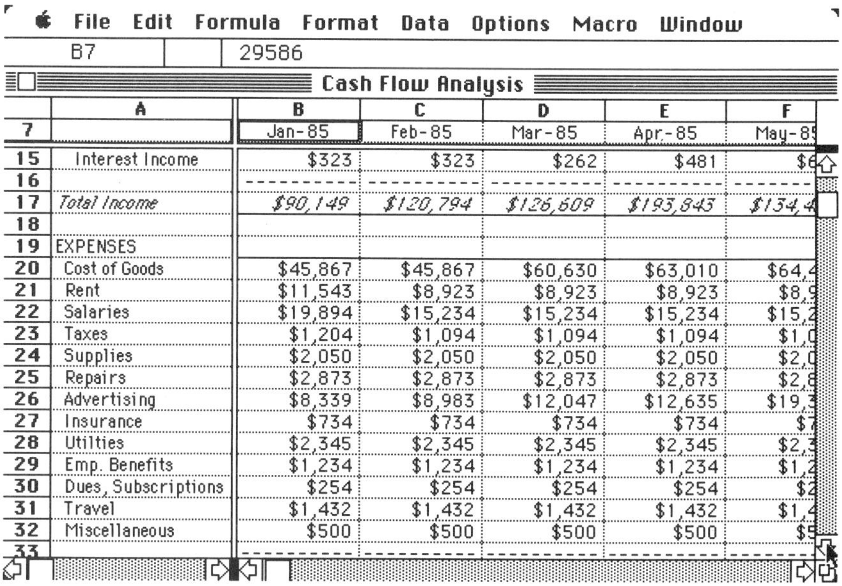

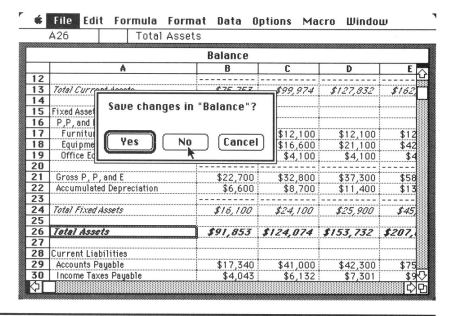

Figure 7.12: *The Cash-Flow Analysis worksheet with panes.*

Figure 7.13: *Quitting Excel*

save them; click No if you want the document to revert back to how it was before you changed it. Excel will then quit, saving the changes if that is what you requested. Once the disk windows are displayed, the easiest way to end your session is to pull down the Special menu and click Shut Down. This will complete your exit and eject the disks.

Summary

You have now learned the basics of creating and using worksheets. By now, you should be opening and closing worksheet windows with confidence. You've also learned how to split windows, open multiple windows, and how to create panes to simplify entering data into large worksheets.

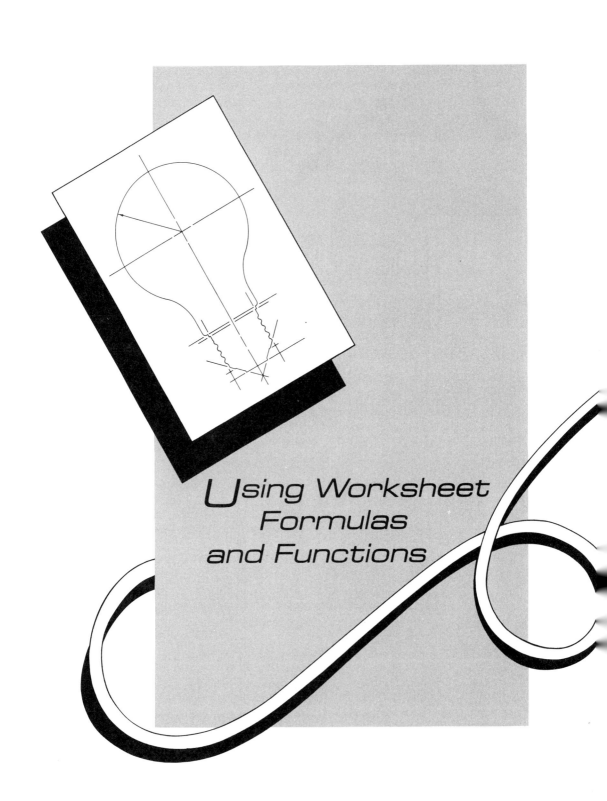

Using Worksheet
Formulas
and Functions

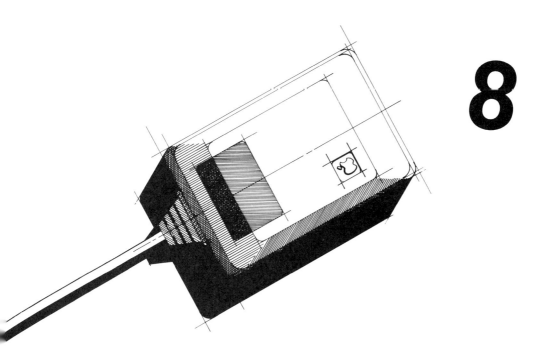

8

Functions are abbreviations of formulas that enable you quickly to perform a task that would take much longer (or could not be done at all) using other operations. Excel provides a total of 86 functions. In most worksheets, you will want to use one or more of these functions to calculate cell values.

In this chapter, you will use some of Excel's functions to create a very useful amortization schedule. Amortizing something means, literally, to put it to death. That is what you do when you pay off a car loan or house mortgage. In amortizing a loan, you make a series of equal payments for a fixed period of time. During this time, however, the proportion that you pay for the principle increases while the proportion that you pay for the interest decreases. If you are purchasing anything on credit, you may need consistently to evaluate your loan to calculate your taxes or to plan for refinancing. In this chapter, you will learn how Excel can help you to perform this evaluation.

However, before you can use this example and Excel's functions, you need to understand some of the basics of cell addressing and how functions work. The first part of this chapter provides that information. After the example, you will find an overview of all of Excel's functions and a summary of how to use each one.

Cell Addressing

With formulas and functions, you can use either relative, mixed, or absolute cell addressing. In the example in this chapter, you will use all three kinds of cell addressing.

Relative Cell Addressing

The Income worksheet that you created in Chapter 3 and the Balance worksheet that you created in Chapters 4 through 6 both used *relative cell addressing.* In Chapter 3, you created the following formula for cell B8:

= (B5 + B6)

What you really stored in cell B8 was a formula that said "Add the value of the cell three cells up to the value of the cell two cells up." This is why you could copy the formula to other cells and it would still work correctly. Relative cell addresses store references to other cells by their position in relation to the active cell.

You can enter relative cell addresses into formulas by typing them in from the keyboard or by clicking the appropriate cells on the worksheet.

Absolute Cell Addressing

There may be times when you want to store a reference in a cell that will not change with a copy, move, or fill operation. In other words, if you used B5 as a part of a formula and then copied it into another cell, it should still be B5 in the formula in that cell. The concept of using a specific cell reference that does not change as a part of a formula or function is called *absolute cell addressing.*

To indicate this kind of addressing, you must insert a dollar sign before both the row and column designators of the referenced cell, as in:

= $B$5 + $B$6

If you copied, moved, or filled this formula, cells B5 and B6 would still be referenced in the new cell. Absolute cell references must always be entered from the keyboard.

The Cash-Flow Analysis worksheet example in the last chapter, shown in Figure 7.6, uses absolute cell addressing. Near the title, in column L, is a list of assumed parameters that were used in computing the project interest, cost of goods, and advertising costs. The formulas in column C used these parameters. When these formulas were copied into the remainder of the row, it was important that the referenced cells in column L were not changed during the fill or copy operation. Thus, these formulas used absolute cell references—advertising costs, for example, in column C were $L$6*B13. This makes it easy to change the parameter values and see how the entire worksheet is affected. (Column B, however, could not contain these formulas, as each formula references a previous month.)

Mixed Cell Addressing

There may be times when you need to use a combination of absolute and relative cell addressing in a single cell reference. Excel allows you to make either the row or column relative and the other absolute. For examples, B$5 refers to a relative column B and an absolute row 5, and $B5 refers to an absolute column B and a relative row 5. This is called *mixed cell addressing.* Mixed cell references must always be entered from the keyboard.

What Is a Function?

A *function* is an abbreviation of a formula. Functions provide a quick way to calculate the value of a cell that would otherwise use a long formula. In some cases, functions allow you to perform calculations that could not be done at all using formulas. For example, in your Income worksheet of Chapter 3, you used the following formula for cell B8:

= (B5 + B6)

Now suppose that you wanted to use a total that was the sum of many cells, for example:

= (B5 + B6 + B7 + B8 + B9)

You can imagine that it would be difficult to get the entire formula into the cell. Instead, you could use the SUM function and specify a range of cells as the input of the function:

= SUM(B5:B9)

See how much shorter the entry has become?

You can try this now with your Income worksheet. Enter **=SUM(B5:B6)** from the keyboard as the formula for cell B8. You will get the same answer as you did before. The new formula, which uses a function, can be copied or filled into cells C8 and D8, just as you did with the earlier formula. Try it.

You can also use any of the reference operators (see Chapter 4) in defining the input for a function. For example, another way to define the formula for cell B8 is **=SUM(B5,B6)**. This would store the sum of cells B5 and B6 in cell B8.

Instead of cell references in a formula, you can use a constant value of the same type as the cell referenced. For example, B8=SUM(100+B5) would store the value of the contents of cell B5 plus 100 in cell B8.

Function Arguments

Arguments are values that are used as the input to a function to calculate the value of the function. With the SUM function, for example, you can have as many as 14 cells or cell ranges as arguments for the function. The number of arguments used by a particular function depends on the function. Some functions do not use any arguments.

Each function expects each of its arguments to be of a certain type. For example, the SUM function expects all its arguments to be numeric. There are ten argument types that can be used by Excel functions. These are listed in Table 8.1.

The arguments of an Excel function must be in a certain order, which is determined by the function. The appropriate ordering of arguments for each function is listed at the end of this chapter. You cannot change the order of the arguments. Be sure to check the appropriate order because the order of the arguments in an Excel function may be different than the order of the arguments of the same function in other worksheet programs, such as Lotus 1-2-3.

Using Functions

Figure 8.1 shows an example worksheet that you can use to experiment with functions. In this example, $8,000.00 is borrowed at 9%

interest, and Excel is used to calculate the monthly payments, the total amount paid, and the amortization schedule. This example makes extensive use of both the PMT (periodic payment) and PV (present value) functions, which are used frequently for financial analyses. Once you create the worksheet, you can change the amount borrowed, the interest, and the term to see how it affects the schedule. This makes the example much more than a simple

Argument	Definition
Number	Anything that produces a number: numeric value, numeric formula, or a reference to a cell with a numeric value
Numbers	Anything that produces one or more numbers
Text	Anything that produces text: text, a text formula, or a reference to a cell containing text
Logical	Anything that produces a logical value
Logicals	Anything that produces one or more logical values
Ref	Anything that produces a reference
Value	Anything that produces a value
Values	Anything that produces one or more values
Array	Anything that produces an array
Vector	Anything that produces a one-dimensional array

Note: Text arguments must be enclosed in quotation marks.

Table 8.1: *Types of Excel Arguments*

tutorial—you can save it and use it to calculate the schedule whenever you purchase something on credit.

Note that the data-entry area for the user, marked in the upper left of the worksheet, consists of only three cells: B6, B7, and B8. Normally, you would want the rest of the worksheet protected so that users can only change these three cells (worksheet protection is described in Chapter 13). The user enters values into these cells, and Excel automatically calculates all the values on the remainder of the worksheet.

Begin creating the Amortization worksheet by entering the titles in cells C1 and C2. Create the data-entry area in cells A5 through B8 and enter the input values shown in Figure 8.2 into this area. Remember to enter a percent sign each time that you insert a value

AMORTIZATION SCHEDULE BY MONTH
Amortization Payment Schedule by Month

```
************ ********** ************    **
Data Entry Area                         *        8/22/85
  Principle     $8,000.00               *        3:13 PM
  Interest          9.00%               *
  Term             48 Months            *
************ ********** ************    **
Payment:        $199.08
Total Paid    $9,555.86
```

Month	Beginning Balance	Ending Balance	Payment	Total Paid	Tot. Princ. Paid	Tot. Interest Paid
1	$8,000.00	$7,860.92	$199.08	$199.08	$139.08	$60.00
2	$7,860.92	$7,720.80	$199.08	$398.16	$279.20	$118.96
3	$7,720.80	$7,579.62	$199.08	$597.24	$420.38	$176.86
4	$7,579.62	$7,437.39	$199.08	$796.32	$562.61	$233.71
5	$7,437.39	$7,294.09	$199.08	$995.40	$705.91	$289.49
6	$7,294.09	$7,149.71	$199.08	$1,194.48	$850.29	$344.20
7	$7,149.71	$7,004.26	$199.08	$1,393.56	$995.74	$397.82
8	$7,004.26	$6,857.71	$199.08	$1,592.64	$1,142.29	$450.35
9	$6,857.71	$6,710.06	$199.08	$1,791.72	$1,289.94	$501.78
10	$6,710.06	$6,561.31	$199.08	$1,990.80	$1,438.69	$552.11
11	$6,561.31	$6,411.44	$199.08	$2,189.88	$1,588.56	$601.32
12	$6,411.44	$6,260.44	$199.08	$2,388.96	$1,739.56	$649.40
13	$6,260.44	$6,108.31	$199.08	$2,588.04	$1,891.69	$696.36
14	$6,108.31	$5,955.05	$199.08	$2,787.12	$2,044.95	$742.17
15	$5,955.05	$5,800.63	$199.08	$2,986.21	$2,199.37	$786.83
16	$5,800.63	$5,645.05	$199.08	$3,185.29	$2,354.95	$830.34
17	$5,645.05	$5,488.31	$199.08	$3,384.37	$2,511.69	$872.68
18	$5,488.31	$5,330.39	$199.08	$3,583.45	$2,669.61	$913.84
19	$5,330.39	$5,171.29	$199.08	$3,782.53	$2,828.71	$953.82
20	$5,171.29	$5,010.99	$199.08	$3,981.61	$2,989.01	$992.60
21	$5,010.99	$4,849.50	$199.08	$4,180.69	$3,150.50	$1,030.18
22	$4,849.50	$4,686.79	$199.08	$4,379.77	$3,313.21	$1,066.55
23	$4,686.79	$4,522.86	$199.08	$4,578.85	$3,477.14	$1,101.71
24	$4,522.86	$4,357.70	$199.08	$4,777.93	$3,642.30	$1,135.63

Figure 8.1: *The Amortization worksheet.*

for cell B7 so that Excel will calculate the schedule with the cell value as a percent.

Enter **Payment:** into cell A10 and **Total Paid** into cell A11. Use the following formulas and functions below the data-entry area:

Cell	Entry
B10	= PMT($B$7/12,$B$8, – $B$6)
B11	= ($B$8 * $B$10)

Note: | If you have been using Lotus 1-2-3, you will notice that the order of the arguments in Excel is slightly different from the Lotus convention. Excel's financial functions follow the HP-12C Financial Calculator's conventions.

Now, enter the column headings into cells A13 through G14. Then, enter the month numbers into column A.

   File Edit Formula Format Data Options Macro Window

E8

Amortization

	A	B	C	D	E
1			AMORTIZATION SCHEDULE BY MONTH		
2			*Amortization Payment Schedule by Month*		
3					
4	************	**********	***********	**	
5	Data Entry Area			*	8/6/85
6	Principle	$8,000.00		*	9:17 AM
7	Interest	9.00%		*	
8	Term	48	Months	*	
9	************	**********	**********	**	
10	Payment:	$199.08			
11	Total Paid	$9,555.86			
12					
13	Month	Beginning	Ending	Payment	Total Paid	Tot.
14		Balance	Balance			P
15	1	$8,000.00	$7,860.92	$199.08	$199.08
16	2	$7,860.92	$7,720.80	$199.08	$398.16
17	3	$7,720.80	$7,579.62	$199.08	$597.24
18	4	$7,579.62	$7,437.39	$199.08	$796.32
19	5	$7,437.39	$7,294.09	$199.08	$995.40

Figure 8.2: *Creating the Amortization Schedule worksheet.*

Tip:

Chapter 13 describes a quick way to enter the month numbers into column A by using the Series command. Here is a summary if you wish to use this method now: (1) enter **1** into cell A15; (2) select cell A15, pull down the Formula menu, and click Goto; (3) enter A62 into the Reference box, hold down the Shift key, and click OK; (4) pull down the Data menu, click Series, and click OK.

Enter these formulas for the values for the first row:

Cell	Entry
B15	= $B$6
C15	= PV($B$7/12,($B$8 − A15), − $B$10)
D15	= $B$10
E15	= D15
F15	= B15 − C15
G15	= E15 − F15

Enter the following into the second row:

Cell	Entry
B16	= C15
E16	= E15 + D16
F16	= F15 + B16 − C16

Now, you can have Excel calculate the remainder of the amortization schedule by using the Fill Down command on the Edit menu for each column except the first. For columns B, E, and F, you will need to fill from the second row down. On the remaining rows, fill from the first row down. The resulting values should be the same as those shown in Figure 8.1.

Format the worksheet, set up the alignments, and set the styles for the titles, as shown in Figure 8.1. Refer to Chapter 6 if you need help. Now, do one more thing: add a date and time stamp. To do this, add the following function entry into *both* cells E5 and E6:

= NOW( )

Use the Number command on the Format menu to change the format of cell E5 to m/d/yy and the format of cell E6 to h:mm AM/PM. Now, each time that you update the worksheet, the date and time on the worksheet will be updated automatically (if you don't want the date and time to be updated, see the explanation of how to prevent this in Chapter 13).

The NOW function that you used to calculate the date and time is described in the section on date functions later in this chapter. The PMT and PV functions that you used earlier are described in the section on financial functions.

Once you have set up the worksheet, save it using the name **Amortization.** Then, prepare for printing a copy by pulling down the File menu, clicking Page Setup, and setting the Printout Orientation to Sideways. Now, print out the Amortization worksheet.

You can try changing any of the values in the data-entry area to see what happens to the amortization schedule. Remember to use the percent sign when you enter a different interest rate. Notice that Excel calculates the entire schedule in only a few seconds.

This is a rather valuable worksheet. Save it for calculating the schedule whenever you purchase something on credit—a house, automobile, computer, or whatever. It calculates the proper interest for income-tax purposes, as well as giving you the status of the principle in case you wish to refinance a loan.

If you are the adventurous type, you can try to create a pie chart from your Amortization worksheet showing the relative percentages paid of principle and interest on a 48-month loan. Select only cells F62 and G62, which contain the final totals. Pull down the File menu, click New, and then double-click Chart. Use the Gallery menu to change the bar chart that was automatically created into a pie chart. Change the interest on the worksheet, and watch the chart change. If you get stuck, refer to Chapter 10.

Types of Functions

There are 86 functions available to the Excel user. These can be classified in nine types: mathematical, statistical, database, trigonometric, logical, text, financial, date, and special-purpose. Each function is described by type in the remainder of this chapter.

Mathematical Functions

The following are Excel's mathematical functions:

Function	Description
ABS(*number*)	Returns the value of *number*.
EXP(*number*)	Returns e raised to the power of *number*. EXP is the reverse of the *LN* (natural logarithm) function. To calculate the power to other bases, use the exponentiation operator.
INT(*number*)	Returns the largest integer less than or equal to *number*. Example: INT(7.6) is 7.
LN(*number*)	Returns the natural logarithm of *number*. *Number* must be positive. LN is the inverse of EXP.
LOG10(*number*)	Returns the base 10 logarithm of *number*.
MOD(*number, divisor number*)	Returns the remainder after *number* is divided by *divisor number*. The result has the same sign as *divisor number*.
PI( )	Returns the value of pi. There is no argument.
RAND( )	Returns a random number between 0 and 0.999. The value will change each time that the worksheet is recalculated. There is no argument.
ROUND(*number, number of digits*)	Returns *number* rounded to *number of digits*.
SIGN(*number*)	Returns 1 if *number* is positive, 0 if *number* is 0, and -1 if *number* is negative.
SQRT(*number*)	Returns the square root of *number*. *Number* must be positive.

Statistical Functions

Excel has the following statistical functions:

Function	Description
AVERAGE(*numbers 1, numbers 2, . . .*)	Returns the average of the numeric arguments.
COUNT(*numbers 1, numbers 2, . . .*)	Returns the number of numbers in a list of arguments. Example: COUNT(A1:A5,A8) equals 6.
GROWTH(*Y array, X array, x array*)	Returns an array with the y values as the exponential curve of regression y = b*m^x for two variables represented by *X array* and *Y array.*
LINEST(*Y array, X array*)	Returns the horizontal array of two elements, the slope and y intercept of the line of regression for y = mx + b for two variables X and Y represented by *X array* and *Y array.*
LOGEST(*Y array, X array*)	Returns a horizontal array of two elements, the parameters of m and b in the exponential curve of regression y = b*m^x for two variables represented by *X array* and *Y array.*
MAX(*numbers 1, numbers 2, . . .*)	Returns the largest number in a list of arguments.
MIN(*numbers 1, numbers 2, . . .*)	Returns the minimum number in a list of arguments.
STDEV(*numbers 1, numbers 2, . . .*)	Returns the standard deviation of the numbers in a list of arguments.
SUM(*numbers 1, numbers 2, . . .*)	Returns the sum of the numbers in a list of arguments.
TREND(*Y array, X array, x array*)	Returns an array, the y values on the line of regression, y = mx + b, for the two variables X and Y represented by *X array* and *Y array.*

VAR(*numbers 1, numbers 2, . . .*)	Returns the variance of the numbers in the list of arguments.

Database Functions

The following are Excel's database functions:

Function	Description
DAVERAGE(*database, field name, criteria*)	Returns the average of the numbers in a particular field of the database records that meet the specified criteria.
DCOUNT(*database, field name, criteria*)	Returns the count of the numbers in a particular field of a database that meet the specified criteria.
DMAX(*database, field name, criteria*)	Returns the maximum of the numbers in a particular field of a database that meet the specified criteria.
DMIN(*database, field name, criteria*)	Returns the minimum of the numbers in a particular field of a database that meet the specified criteria.
DSTDEV(*database, field name, criteria*)	Returns the standard deviation of the numbers in a particular field of a database that meet the specified criteria.
DSUM(*database, field name, criteria*)	Returns the sum of the numbers in a particular field of a database that meet the specified criteria.
DVAR(*database, field name, criteria*)	Returns the variance of the numbers in a particular field of a database that meet the specified criteria.

Trigonometric Functions

Excel has the following trigonometric functions:

Function	Description
ACOS(*number*)	Returns the arc cosine of *number.*

	The value is returned in radians. To convert to degrees, multiply by 180/PI( ).
ASIN(*number*)	Returns the arc sine of *number* (see ACOS).
ATAN(*number*)	Returns the arc tangent of *number* (see ACOS).
ATAN2(*x number, y number*)	Returns the arc tangent of *x number* and *y number*.
COS(*number*)	Returns the cosine of *number*.
SIN(*number*)	Returns the sine of *number*.
TAN(*number*)	Returns the tangent of *number*.

Logical Functions

The following are Excel's logical functions:

Function	Description
AND(*logicals 1, logicals 2, . . .*)	Returns TRUE if all logical values in the list of arguments are true. If any of the values are false, the function will return a value of FALSE.
CHOOSE(*index, value 1, value 2, . . .*)	Returns the value from the list of arguments based on the value of *index*. If *index* is 1, *value 1* is returned.
FALSE( )	Returns the value of FALSE. Useful as an argument in the CHOOSE function.
IF(*logical, value if true, value if false*)	Returns *value if true* if *logical* is TRUE, otherwise returns *value if false*.
ISERROR(*value*)	Returns TRUE if *value* is any Excel error value, otherwise returns FALSE.

ISNA(*value*)	Returns TRUE if *value* is #N/A, (not available—see Appendix D), otherwise returns FALSE.
ISREF(*value*)	Returns TRUE if *value* is a reference or reference formula, otherwise returns FALSE.
NOT(*logical*)	Returns FALSE if *logical* is TRUE, TRUE if *logical* is FALSE.
OR(*logicals 1, logicals 2, . . .*)	Returns TRUE if any of the logical values in the list of arguments is TRUE. If all logical values in the list are FALSE, it returns FALSE.
TRUE( )	Returns a logical value of TRUE. Used with CHOOSE function. There is no argument.

Text Functions

The following are Excel's text functions:

Function	Description
DOLLAR(*number, number of digits*)	Rounds *number* to *number of digits,* formats it to currency format, and returns a text result.
FIXED(*number, number of digits*)	Rounds *number* to *number of digits,* formats to a decimal format with commas, and returns a text result.
LEN(*text*)	Returns a number equal to the length of *text.*
MID(*text, start position, number of characters*)	Extracts *number of characters* from *text,* starting with *start position.*
REPT(*text, number of times*)	Repeats *text* for *number of times.*
TEXT(*number, format text*)	Formats *number* to *format text* and returns it as text.

| VALUE(*text*) | Converts *text* to a number. (Not necessary to use in a formula, as Excel converts it automatically if necessary.) |

Financial Functions

The following are Excel's financial functions:

Function	Description
FV(*rate, nper, pmt, pv, type*)	Returns the future value of an investment (see PV).
IRR(*values, guess*)	Returns internal rate of return of a series of cash flows, represented by values. *Guess* is an optional argument, specifying the starting point for the iteration. If *guess* is omitted, it is assumed to be 0.1 or 10%. *Values* should be an array or reference that contains numbers.
MIRR(*values, safe, risk*)	Returns a modified internal rate of return of a series of cash flows, represented by the numbers in *values*, given *safe* and *risk*. *Safe* is the rate returned by the investment that will finance the negative cash flows. *Risk* is the rate at which the positive cash flows can be reinvested.
NPER(*rate, pmt, pv, fv, type*)	Returns the number of periods of an investment involving constant cash flows (see PV).
NPV(*rate, values 1, values 2, . . .*)	Returns net present value of a series of future cash flows, represented by the numbers in the list of values, discounted at a constant interest rate specified by *rate*.
PMT(*rate, nper, pv, fv, type*)	Returns the periodic payment on an investment involving constant

cash flows (see PV and the example in this chapter).

PV(*rate, nper, pmt, fv, type*)	Returns the present value. The arguments are as follows:
	rate: interest rate per period
	nper: number of periods
	pmt: periodic payment
	fv: future value
	type: indicates whether payments occur at the beginning or end of the period. If *type* = 0, first payment is at the end of the first period. If *type* = 1, payment is at beginning. If argument is omitted, it is assumed to be 0.
RATE(*nper, pmt, pv, fv, type, guess*)	Returns the interest rate per period of an investment involving constant cash flows. (See PV.) *Guess* is an optional argument that specifies the starting value for the iteration. If omitted, it is assumed to be 0.1 or 10%.

The functions PV, FV, NPER, PMT, and RATE are all interrelated; you can calculate one given the value of the others. See the example in this chapter.

Date Functions

The following are Excel's date functions:

Function	Description
DATE(*year, month, day*)	Returns the serial number of the specified day.
DAY(*serial number*)	Converts *serial number* to the day of the month.
HOUR(*serial number*)	Converts *serial number* to an hour of the day.

MINUTE(*serial number*)	Converts *serial number* to a minute.
MONTH(*serial number*)	Converts *serial number* to a month of the year.
NOW( )	Returns the *serial number* of the current date and time. There is no argument.
SECOND(*serial number*)	Converts *serial number* to second.
TIME(*hour, minute, second*)	Returns the *serial number* for the specified time.
WEEKDAY(*serial number*)	Converts *serial number* to the day of the week.
YEAR(*serial number*)	Converts *serial number* to a year.

Special-Purpose Functions

Excel's special-purpose functions are the following:

Function	**Description**
AREAS(*ref*)	Returns the number of areas in *ref*. *Ref* can refer to multiple areas. Example: AREAS(A1:A5,B1) equals 2.
COLUMN(*ref*)	Returns the column number of *ref*. If *ref* is omitted, it returns the column number of the current cell. *Ref* cannot refer to multiple areas.
COLUMNS(*array*)	Returns the number of columns in *array*.
HLOOKUP(*lookup value, compare array, index number*)	Searches the first row of *compare array* for the largest value that is less than or equal to *lookup value*. The function moves down the column by the amount specified by *index number* and returns the value found there.

INDEX(*ref, row, column, area*)	Returns the cell that is defined in *ref* by row and column. If *ref* refers to multiple areas, *area* defines the areas from which the cell is to be obtained.
INDEX(*array, row, column*)	Returns the value of a single element within *array,* selected by *row* and *column.*
LOOKUP(*lookup value, compare vector, result vector*)	Searches *compare vector* for largest value less than or equal to *lookup value.* The function returns the corresponding value of *result vector.* The values in *compare vector* can be text, numbers, or logical, but they must be in ascending order. Microsoft recommends using this version of LOOKUP rather than the next one.
LOOKUP(*lookup value, compare array*)	Searches first row or column of *compare array* for largest value that is less than or equal to *lookup value.* The function returns the corresponding value in the last row or column of *compare array.* Whether the first row or column is searched depends on the size of the array. If it is square or has more rows than columns, LOOKUP searches the first column and gives a value from the corresponding last column. If there are more columns than rows, the first row is searched and LOOKUP gives the value of the corresponding cell in the last row. The values in the array can be text, numbers, or logical, but they must be in ascending order.
MATCH(*lookup value, compare vector, type*)	Returns the corresponding number of the comparison value in *compare vector* that matches *lookup*

	value. Example: If the look-up value matches the second comparison value, MATCH returns a 2.
NA( )	Returns the error value of #N/A (value not available—see Appendix D). There is no argument.
ROW(*ref*)	Returns the row number of *ref* if *ref* references a single cell. If *ref* refers to a range of cells, a vertical array is returned. If the argument is omitted, the row of the current cell is returned. ROW cannot refer to multiple areas.
ROWS(*array*)	Returns the number of rows in *array*.
TRANSPOSE(*array*)	Returns an array that is the transpose of *array*.
TYPE(*value*)	Returns a code defining the type of *value:* 1 for number, 2 for text, 4 for logical, and 16 for error.
VLOOKUP(*lookup value, compare array, index number*)	Identical to HLOOKUP, except that it searches the first column of *compare array*, moving right in that row by the amount specified by *index number*.

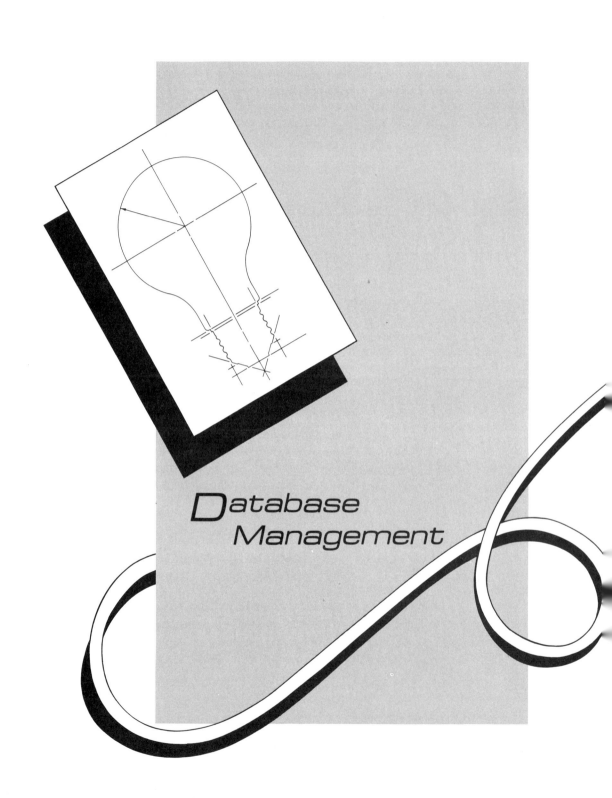

Database
Management

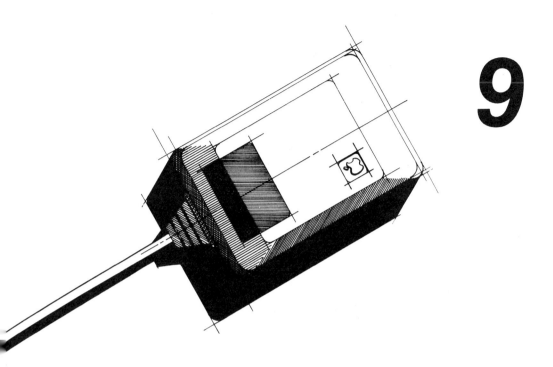

9

Excel can also be used for database management, which is useful when you need to rearrange the order of the data or to extract data based on certain criteria. Typical applications include mailing lists, prospect lists, and personnel registers.

Excel contains an on-screen database-management capability. That is, a database can be created as part of a worksheet and used to calculate cell values in other parts of the worksheet.

The first part of this chapter discusses the fundamentals of database management: applications for databases, database components, and how to work with your databases. In the second part of the chapter, you will create a database and extract specific information from it. In later chapters, this same database example will be used to create complex reports and charts.

On-Screen Database Management

The Excel on-screen database-management system can be viewed much like an electronic filing system for records. A record is a collection of data about a single item—a person, a product, an inventory part, an event—anything that you would like to store information about. You can store any number of pieces of information about each item. For an inventory part, for example, you might store the part number, a description, the cost, and the quantity on hand. The primary use of a database is to sort data in a particular order or to extract data that meet specific criteria.

Database Applications

You should be aware that databases created with Excel are different from databases created with single-application database-management systems, such as dBASE III or R:base 5000. In single-application database-management systems, data are stored on the disk and listed or extracted from the disk. The amount of data that can be stored in the database is limited only by the size of the disk storage. When you are working with Excel's database, *all* the database data are stored in the computer memory at the same time. As a result, the size of the database that you can create is limited by the amount of computer memory available. (When Excel is not in use, data are stored in a file on the disk, just as in a single-application system.) However, there is a benefit from the way Excel stores databases: Because the entire database is in memory, database operations are much faster than in comparable single-application products.

If you are working with an application in which the database is very large, you might wish to consider using an external database-management system to store the data and using Excel to manage a portion of the database. As an example, suppose that you are managing a pension fund for a company. You could keep the annual data for each employee in an Excel database and use an Excel worksheet to calculate the earnings for the year for each employee. After you've calculated the earnings for the year using Excel, you could transfer the results to an external database (using the procedure described in Chapter 20), which would store all the historical information and produce summary reports.

For many applications that involve relatively small databases, Excel's database-management system is ideal because of its ease of use, its capability to interface with worksheet data, and its fast response. Here are some typical applications for Excel's database:

- Financial: General ledgers and accounts-receivable and accounts-payable systems

- Sales and marketing: Contract management, sales projections, expense accounts, and prospect lists

- Business: Personnel registers, telephone-extension directories, inventory listings, low-inventory reports, and material-requirement planning

- Home: Cataloging of books, records, and tapes; nutrition analyses; mailing lists; and address management

Database Components

In Excel, a *database* is two or more rows of cells that span at least one column. Each row represents a single *record*. You can put as many as 16,383 records in an Excel database (the top row must be used for the field names).

Each piece of data that you store about an item is called a *field*. For an inventory part, the number, description, cost, and quantity on hand would each be fields. In the worksheet analogy, the records are rows and the fields are columns, as shown in Figure 9.1.

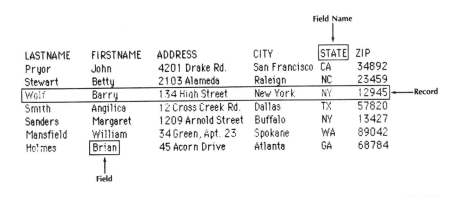

Figure 9.1: *The database components.*

Working with Databases

It is the fact that an on-screen database looks very much like a worksheet that makes the Excel database so easy to use. There are only two primary differences between the database and the worksheet: in a database, the rows no longer have a title and each of the columns (including the first) has a name that represents a field name.

The features and commands that are available for working with worksheets are the same as those available for databases. The menu bar at the top of the screen also remains the same. You can define any part of a worksheet for a database and use the remainder for worksheet functions, or you can define the entire worksheet as a database. You can add, edit, and delete items and fields in a database in the same way that you work with cells in a worksheet. You can move data from a database to somewhere else on the worksheet (or from somewhere else on the worksheet to the database) using the familiar Copy, Cut, and Paste commands.

A database can be sorted so that the rows are in any desired order. For example, a mailing list might be sorted in zip-code order to prepare some mailing labels, then sorted again alphabetically by names to print an alphabetical directory. You can also extract information based on a particular criterion; for example, from a mailing list, you could extract all the addresses that are local. In this chapter, you will learn how to create a database, sort it, and extract information based on particular criteria. Later, you will learn how you can link databases with worksheets or other databases, how to create charts from databases, and how to use macros to execute repetitive database operations.

Creating and Using a Database

Widget Manufacturing had a staff of sales representatives in four areas of the country. Each sales representative had a sales target, and the sum of the targets for the representatives in each area represented the sales target for that particular area. Widget also tracked sales performance by representative during each three-month cycle. These data were recorded in a database and used for a variety of reports. Management used these reports to track the sales performance of representatives and the performance of each sales area. The sales target for each of the sales representatives is shown in Figure 9.2. Notice that the records (rows) do not have titles, but each field (column), including the first, has a name.

Now, you can create the Sales Projections database. There are four steps involved in creating and using a database:

1. Defining the fields and entering the data

	A	B	C	D
1				
2				
3				
4				
5				
6				
7				
8				
9				
10				
11	LAST	FIRST	TARGET	REGION
12	Adams	Chuck	$118,000	South
13	Allen	Ellen	$90,000	East
14	Atkins	Lee	$113,000	East
15	Conners	Paul	$142,000	West
16	Ford	Carl	$191,000	Midwest
17	Glenn	John	$80,000	South
18	Harris	Ken	$176,000	West
19	Jackson	Robert	$112,000	East
20	Keller	Janet	$105,000	West
21	Kennedy	Sandra	$135,000	East
22	Linn	Vera	$80,000	Midwest
23	Parker	Greg	$196,000	South
24	Peterson	Tom	$98,000	Midwest
25	Stevens	Carla	$110,000	East
26	Ellis	Nancy	$122,000	East

Figure 9.2: *Widget sales targets.*

2. Defining the database range, which is that part of the worksheet that will be used as the database

3. Creating the criteria for the search

4. Searching the database for the desired records

Defining the Fields and Entering the Data

First, open a new worksheet for the database. Pull down the File menu and click New. You will see the New dialog box, as shown in Figure 9.3. Leave Worksheet selected (because a database is a part of a worksheet) and click OK. Excel displays an empty worksheet. Enter the records and field names shown in Figure 9.2. Start in row 11, as you will need some working space at the top later.

Defining the Database Range

Now, you must define the area of the worksheet that will serve as your database:

1. Click cell A11 and scroll to row 26.

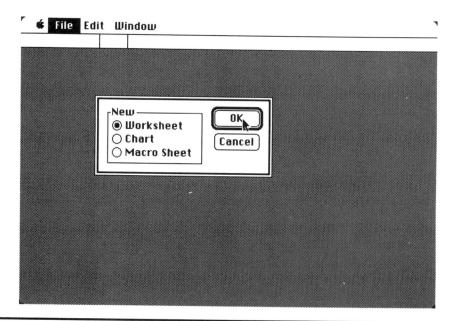

Figure 9.3: *Opening a worksheet window for a database.*

2. Hold down the Shift key and click cell D26. You have now selected the entire database area, including the field names.

3. Pull down the Data menu and click Set Database. This assigns the name Database to the worksheet area that you defined. (You can use the name Database in commands and in formulas, as described in Chapter 11.)

Defining the Criteria

The next step is to define the criteria for the database:

1. Click cell A11 and drag to cell D11.

2. Pull down the Edit menu, click Copy, and click cell A3.

3. Pull down the Edit menu and click Paste. The field names are now copied to a new area of the worksheet.

4. Under the word REGION (in cell D3), enter **West** into cell D4, as shown in Figure 9.4.

5. Click cell A3 and drag to cell D4. This defines the criteria area on the worksheet. You will enter all criteria for searches into this area.

6. Pull down the Data menu and click Set Criteria. This assigns the name Criteria to the worksheet area that you just defined. (You can use the name Criteria in formulas and commands, as described in Chapter 11.)

Finding Records Using the Criteria

Once the criteria are set, you can find any records that meet them. Pull down the Data menu and click Find. Excel will then display the first record in the database that meets the specified criterion, as shown in Figure 9.5. Notice that the scroll boxes have changed—they are now striped instead of white. The number of the record in the database is displayed in the upper left where the active-cell designator is normally displayed. The scroll arrows now permit you to move through the database to the next or previous record that meets the specified criterion. If you move the scroll box at the right all the way to the end of the scroll bar, Excel will display the last record in the database that matches the criterion.

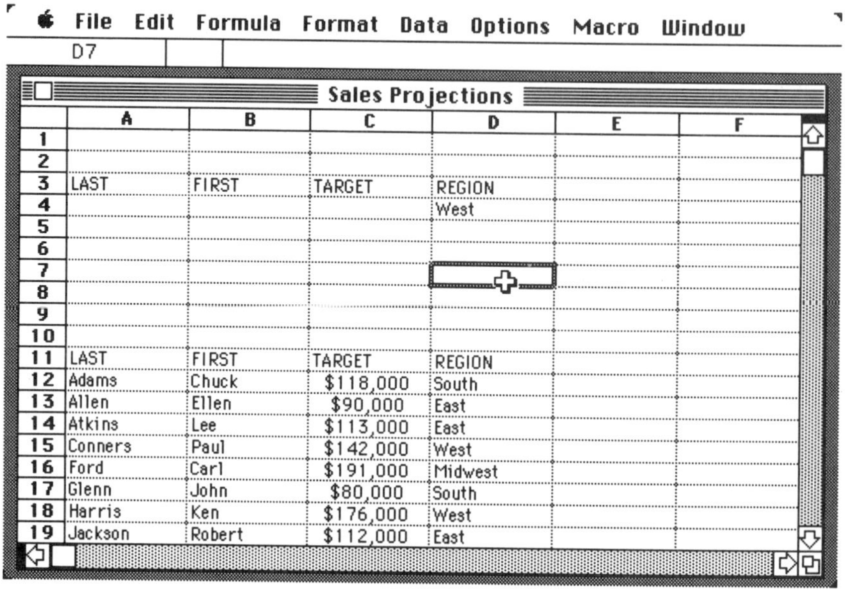

Figure 9.4: *Creating the criteria area.*

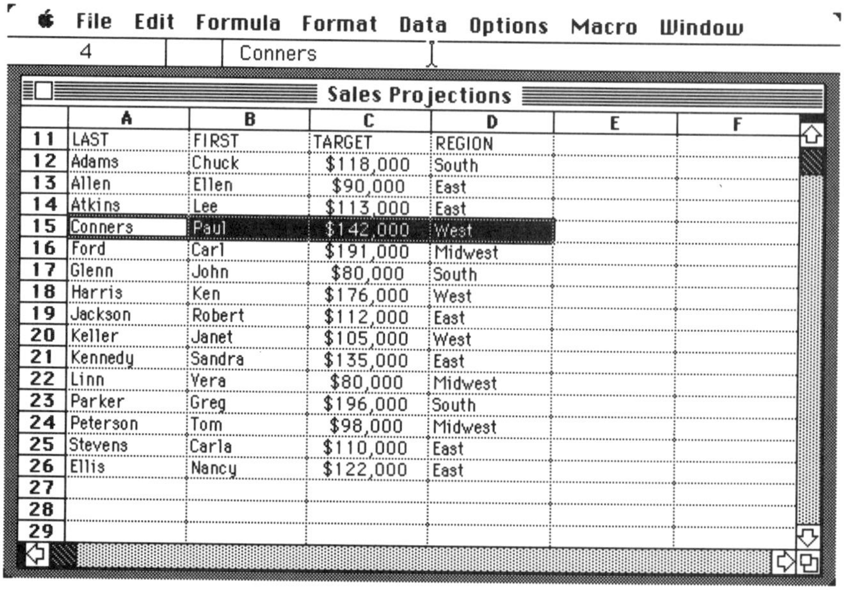

Figure 9.5: *Finding the first record matching the criterion.*

To exit the search, pull down the Data menu and click Exit Find. The scroll boxes return to normal. You can now specify another criterion and search the database again. Enter <**100000** in cell C4, leaving West in cell D4, and repeat the find operation. Notice that the two conditions are combined; you will find the first record where the region is West and the target is less then $100,000. It is not necessary to click Set Criteria again. As long as the cell range used for criteria entry is not changed, you can continue to repeat searches using other criteria.

Notice that you now have two areas on the worksheet: the database area and the criteria area. You can use the remainder of the worksheet for normal worksheet applications: formulas, text, or whatever you wish.

Creating criteria is discussed further at the end of this chapter.

Sorting the Database

You can sort a database by rows or columns, with up to three fields, called *keys,* controlling the sort. Each field can be used to sort in ascending or descending order.

Now, sort the Sales Projections database by region:

1. Select the range of cells A12 to D26. (This time, do not include the field names.)

2. Pull down the Data menu and click Sort. The Sort window shown in Figure 9.6 appears. This is actually a window, not just a dialog box, and it can be moved but not resized.

3. Click the title bar and move the window so that you can see cell D12.

4. Click cell D12 (to sort by region), and this cell reference will be entered into the Sort window as the first key. Click OK. The items are now sorted by region, as shown in Figure 9.7.

Tip:

You cannot undo a sort. If you think you might need to recover a sort, before you sort the database again, add a new field (column) that contains the database's record (row) numbers. After you've sorted the database again, you can easily recover the previous order by sorting the database using the record-number field as the key.

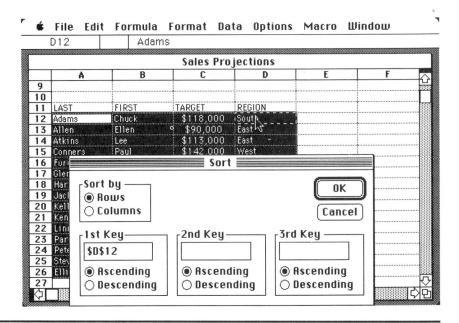

Figure 9.6: *The Sort window.*

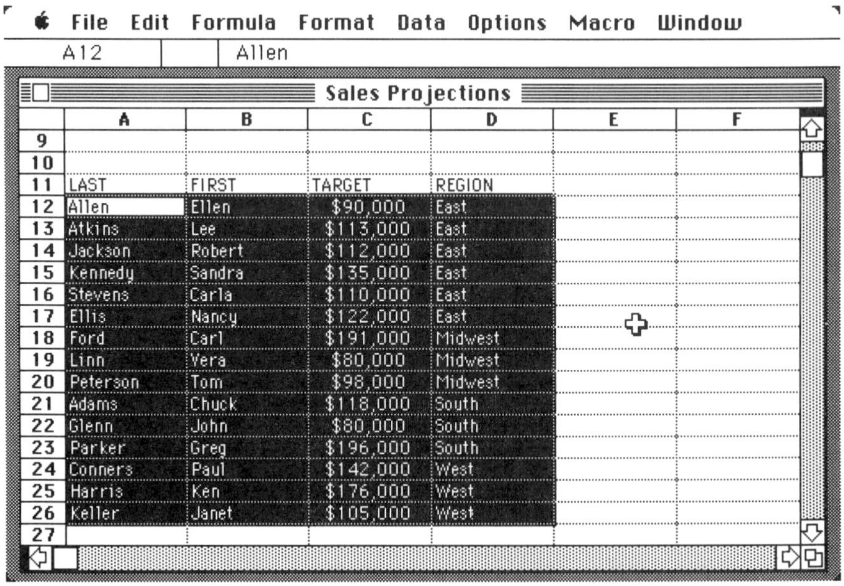

Figure 9.7: *The database after sorting.*

Using Database Functions

You use database functions in the same way that you use worksheet functions. Let's experiment with your Sales Projections database:

1. In the criteria area, enter **East** into cell D4. Be sure that cells A4, B4, and C4 are clear.

2. Click cell E6 to select it.

3. Pull down the Formula menu and click Paste Function.

4. The Paste Function dialog box shown in Figure 9.8 appears. Scroll this dialog box until DSUM() is displayed, then double-click this function. The function name is now entered into the formula bar with an equal sign before it, as shown in Figure 9.9. The cursor is in the formula bar, ready for you to enter the first argument.

5. Pull down the Formula menu and click Paste Name. When the Paste Name dialog box shown in Figure 9.10 appears, double-click Database (the name of your database). It is now entered into the formula bar.

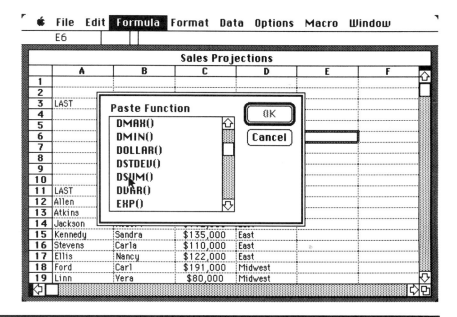

Figure 9.8: *Pasting a function name.*

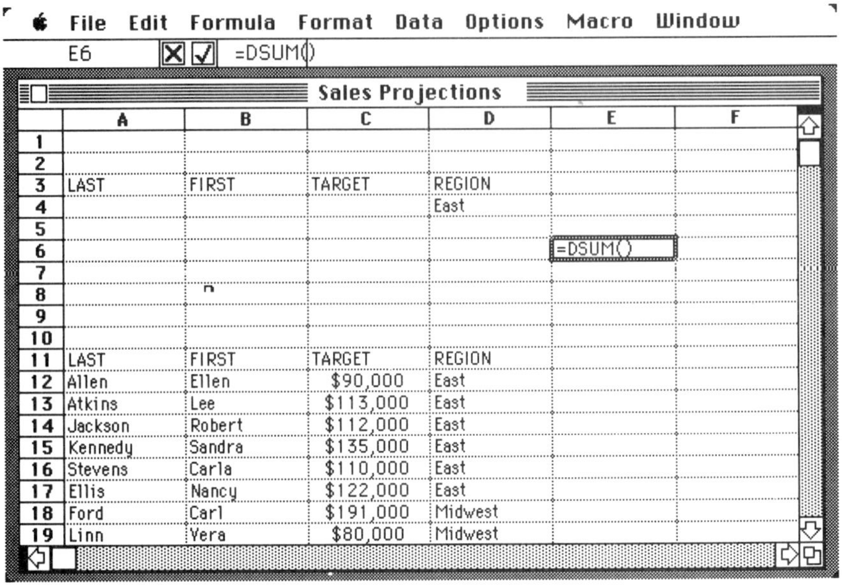

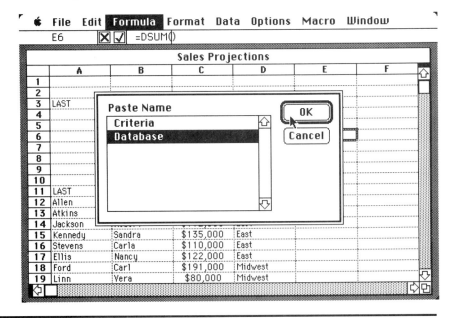

Figure 9.9: *Starting the formula entry.*

Figure 9.10: *Pasting a name.*

6. Type a comma, **"Target"** (with quotation marks), and another comma from the keyboard.

7. Pull down the Formula menu again and click Paste Name.

8. Double-click Criteria, and it is entered into the formula bar.

9. Click the enter box (check) to complete the entry.

You now have a complete formula:

= DSUM(Database,"Target",Criteria)

The sum of the eastern sales targets is now displayed in cell E6: 682,000. Enter **West** into cell D4, and the sum changes to 423,000, the sum of the western sales targets. You can specify any region, and cell E6 will automatically change to reflect those target totals.

Before you continue, turn back to Chapter 8 and review the database functions, particularly DSUM. Although you created the formula by pasting the function and name, you could have entered the entire formula from the keyboard.

Before leaving this section, add a small worksheet area under the criteria area. In cell B6, enter the sum of the eastern regions as **= SUM(C12:C17).** Continue with the other sums:

Region	Cell	Formula
East	B6	= SUM(C12:C17)
Midwest	B7	= SUM(C18:C20)
South	B8	= SUM(C21:C23)
West	B9	= SUM(C24:C26)

Add the row titles **East, Midwest, South,** and **West** in cells A6 through A9 and the worksheet title **Sales Projections,** as shown in Figure 9.11. In Chapter 12, you will learn a better way to create this same worksheet. For now, save the Sales Projections worksheet for exercises in other chapters.

Deleting Records

To delete records from a database, first select the criteria for the deletion. Next, pull down the Data menu and click Delete, then click OK. Excel automatically deletes the selected records and moves up the remaining records to close the space.

Note:

Data
Exit Find	⌘F
Extract...	⌘E
Delete	
Set Database	
Set Criteria	
Sort...	
Series...	
Table...	

You won't see a warning message or dialog box when you delete records. A database deletion cannot be undone. Be sure that the database is saved before you delete any part of it. If you delete a record of the Sales Projections database, the totals in cells B6 through B9 will be in error. In Chapter 12, you will learn how to use the Table command to avoid this problem.

SALES PROJECTIONS

LAST	FIRST	TARGET	REGION	
			West	
East	$682,000			$423,000
Midwest	$369,000			
South	$394,000			
West	$423,000			

LAST	FIRST	TARGET	REGION
Allen	Ellen	$90,000	East
Atkins	Lee	$113,000	East
Jackson	Robert	$112,000	East
Kennedy	Sandra	$135,000	East
Stevens	Carla	$110,000	East
Ellis	Nancy	$122,000	East
Ford	Carl	$191,000	Midwest
Linn	Vera	$80,000	Midwest
Peterson	Tom	$98,000	Midwest
Adams	Chuck	$118,000	South
Glenn	John	$80,000	South
Parker	Greg	$196,000	South
Conners	Paul	$142,000	West
Harris	Ken	$176,000	West
Keller	Janet	$105,000	West

Figure 9.11: *Adding the regional sums.*

Extracting Records

You can also extract the part of your database that matches specified criteria and place it in another area of the worksheet or in another worksheet. To do this, first copy the cells that contain the field names into a new area of the worksheet with sufficient room or into another worksheet. You may delete any field names that are not needed in the extracted database. Be sure that the proper criteria are selected. Select the field names for the area in which you want to copy the extracted records. Pull down the Data menu and click Extract. You will then see the Extract dialog box shown in Figure 9.12. Notice that you can select Unique Records Only if you wish the extracted file to contain no duplicates. Click OK. The extracted records will be copied into the new worksheet area, as shown in Figure 9.13.

Data

Exit Find ⌘F
Extract... ⌘E
Delete
Set Database
Set Criteria

Sort...

Series...
Table...

C reating Criteria

The criteria area of the worksheet is used to define which records in the database are to be found, deleted, or extracted. You may create several criteria areas on the worksheet, but only one of them can be made active at a time by using the Set Criteria command. The criteria area consists of a row of field names called the *criteria name row* and one or more additional rows into which the criteria are entered.

You can use numbers, labels, or formulas to define the criteria. The criteria must always be positioned directly below the field name to which they correspond in the criteria name row. Criteria entered into the same row are ANDed together, criteria entered into separate rows are ORed together. In an AND operation, the search will find only

Extract

☐ **Unique Records Only**

OK

Cancel

Figure 9.12: *The Extract dialog box.*

those records that meet *both* criteria; an OR operation finds those records that meet *either* of the criteria. Using this rule, you can create complex criteria with Boolean operations (AND, OR, etc.).

Finding Exact Matches

To find records that exactly match a specific criterion, enter the criterion value under the field name in the criteria name row. Do not use quotation marks or an equal sign. You may use wild-card entries in specifying the search: a question mark for any single character or an asterisk for a group of characters. For example, SM∗ under the field name Last would find all records with the last name beginning with SM.

As an example of ANDing and using comparison operators, enter <**100,000** under TARGET and **East** under REGION. The total in cell E6 is 90,000, the sum of the eastern targets that are less than $100,000.

🍎	File	Edit	Formula	Format	Data	Options	Macro	Window

E26

Sales Projection

	A	B	C	D	E	F
14	Jackson	Robert	$112,000	East		
15	Kennedy	Sandra	$135,000	East		
16	Stevens	Carla	$110,000	East		
17	Ellis	Nancy	$122,000	East		
18	Ford	Carl	$191,000	Midwest		
19	Linn	Vera	$80,000	Midwest		
20	Peterson	Tom	$98,000	Midwest		
21	Adams	Chuck	$118,000	South		
22	Glenn	John	$80,000	South		
23	Parker	Greg	$196,000	South		
24	Conners	Paul	$142,000	West		
25	Harris	Ken	$176,000	West		
26	Keller	Janet	$105,000	West		
27						
28	LAST	FIRST	TARGET			
29	Conners	Paul	$142,000			
30	Harris	Ken	$176,000			
31	Keller	Janet	$105,000			
32						

Figure 9.13: *The new extracted database.*

Finding Records Within Limits

If you want to find all records within a specific limit, use the comparison operators (see Chapter 4) to specify the range. For example, = >100,000 under TARGET would find all records in which the target sales value is greater than or equal to $100,000.

To find records within a given range, set up two columns in the criteria name row with the same field name and put one limit under one and the second limit under the other. For example:

TARGET	TARGET
>100000	<150000

would find all records with a target sales value between $100,000 and $150,000.

Using Formulas in Criteria

You can also use formulas in creating criteria. For example, in Figure 9.14, a few actual sales figures have been added to compare with

	File	**Edit**	**Formula**	**Format**	**Data**	**Options**	**Macro**	**Window**

E3

Sales Projection

	A	B	C	D	E	
1	ACTUAL/SALES=>1					
2	TRUE					
3						
4						
5						
6						
7						
8						
9						
10						
11	LAST	FIRST	TARGET	REGION	ACTUAL	
12	Allen	Ellen	$90,000	East	$80,000	
13	Atkins	Lee	$113,000	East	$120,000	
14	Jackson	Robert	$112,000	East	$110,000	
15	Kennedy	Sandra	$135,000	East	$140,000	
16	Stevens	Carla	$110,000	East		
17	Ellis	Nancy	$122,000	East		
18	Ford	Carl	$191,000	Midwest		
19	Linn	Vera	$80,000	Midwest		

Figure 9.14: *Using a formula in a criterion.*

the targets. The criteria area includes a formula in the criteria name row that defines an extraction if sales were equal to or greater than the target value. Another example of this might be an inventory database in which the fields include a quantity on hand and cost. You could extract records in which the quantity on hand times the cost exceeds a specified amount.

Summary

You have now created an on-screen database and used the database to calculate the totals for the worksheet part of the same document. Save this worksheet—you will use it in many examples while you are exploring the more advanced features of Excel.

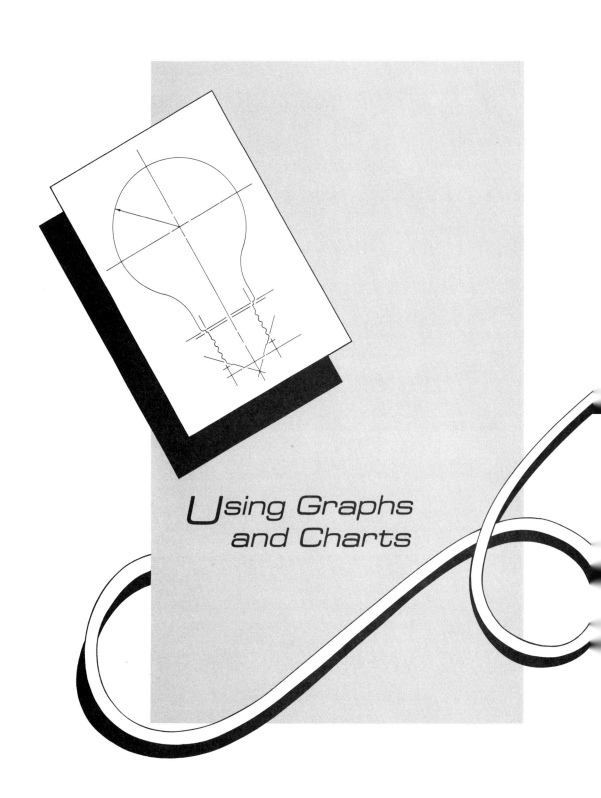

Using Graphs
and Charts

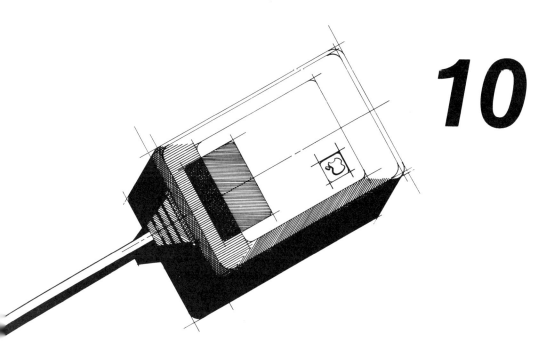

10

Excel's graphics application gives you a quick and easy way to illustrate the results of your worksheet and database analyses. Graphs convey the full significance of what you are presenting in a concise and persuasive manner. You can use them to show relationships, comparisons, and trends.

Using Excel, you can create a graphic representation of your data with only a few clicks of the mouse. The graphs will be dynamically linked to your data—whenever the data change, your graphs will change, too. With Excel, you also have a wide choice of formats and features to use with your graphs. You can choose from 42 different types of graphs to present your data. You can alter fonts on any part of the graph, add arrows, and include comments to add clarity.

In this chapter, you will produce a simple graph from a worksheet that you created earlier. While you're working with this simple graph, you will quickly see the advantages of adding graphic presentations to your reports.

Graphs and Charts

Graphs and charts show visual relationships. They are especially useful for relaying information to busy people who don't have the time to pore over tables of numbers. Although the Excel documentation uses *chart* and *graph* interchangeably, I make a distinction between the two terms. A graph is a visual presentation of one or more sets of data. A chart is a single document that displays graphics. You could create *one* chart from *several* graphs.

Figure 10.1 shows the various components of a chart. These components are described below:

- Axes: The straight lines used on the graph for measurement and reference. A pie chart has no real axis, all other types have two: the x axis (the horizontal line) and the y axis (the vertical line). The x axis shows the data classification, and the y axis shows the quantity or unit of measure.

- Markers: The type of indicator used on the graph to represent the data. A column graph uses vertical bars filled with a pattern for markers. A line graph uses small symbols.

- Tick marks: The small vertical lines that divide the axes. They are used to indicate categories (e.g., quantities or regions) and scales (e.g., dollars or another type of measurement).

- Plot area: The area bounded by the axes or, in the case of a pie chart, the area within the circle.

- Scale: The range of values covered by the y axis of the chart.

- Legend: The symbols and labels used to identify the different types of data on the chart.

- X-axis label: The title for the x axis.

- Y-axis label: The title for the y axis.

- Chart title: The text that is the title of the graph or chart.

- Grid lines: Optional horizontal or vertical lines in the plot area that help the viewer to determine the value of a marker.

Each marker on a graph represents a *data point*. A set of related markers is a *data series*. With all types of graphs, except the pie

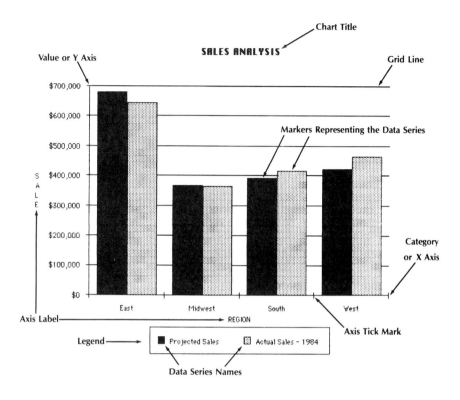

Figure 10.1: *The chart components.*

chart, you can plot several data series on a single graph by using different types of markers, as shown in Figure 10.2. In a pie chart, you can represent only a single data series.

*T*ypes of Graphs

The type of graph that you should use for a particular presentation depends upon what you are trying to communicate. With Excel, you can create any of 42 different kinds of graphs. These can be divided into six general types:

- Column graphs: Useful for representing quantitative information, particularly for making comparisons between groups of

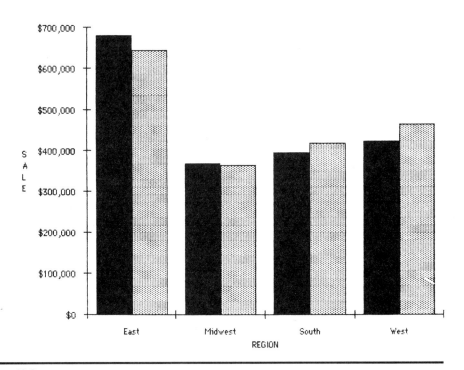

SALES ANALYSIS

Figure 10.2: *Graphing two data series on one chart.*

data. Examples of column graphs are shown in Figures 10.1 and 10.2.

- Bar graphs: The same as column graphs, except that they are rotated 90 degrees so that the categories are on the vertical axis and the values are on the horizontal axis. Figure 10.3 shows a bar graph that is used to compare sales-forecast figures with actual sales.

- Line graphs: Useful for describing and comparing numerical information, especially for showing trends or changes over time. Figure 10.4 shows a line graph that is used to indicate the growth in sales of a product over a period of time.

- Pie charts: Useful for showing the relationship of quantitative data as they relate to the whole. Figure 10.5 shows a pie chart created from the same data that was used for the bar chart in Figure 10.1.

- Area graphs: Useful for showing the relative importance of different data. Figure 10.6 shows an area graph that compares the sales of two products.

- Scatter graphs: Useful for showing the relationship between two variables. The individual data points are marked, but the relationship between these points is left to the observer. Figure 10.7 shows a scatter graph with points representing income and sales figures.

You may create a chart and then decide that the type of graph that you selected does not suit the chart's purpose. This is not a problem—you will find it very easy to convert one type of Excel graph to another, often with only a few clicks of the mouse. You should feel free to experiment with the different types until you've created a chart that communicates what you intended.

Creating a Chart

Now, you can create a chart. Start Excel with the Sales Projections worksheet that you created in Chapter 9 by double-clicking the

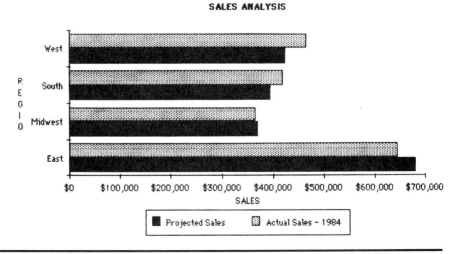

Figure 10.3: *A bar graph.*

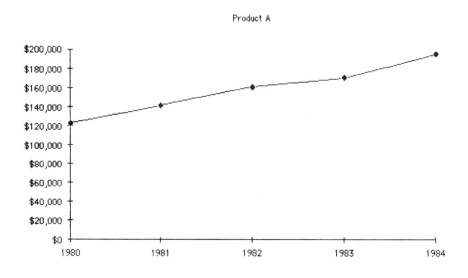

Figure 10.4: *A line graph.*

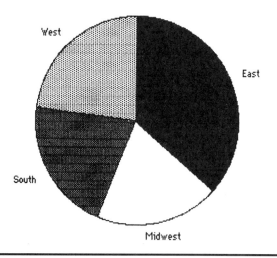

Figure 10.5: *A pie chart.*

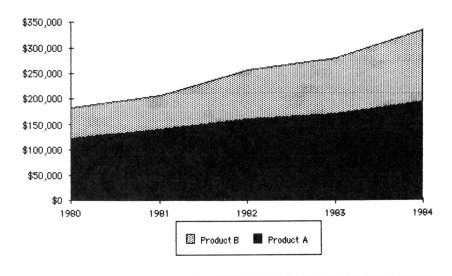

Figure 10.6: *An area graph.*

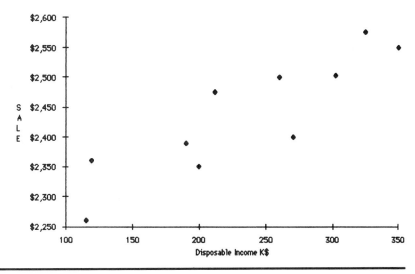

Figure 10.7: *A scatter graph.*

Sales Projections icon. You should see the worksheet shown in Figure 10.8. You'll chart the regional sales as a column graph:

1. Identify the data series that you want to show on the graph by clicking cell A6 and dragging to cell B9.

2. Pull down the File menu and click New.

3. When the New dialog box shown in Figure 10.9 is displayed, click Chart, then click OK.

You should now see the chart shown in Figure 10.10. Notice that Excel automatically scales the y axis, creates the column categories,

LAST	FIRST	TARGET	REGION
			West
East	$682,000		$423,000
Midwest	$369,000		
South	$394,000		
West	$423,000		

LAST	FIRST	TARGET	REGION
Allen	Ellen	$90,000	East
Atkins	Lee	$113,000	East
Jackson	Robert	$112,000	East
Kennedy	Sandra	$135,000	East
Stevens	Carla	$110,000	East
Ellis	Nancy	$122,000	East
Ford	Carl	$191,000	Midwest
Linn	Vera	$80,000	Midwest
Peterson	Tom	$98,000	Midwest
Adams	Chuck	$118,000	South
Glenn	John	$80,000	South
Parker	Greg	$196,000	South
Conners	Paul	$142,000	West
Harris	Ken	$176,000	West
Keller	Janet	$105,000	West

Figure 10.8: *The Sales Projections worksheet.*

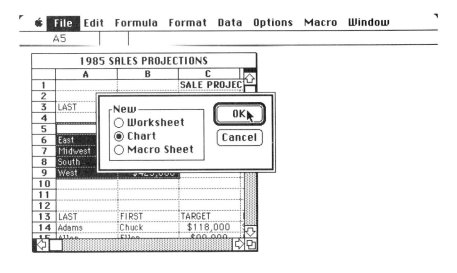

Figure 10.9: *The New dialog box.*

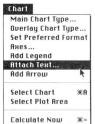

and labels the columns. You also will see a new menu bar at the top of the screen.

The chart still needs a title and axes labels. You can create these by following the steps below:

1. Add a title. Pull down the Chart menu and click Attach Text. When the Attach Text dialog box shown in Figure 10.11 is displayed, click 'OK. Enter the title **1985 SALES PROJECTIONS** from the keyboard. Press Enter or click the enter box.

2. Put the title in boldface and larger print. Click the title, pull down the Format menu, and click Text. When the dialog box shown in Figure 10.12 is displayed, click Bold in the Style box, click 12 for the font size, and then click OK.

3. Add a label for the y axis. Pull down the Chart menu and click Attach Text. When the dialog box appears, click Value Axis, then click OK, as shown in Figure 10.13. Enter **SALES.** Press Enter or click the enter box.

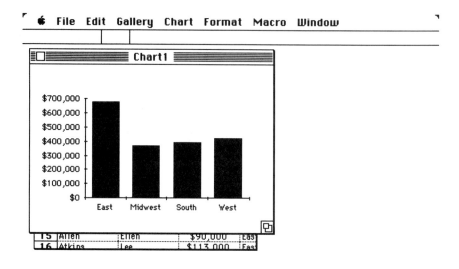

Figure 10.10: *The chart after the initial plot.*

4. Format the y-axis label so that it appears vertically. Click the y-axis label. Pull down the Format menu and click Text. Click Vertical in the Orientation box when the dialog box appears (see Figure 10.12), then click OK.

5. Add a label for the x axis. Pull down the Chart menu and click Attach Text. Click Category Axis in the dialog box (see Figure 10.13), then click OK. Enter the title **REGION.** Press Enter or click the enter box.

When you've finished creating the chart, you can print it. Pull down the File menu, click Print, then click OK in the dialog box (see Figure 10.14). The final printout is shown in Figure 10.15. You should also save the chart. Select the chart, pull down the File menu, and click Save As. In the dialog box shown in Figure 10.16, enter **1985 SALES CHART,** then click OK.

Working with Charts

Once you have created a chart, you can change its size, data-point values, and category names. After you use the sizing box to make

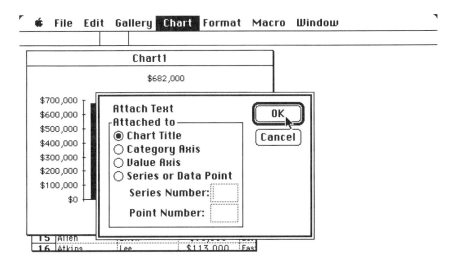

Figure 10.11: *Adding the title.*

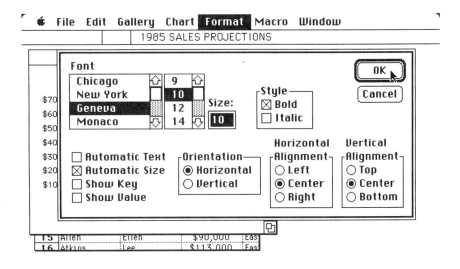

Figure 10.12: *Enlarging and boldfacing the title.*

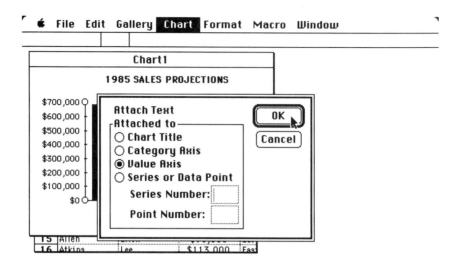

Figure 10.13: *Labeling the y axis.*

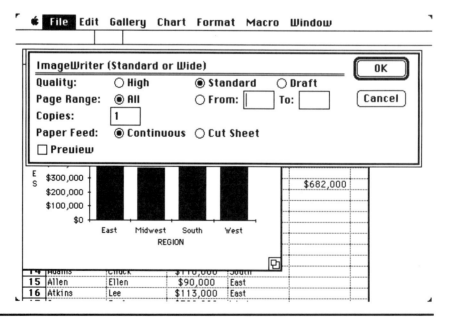

Figure 10.14: *The Print dialog box.*

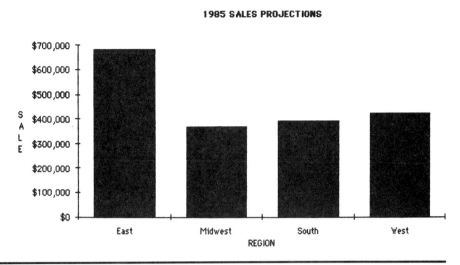

Figure 10.15: *The final chart.*

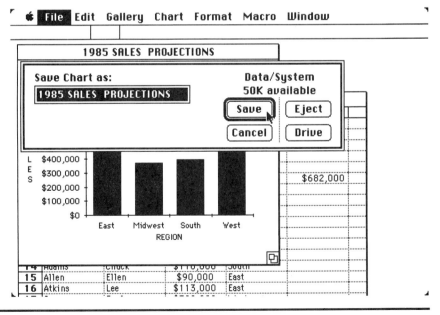

Figure 10.16: *Saving the chart.*

the window smaller, you can try the following experiments to see how these changes affect your chart:

1. Select the worksheet, then the chart. What happens to the menu bar?

2. Change the width of the chart, then the height using the sizing window. What happens? The scaling automatically adjusts, and the category labels take two lines if necessary. Adjust the windows so that you can see the target value for the second person in the eastern region on the database, as well as the chart, as shown in Figure 10.17.

3. Change a data-point value. Select cell C13 and change the value to zero. What happens this time? The scaling on the chart changes, and the columns are redrawn, as shown in Figure 10.18.

4. Change a category name. Select cell A6 and change the value to **Europe.** What happens to the chart? The category labels change, and the chart is redrawn, as shown in Figure 10.19.

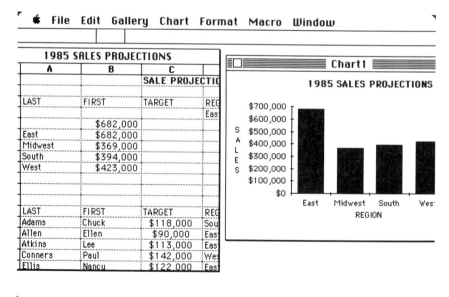

Figure 10.17: *Displaying both windows.*

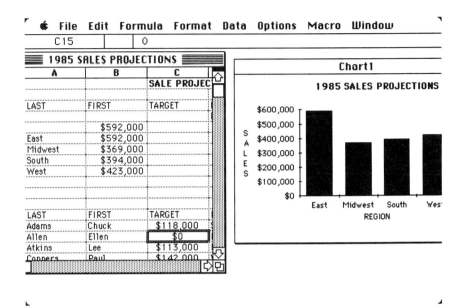

Figure 10.18: *Changing a data-point value.*

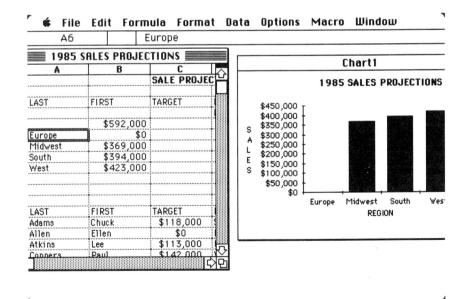

Figure 10.19: *Changing a category name.*

As you can see, Excel quickly responds to any changes that you make to the chart or to the worksheet cells that contain the data on which the graph is based. It also can change the chart to an entirely different type just as quickly, as described below.

Changing Chart Types

Before continuing, create the chart shown in Figure 10.10 again by closing the existing windows, opening the Sales Projections worksheet, selecting cells A6 to B9, and clicking Open on the File menu.

Once you've recreated the chart, you can practice changing the type, legend, and other features. This is how you would change it into a pie chart:

1. Be sure that the chart window is selected, then pull down the Gallery menu and click Pie. The Pie dialog box shown in Figure 10.20 is displayed.

2. Double-click box 5 in the lower left of the dialog box (or click the box and then click OK). Excel displays a pie chart, as

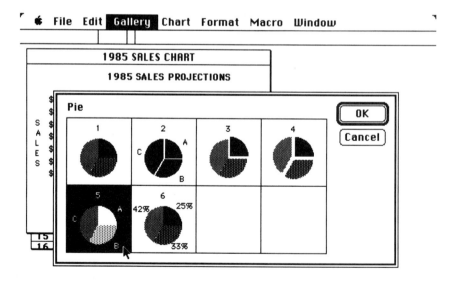

Figure 10.20: *The Pie dialog box.*

shown in Figure 10.21, using the same data that were plotted on your original bar chart.

Before going on, you may wish to experiment with other options on the various menus on the chart menu bar and try creating other types of graphs. Be sure when you have finished that you close all windows, but do not save the chart or worksheet again.

Summary

In this chapter, you have created a simple chart and experimented with a few of Excel's chart features. In Chapter 14, you will learn more about linking charts to worksheets. Chapter 15 provides information about advanced charting techniques.

1985 SALES PROJECTIONS

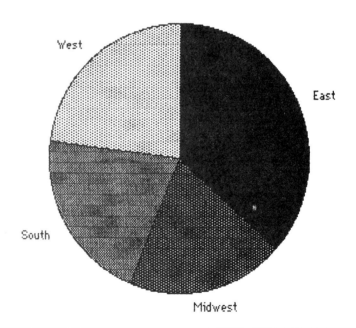

Figure 10.21: *The Bar chart changed into a pie chart.*

Advanced Excel

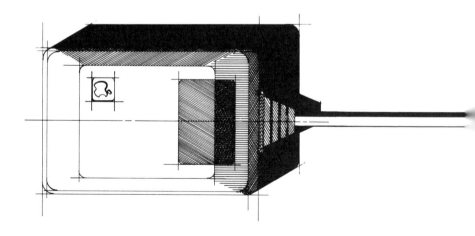

Part 2

Excel has many advanced features that make creating worksheets and performing calculations even easier. Along with many special commands, Excel includes the capability of naming cells and cell ranges, linking worksheets, using arrays, and creating and using macros. There are also many additional charting features that you can use to produce high-quality graphics. This part describes these features and how to use them.

Many of the exercises in this part will use examples created in Part 1. For this reason, be sure that you have completed the exercises in the first part before you continue. You will also create a new linear-regression example, which shows how Excel can be used to make projections. The exercises in this part do not include detailed instructions for any of the basic procedures described in Part 1. If you need help, refer to the earlier chapters.

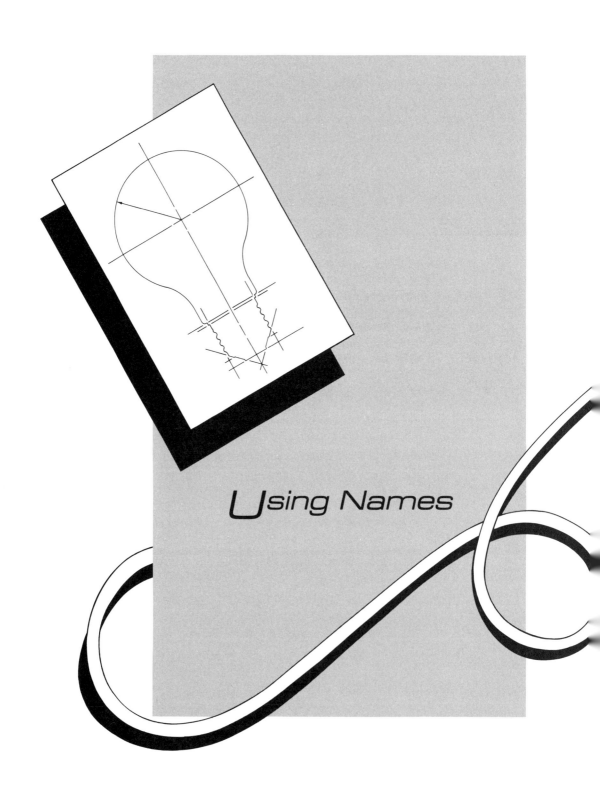

Using Names

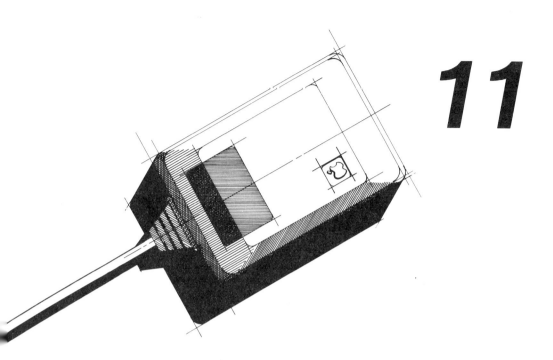

11

When you're creating worksheets, you may often find it an advantage to use names to identify a cell or cell range. Names make the worksheet and formulas easier to work with and read.

Once you have defined a name, you can use it in functions and formulas, just as you would use a cell or cell range reference. Some functions, such as the database ones, *require* the use of names. You can also use names with the Goto command to simplify moving to a cell or cell range.

In this chapter, you will learn how to define and paste names by using the simple Income worksheet that you created in Chapter 3. The same techniques can be applied to more complex worksheets of any type.

Naming Cells

It is possible with Excel to assign names to cells or cell ranges. You will find it much easier to read formulas and function arguments when you use names. Using names reduces user errors because names make the purpose of calculations so much clearer.

In almost all of the examples that you have worked through so far, cells and cell ranges have been designated by their row and column references. However, there was one example in which you used names: the database example in Chapter 9. In that chapter, you defined two names—Database and Criteria—and used them as arguments with the DSUM function. You may wish to review that example briefly before continuing.

Names can be used to refer to absolute, relative, or mixed cell references. Generally, names are used to refer to absolute cell references. For example, the Cash-Flow Analysis worksheet that you created in Chapter 7 used a series of constants in column L (near the top of the page) that were part of the worksheet calculations for each month (see Figure 7.6). These could be named Interest, Cost_of_Goods_Ratio, and Advertising_Ratio. The formula for cell C26, the advertising cost for February, would be:

= Advertising_Ratio * B12

where B12 is the previous month's sale of goods. You could also give cell B12 a name, but you would have to use relative cell addressing in defining that name if you wanted to use a Copy or Fill command to copy the formula into other cells.

Defining Names

There are three different methods that you can use to define names for cells or cell ranges:

- Use the Create Names command on the Formula menu to designate row or column titles as names.

- Use the Define Name command on the Formula menu to create a name for any cell or cell range.

• Use the Define Name window to assign a name to a constant used in formulas.

Naming Rows and Columns

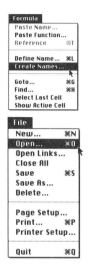

The easiest way to define a name is to use a row or column title as a name for all the cells in a row or column. First, select the entire row or column. Then, pull down the Formula menu and click Create Names. The Create Names dialog box shown in Figure 11.1 appears. Click Top Row if you wish to use column titles as names; click Left Column if you wish to use row titles as names. You can use both row and column titles by clicking both Top Row and Left Column. After you've made your selection, click OK.

As an example, let's use the simple Income worksheet that you created in Chapter 3. Double-click the Income icon, or use the Open command on the File menu if Excel is already started, and open this worksheet. Figure 11.2 shows the Income worksheet.

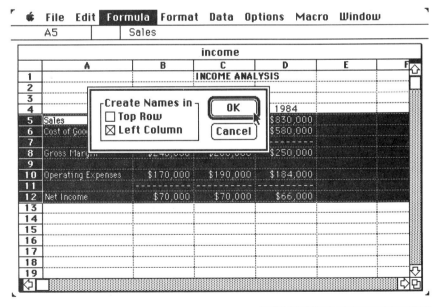

Figure 11.1: *The Create Names dialog box.*

	A	B	C	D
1			INCOME ANALYSIS	
2				
3				
4		1982	1983	1984
5	Sales	$800,000	$850,000	$830,000
6	Cost of Goods Sold	$560,000	$590,000	$580,000
7		- - - - - - - - -	- - - - - - - - -	- - - - - - - - -
8	Gross Margin	$240,000	$260,000	$250,000
9				
10	Operating Expenses	$170,000	$190,000	$184,000
11		- - - - - - - - -	- - - - - - - - -	- - - - - - - - -
12	Net Income	$70,000	$70,000	$66,000

Figure 11.2: *The Income worksheet.*

Now try the following exercise:

1. Select rows 5 through 12 by clicking the designator for row 5 and dragging to row 12. Be sure that the entire rows are selected.

2. Pull down the Formula menu and click Create Names.

3. When the Create Names dialog box shown in Figure 11.2 is displayed, click Left Column, then click OK.

4. Click cell B8. The cell's current formula is displayed in the formula bar, as shown in Figure 11.3.

5. Pull down the Formula menu and click Paste Name. The Paste Name dialog box shown in Figure 11.4 appears. It lists the names that are currently available. These names are the row titles that you selected in step 1. Notice that Excel automatically converted all the spaces that were in the names into underlines. This is because you cannot use spaces in names.

6. Double-click Sales. The formula bar clears, and an equal sign and the name Sales are entered into the formula bar, as shown in Figure 11.5.

7. Enter a minus sign into the formula bar from the keyboard.

8. Pull down the Formula menu again and click Paste Name. When the Paste Name dialog box (Figure 11.4) appears, double-click Cost_of_Goods_Sold. This name will appear in the formula bar, as shown in Figure 11.6.

9. Click the enter box in the formula bar, and the correct total will appear in cell B8.

You can use the Option key to enter the same formula into a range of cells. For example, select cells B8 to D8. Repeat the above steps starting with step 4, with the only difference being that when you reach step 9, hold down the Option key before you click the enter box. The new formula will be entered for the entire range. Select cells C8 and D8 and examine their current formulas. Now, enter the formulas for row 12 using the same procedure.

** File Edit Formula Format Data Options Macro Window**

	B8		=B5-B6			

income

	A	B	C	D	E	F
1			INCOME ANALYSIS			
2						
3						
4		1982	1983	1984		
5	Sales	$800,000	$850,000	$830,000		
6	Cost of Goods Sold	$560,000	$590,000	$580,000		
7						
8	Gross Margin	$240,000	$260,000	$250,000		
9						
10	Operating Expenses	$170,000	$190,000	$184,000		
11						
12	Net Income	$70,000	$70,000	$66,000		
13						
14						
15						
16						
17						
18						
19						

Figure 11.3: *The selected cell's current formula displayed in the formula bar.*

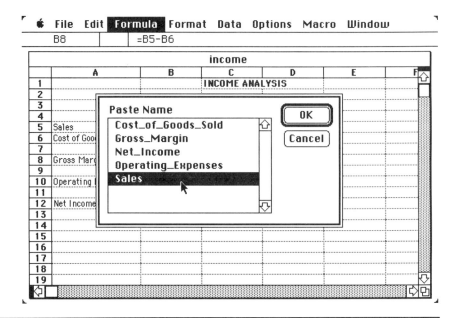

Figure 11.4: *The names available for pasting.*

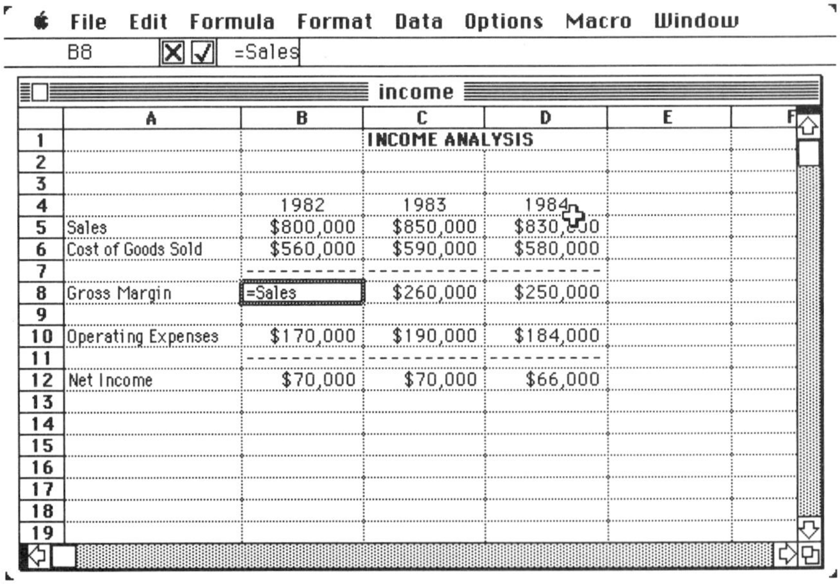

Figure 11.5: *Pasting a name in a formula.*

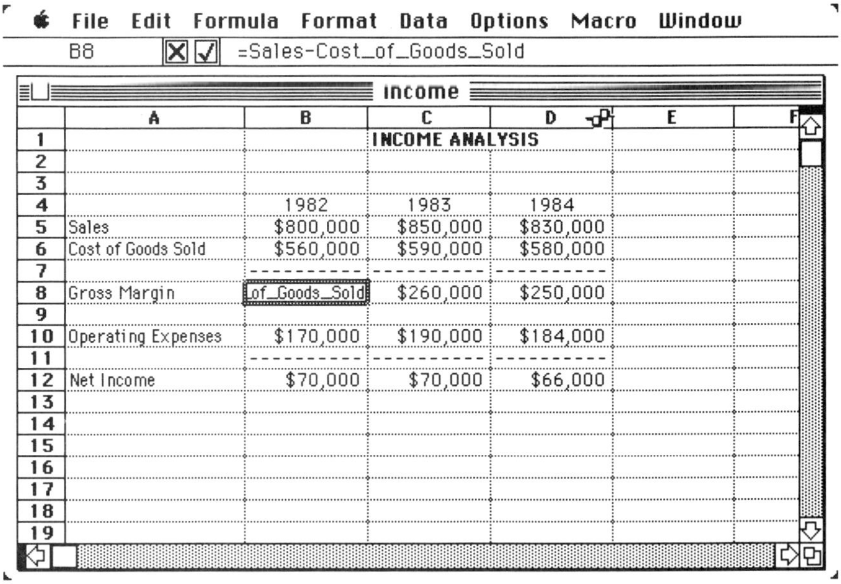

```
  🍎  File   Edit   Formula   Format   Data   Options   Macro   Window
      B8        ☒ ☑   =Sales-Cost_of_Goods_Sold
```

	A	B	C	D	E	F
1			**INCOME ANALYSIS**			
2						
3						
4		1982	1983	1984		
5	Sales	$800,000	$850,000	$830,000		
6	Cost of Goods Sold	$560,000	$590,000	$580,000		
7						
8	Gross Margin	of_Goods_Sold	$260,000	$250,000		
9						
10	Operating Expenses	$170,000	$190,000	$184,000		
11						
12	Net Income	$70,000	$70,000	$66,000		
13						
14						
15						
16						
17						
18						
19						

The window title bar reads: **income**

Figure 11.6: *The formula bar after the second name is pasted.*

Creating a Name

You can also assign a name to a cell or cell range that is not a row or column title by using the Define Name command on the Formula menu. You can choose a name and assign it to any type of worksheet range. For example, in Chapter 9, an entire section of the worksheet was assigned the name Database, and another portion was assigned the name Criteria.

Try creating a name now by naming row 8 of your Income worksheet:

```
Formula
Paste Name...
Paste Function...
Reference       ⌘T

Define Name...  ⌘L
Create Names...

Goto...         ⌘G
Find...         ⌘H
Select Last Cell
Show Active Cell
```

1. Select the range to name by clicking the row 8 designator.

2. Pull down the Formula menu and click Define Name.

3. The Define Name window shown in Figure 11.7 is now displayed. It lists the names that are currently active and shows the cell range that you just selected in the Refers To box. Enter **Gross_Sales** at the cursor location in the Name box, then

press Enter or click OK. Remember to use an underline rather than a space to separate the two words.

The new name has been added to the name list. You can see the name by pulling down the Formula menu and clicking Define Name again. Notice that what appears (Figure 11.7) is actually a window, not just a dialog box. You can move it around on the screen, but you cannot resize it. It also does not have a close box. Click Cancel to return to your worksheet.

The following rules are applicable to creating names:

- Only one name can be defined each time that the Define Name command is used.

- The first character must be a letter.

- Spaces are not allowed.

- With the exception of the first character, letters, digits, periods, and underlines can be used.

- Names can be up to 255 characters long.

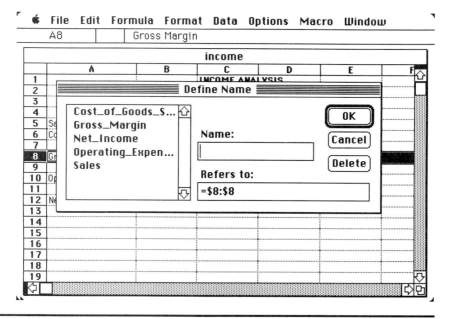

Figure 11.7: *Defining a name.*

- Uppercase or lowercase letters can be used.

- The name cannot look like an absolute, relative, or mixed cell reference.

If you try to use a name that breaks any of these rules, Excel will display an "illegal name" message.

Using the Define Name Window

Instead of selecting a cell or cell range, you can use the Refers To box on the Define Name window to define the range to which a name refers. You can even enter formulas or other names as a part of the reference.

Any cells that you select before you use the Define Name command will appear in the Refers To box when the window is displayed. You can change that entry, and your new cell or cell range will replace the previous selection. You can clear the Refers To box by placing the cursor at the end of the current entry and backspacing to the beginning.

You can enter the cell or cell range into the Refers To box by typing it in from the keyboard, by using the Paste Name command, or by clicking the cell that you want to reference in the worksheet. If you click a cell to enter its reference into the Refers To box, it will be entered as an *absolute cell reference.* (The opposite is true when you click a cell to reference it in the formula bar—then it is a relative cell reference.) You can, of course, enter a cell reference from the keyboard as an absolute, relative, or mixed cell address when defining a name.

The commands on the Edit menu are not available for editing the Define Name window. Although you can mark a portion for cutting or moving, you will not be able to execute any operation because you cannot make any selections from the Edit menu.

Try pasting a new name into the Refers To box to see how this method works. Select a row, pull down the Formula menu, and click Define Name. When the Define Name window appears, click the cursor on the Refers To box. Now pull down the Formula menu, click Paste Name, and then double-click a name to paste it into the box. Practice using both the Name and Refers To boxes on the Define Name window. When you have finished, close the window by clicking Cancel.

Working with Names

Once you have named a cell or cell range, you can work with that name in many ways. You can use cut, copy, and fill operations in the same way that you used them with other types of cell referencing. You can also use the Paste Name command on the Formula menu to enter names into formulas, and you can use names with the Goto command.

Pasting Names

As you just discovered, you can insert any of the names that you have already defined into the Define Name window by using the Paste Name command. You can also paste names into formulas by using the following procedure:

1. Click the cursor on the insertion point in the formula bar.

2. Pull down the Formula menu and click Paste Name. The Paste Name dialog box shown in Figure 11.4 will then be displayed. Scroll through the box until the name that you want to use is visible.

3. Double-click the name, or click the name and then click OK.

Names in one worksheet can also be pasted into formulas in other worksheets. The reference to the other worksheet can be entered in either of two ways:

- You can enter the name from the keyboard by preceding it with the worksheet name and an exclamation point, such as:

BALANCE!CASH

- You can select the cell or cell range that will contain the formula on the other worksheet. With the other worksheet active, use the Paste Name command to point at a name in the alternate worksheet's Paste Name dialog box. The name will be entered into the formula bar of the original worksheet, preceded by the worksheet name and an exclamation point, as in the example above.

When you use the Paste Name command to enter a name into a formula, an equal sign is entered into the formula bar automatically on the first paste. On subsequent pastes, if no operator precedes the cursor location, a plus sign will be added before the name. If an operator precedes the cursor location, a plus sign will not be added.

Using Names with the Goto Command

You can also use names with the Goto command. This command moves you directly to any specific cell or cell range.

You can try using the Goto command with your Income worksheet, with the row titles defined as names. Pull down the Formula menu and click Goto. When the Goto dialog box shown in Figure 11.8 is displayed, double-click Net Income. The cursor will move to this row on the screen.

Editing and Deleting Names

To edit a name that you have already defined, pull down the Formula menu and click Define Name. The Define Name window

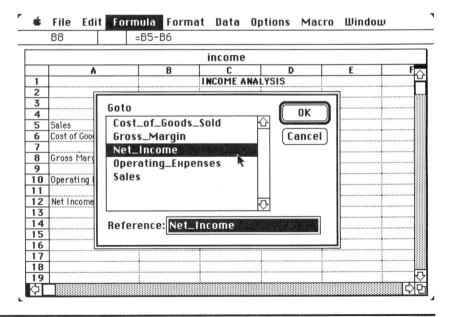

Figure 11.8: *The Goto dialog box.*

(Figure 11.7) will be displayed. Scroll until the name that you want to edit is visible, then click it. The current name will be displayed in the Name box, and the current reference will be in the Refers To box. The contents of either box can be edited. Click OK when you have completed your editing.

If you want to delete a name that you previously defined, use the following procedure:

1. Pull down the Formula menu and click Define Name.

2. When the Define Name window is displayed, click the desired name.

3. Click Delete.

As an exercise, delete the Gross_Sales name that you defined earlier.

Summary

You have now defined and pasted names using a simple worksheet. The same techniques can be applied to any type of document. You will probably use names quite often to clarify your worksheet formulas and function arguments.

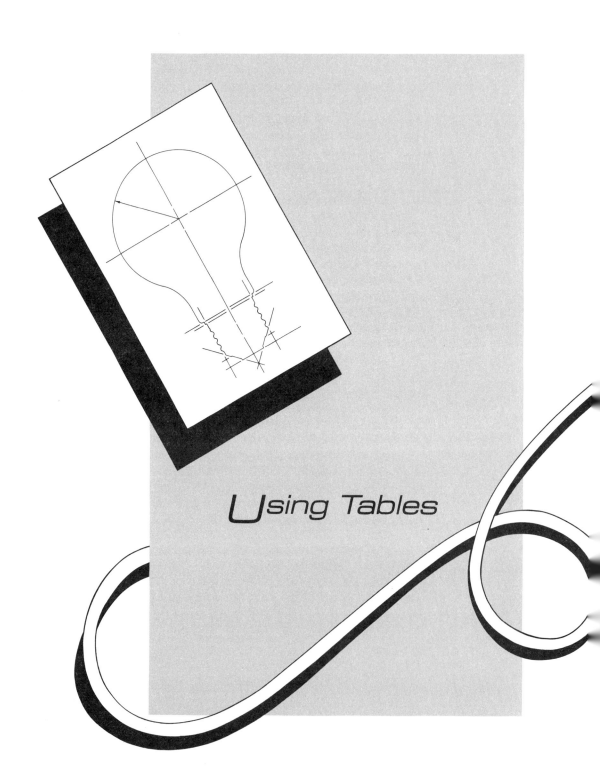

Using Tables

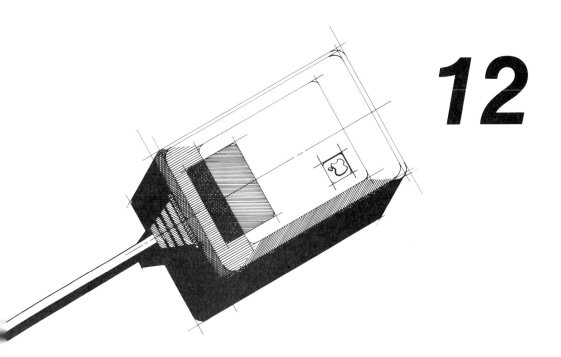

12

There may be times when you want to change certain constant values on your worksheet to see how the different values affect the rest of the values on the worksheet. For example, in Chapter 9, you created a database of sales targets and then searched this database using a criterion. You could only use one criterion at a time, which is somewhat cumbersome if you want to use a series of criteria and then create a table or chart showing the results of each analysis. You did create a short worksheet portion showing the totals for each region, which were calculated using the SUM function. However, the calculations were only correct if the database was sorted by region.

In this chapter, you will learn how to use the Table command to avoid all of these problems. You will take this same example (the Sales Projections database and worksheet) and use a table to search the database based on a series of criteria. You will see that tables are useful for what-if analyses with worksheets because they allow you to perform multiple analyses with a series of input values.

You will also learn how to use look-up tables. These types of tables work with the LOOKUP, VLOOKUP, and HLOOKUP functions, rather than with the Table command. They provide a quick way to find certain values in your worksheets.

*O*ne-Input Tables

You use a *one-input table* to see how changes in one cell affect the values calculated by one or more formulas.

Designing a One-Input Table

To design a one-input table, you need three things:

- A single-input cell to contain the value that you wish to change.

- A column or row containing the values that will be applied successively to the input cell.

- One or more columns or rows that contain cells for the resulting values, with the formulas used as headings for each column or row. You can use formulas that refer directly to the input cell or to other cells on the worksheet.

If you have defined the three areas listed above, you can use a one-input table. First, select the range containing the input values for the input cell and the columns or rows, with the formula headings, for the output values. Pull down the Data menu and click Table. The Table window shown in Figure 12.1 is displayed. Like the Define Name window, the Table window can be moved, but it cannot be resized, and it does not have a close box. If the input values are in a row, enter the input cell reference in the Row Input Cell box. If the input values are in a column, enter the input cell reference in the Column Input Cell box. After you've entered the input cell, click OK.

Note: The input cell for the formula must be a *single cell*. The *Column* and *Row* next to the input cell box in the Table window refer to the column or row that contains the values for this input cell, not to the location of the input cell.

Creating a One-Input Table

So that you can understand how a one-input table is used, let's experiment with the Sales Projections database that you created in

Chapter 9. You'll set up a one-input table to search the database based on a series of criteria.

First, open the Sales Projections database and worksheet, shown in Figure 12.2. Our particular area of interest is the worksheet portion—rows 6 through 9—which contain the sales totals by region. These totals were obtained using the SUM function.

See how the SUM function works by adding a row to the database portion (rows 12 through 26), then deleting a database row. You will notice that, if you do it carefully (that is, keeping the database in region order), the formulas for the totals in rows 6 through 9 will change to reflect your additions and deletions.

Now, sort the database in name order (refer to Chapter 9 if you need help). The database is now alphabetized by name. The totals in the worksheet cells B6 through B9 have also changed, and now they are incorrect, as shown in Figure 12.3. This is because the formulas for these cells did not change to reflect the new order.

Notice, however, that the total in cell E6 did not change when you sorted the database. This is because this total was calculated using the DSUM function. Examine the formula for this cell, and you will

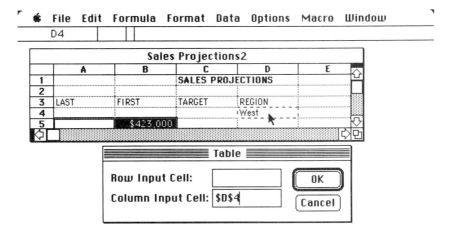

Figure 12.1: *The Table window.*

see that the total is based on a criterion:

= DSUM(Database,"Target",Criteria)

Although the DSUM function gives the correct value, the problem with using it is that you can only use a single criterion at a time. The benefit of a table is that you can use multiple criteria.

Now, let's change the formulas for cells B6 and B9 so that the values are calculated using a table and the DSUM function. Follow these steps:

1. Close the current worksheet and reopen the Sales Projections database and worksheet so that the data are correct. Clear cell D4.

	A	B	C	D	E
1			SALES PROJECTIONS		
2					
3	LAST	FIRST	TARGET	REGION	
4				West	
5					
6	East	$682,000			$423,000
7	Midwest	$369,000			
8	South	$394,000			
9	West	$423,000			
10					
11	LAST	FIRST	TARGET	REGION	
12	Allen	Ellen	$90,000	East	
13	Atkins	Lee	$113,000	East	
14	Jackson	Robert	$112,000	East	
15	Kennedy	Sandra	$135,000	East	
16	Stevens	Carla	$110,000	East	
17	Ellis	Nancy	$122,000	East	
18	Ford	Carl	$191,000	Midwest	
19	Linn	Vera	$80,000	Midwest	
20	Peterson	Tom	$98,000	Midwest	
21	Adams	Chuck	$118,000	South	
22	Glenn	John	$80,000	South	
23	Parker	Greg	$196,000	South	
24	Conners	Paul	$142,000	West	
25	Harris	Ken	$176,000	West	
26	Keller	Janet	$105,000	West	

Figure 12.2: *The Sales Projections database and worksheet.*

2. Be sure that the database is defined as well as the criteria. Pull down the Formula menu, click Define Names. You should see both Database and Criteria listed in the window. (If they are not, refer to Chapter 9.) Click Cancel to close the Define Names window.

3. Create a row containing the formula that will be used for the table by copying cell E6 into cell B5. The formula must be in the first row of the table. The resulting worksheet is shown in Figure 12.4.

	A	B	C	D	E
1			SALES PROJECTIONS		
2					
3	LAST	FIRST	TARGET	REGION	
4				West	
5					
6	East	$776,000			$423,000
7	Midwest	$368,000			
8	South	$320,000			
9	West	$404,000			
10					
11	LAST	FIRST	TARGET	REGION	
12	Adams	Chuck	$118,000	South	
13	Allen	Ellen	$90,000	East	
14	Atkins	Lee	$113,000	East	
15	Conners	Paul	$142,000	West	
16	Ellis	Nancy	$122,000	East	
17	Ford	Carl	$191,000	Midwest	
18	Glenn	John	$80,000	South	
19	Harris	Ken	$176,000	West	
20	Jackson	Robert	$112,000	East	
21	Keller	Janet	$105,000	West	
22	Kennedy	Sandra	$135,000	East	
23	Linn	Vera	$80,000	Midwest	
24	Parker	Greg	$196,000	South	
25	Peterson	Tom	$98,000	Midwest	
26	Stevens	Carla	$110,000	East	

Figure 12.3: *Database after sorting, with the incorrect worksheet totals.*

4. Select the table area with the formula in the first row by clicking cell A5 and dragging to cell B9.

5. Pull down the Data menu and click Table. The Table window (Figure 12.1) should be displayed. Move the window so that cell D4 is visible.

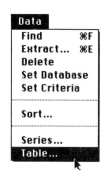

6. Click Column Input Cell on the Table window because the criteria will be from a column.

7. Click cell D4. This indicates that the selected values in column A (cells A6 through A9) will be applied sequentially as the value of cell D4. The value of $D$4 is now displayed in the Table window.

8. Click OK.

The totals for cells B6 through B9 remain the same, but the formula for each cell is now different. Examine their formulas. What has happened? Each title in cells A6 through A9 is applied successively to cell D4. The formula in the first row of column B of the selected range is then used to evaluate the cell in column B that corresponds with the name in column A. The results are shown in Figure 12.5. Compare this figure with Figure 12.2 and the erroneous Figure 12.3.

Now sort your database again by name:

1. Select rows 12 through 26. Be careful not to select row 11, which contains the database field names.

	A	B	C	D	E	F
1			SALES PROJECTIONS			
2						
3	LAST	FIRST	TARGET	REGION		
4				West		
5		$423,000				
6	East	$776,000			$423,000	
7	Midwest	$368,000				
8	South	$320,000				
9	West	$404,000				

Figure 12.4: *Worksheet after copying the formula.*

2. Pull down the Data menu and click Sort.

3. The Sort window shown in Figure 12.6 is displayed. It can be moved, but it doesn't have a close box, a resizing box, or scroll bars. Move the window so that you can see the totals in column B easily, then click OK.

This time, the totals did not change. You can edit, resort, or otherwise modify the database, and the worksheet totals will always remain accurate.

	A	B	C	D	E
1					
2					
3	LAST	FIRST	TARGET	REGION	
4				West	
5		$423,000			
6	East	$682,000			$423,000
7	Midwest	$369,000			
8	South	$394,000			
9	West	$423,000			
10					
11					
12					
13	LAST	FIRST	TARGET	REGION	
14	Adams	Chuck	$118,000	South	
15	Allen	Ellen	$90,000	East	
16	Atkins	Lee	$113,000	East	
17	Conners	Paul	$142,000	West	
18	Ellis	Nancy	$122,000	East	
19	Ford	Carl	$191,000	Midwest	
20	Glenn	John	$80,000	South	
21	Harris	Ken	$176,000	West	
22	Jackson	Robert	$112,000	East	
23	Keller	Janet	$105,000	West	
24	Kennedy	Sandra	$135,000	East	
25	Linn	Vera	$80,000	Midwest	
26	Parker	Greg	$196,000	South	
27	Peterson	Tom	$98,000	Midwest	
28	Stevens	Carla	$110,000	East	

Figure 12.5: *The worksheet values calculated with the Table command.*

Note: If you add or insert rows within the database range, your entries will be formatted correctly, and the database totals will be updated to reflect the changes. If you add data at the end of the database, you will need to redefine the database area in order for the totals to be correct. You will also need to format the new entries at the end of the database (by pulling down the Format menu and clicking Number).

Calculating Two Columns

Using the Table command, you can use multiple formulas and calculate the values for more than one column or row. For example, save the Sales Projections worksheet and then try the following experiment. Assume that you now have a few actual sales figures, and you want to create a separate field for them in your database. Then, you want to recalculate the worksheet values using the Table command. Follow these steps:

1. Add a new field to your database titled **ACTUAL,** as shown in Figure 12.7.

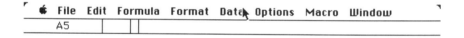

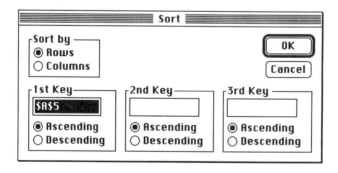

Figure 12.6: *The Sort window.*

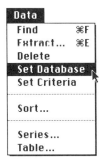

2. Enter the values shown in Figure 12.7 into this field.

3. Redefine your database area by selecting the range with the field names, pulling down the Data menu, and clicking Set Database.

4. Add the new field to your criteria area, as shown in Figure 12.8.

5. Redefine your criteria area by selecting the range, pulling down the Data menu, and clicking Set Criteria.

6. Copy the formula in cell B5 into cell B6, except change the word TARGET to **ACTUAL.**

7. Select cells B5 through C9.

8. Pull down the Data menu and click Table.

9. Click the Column Input Cell and cell D4, just as you did before, then click OK.

Now, both columns will be calculated, and the results will be displayed, as shown in Figure 12.8. Before continuing, save the database that you just created (Figure 12.7) as **Actual Sales.**

File   Edit   Formula   Format   Data   Options   Macro   Window

| C5 | =DSUM(Database,"Actual",Criteria) |

ACTUAL SALES

	A	B	C	D	E
13	LAST	FIRST	TARGET	REGION	ACTUAL
14	Adams	Chuck	$118,000	South	$110,000
15	Allen	Ellen	$90,000	East	$95,000
16	Atkins	Lee	$113,000	East	$80,000
17	Conners	Paul	$142,000	West	$165,000
18	Ellis	Nancy	$122,000	East	$115,000
19	Ford	Carl	$191,000	Midwest	$185,000
20	Glenn	John	$80,000	South	$95,000
21	Harris	Ken	$176,000	West	$190,000
22	Jackson	Robert	$112,000	East	$110,000
23	Keller	Janet	$105,000	West	$110,000
24	Kennedy	Sandra	$135,000	East	$125,000
25	Linn	Vera	$80,000	Midwest	$85,000
26	Parker	Greg	$196,000	South	$213,000
27	Peterson	Tom	$98,000	Midwest	$95,000
28	Stevens	Carla	$110,000	East	$120,000
29					
30					
31					

Figure 12.7: *The new actual sales field.*

Two-Input Tables

In a one-input table, a single input cell is used to calculate the values for one or more columns or rows. In a two-input table—as its name implies—two input cells are used to calculate the values for one or more columns or rows.

Designing a Two-Input Table

To design a two-input table, you need to define the following four areas on your worksheet:

- Two input cells to contain the values that you wish to change.

- A row containing the values that will be applied successively to one of the input cells.

- A column containing the values that will be applied successively to the other input cell.

- One or more columns or rows that contain cells for the resulting values, with the formulas used as headings for each column or row. You can use formulas that refer directly to the input cell or to other cells on the worksheet.

Once you have set up these areas on your worksheet, you can use a two-input table, as described below.

Creating a Two-Input Table

You create a two-input table by following the same procedure that you used to create a one-input table, except that you will have both a row input cell and a column input cell. First, select the range of cells containing the input rows or columns and the output rows or columns with the formulas. Then, pull down the Data menu and click Table. In the Row Input Cell box, enter the reference to the input cell for which you wish the row to be calculated. In the Column Input Cell box, enter the reference to the input cell for which you wish the column to be calculated. Then click OK. Excel will then calculate the values for both input cells.

Editing What-If Tables

You can edit the values used for input cells or the formulas of a table by using the commands on the Edit menu. After you make any changes, the table will be automatically updated using the new input values or formulas. However, you *cannot* edit the output columns or rows of a table (such as cells B6 through B9 in the Sales Projections database and worksheet example). For example, try changing Midwest to Europe on your worksheet—select cell A7 and enter **Europe.** Since there are no records that match this criterion, the

	A	B	C	D	E
1					
2					
3	LAST	FIRST	TARGET	REGION	ACTUAL
4					
5		$1,868,000	$1,893,000		
6	East	$682,000	$645,000		
7	Midwest	$369,000	$365,000		
8	South	$394,000	$418,000		
9	West	$423,000	$465,000		
10					
11					
12					
13	LAST	FIRST	TARGET	REGION	ACTUAL
14	Adams	Chuck	$118,000	South	$110,000
15	Allen	Ellen	$90,000	East	$95,000
16	Atkins	Lee	$113,000	East	$80,000
17	Conners	Paul	$142,000	West	$165,000
18	Ellis	Nancy	$122,000	East	$115,000
19	Ford	Carl	$191,000	Midwest	$185,000
20	Glenn	John	$80,000	South	$95,000
21	Harris	Ken	$176,000	West	$190,000
22	Jackson	Robert	$112,000	East	$110,000
23	Keller	Janet	$105,000	West	$110,000
24	Kennedy	Sandra	$135,000	East	$125,000
25	Linn	Vera	$80,000	Midwest	$85,000
26	Parker	Greg	$196,000	South	$213,000
27	Peterson	Tom	$98,000	Midwest	$95,000
28	Stevens	Carla	$110,000	East	$120,000

Figure 12.8: *The worksheet showing actual sales results by region.*

value in cell B7 becomes zero. You will not be able to edit the individual cells B6 through B9 or even to clear them. You cannot clear a portion of a table; you must clear the entire table.

If you wish to use the Cut and Paste commands to move a table or the Copy and Paste commands to copy a table, you must first select the *entire* table. You cannot move or copy a portion of a table. (The *table,* in this case, refers to the output rows and columns. You can copy or move the input values for the table.) To select an entire table, double-click anywhere within the table.

If you copy a value from an output row or column into another cell of the worksheet, the new cell will contain only the value, not the formula.

When you select cells in the output columns or rows, the formula bar will display the table reference with braces to indicate that the cell is one of a series of cells. For example, the formula bar for cells B6, B7, B8, and B9 shows:

$$\{ = \text{TABLE}(,D4)\}$$

The braces indicate that the formula is part of a table. The same formula will appear when you select any of the cells whose values are calculated by the table.

Using the Table Command

The Table command should be used whenever you need to apply a series of input values to one or two cells in a worksheet to create a series of output values in one or more columns or rows. The following notes apply to using the Table command:

- You enter the formula for the output into the first cell in each column or row that will contain the output values.

- There is no limit to how many tables you can have active at one time.

- Once you have defined a range as a table, the entire range must be cleared or edited as a unit—tables cannot be partially cleared.

Using Look-Up Tables

Another application for tables is to use them as a substitute for formulas to produce an output value from an input value. Such tables are called *look-up tables*. You can create look-up tables anywhere on a worksheet.

You can access your look-up tables by using the LOOKUP, VLOOKUP, and HLOOKUP functions, which are described in Chapter 8. These functions permit you to locate a value in a table based on the value of a test variable. The first argument in each function is called the test variable. The second argument defines the look-up table as an array (see Chapter 16).

The LOOKUP, VLOOKUP, and HLOOKUP functions search the first row or column of the table and return the largest value that is equal to or less than the test value. The table values must be in ascending order. For example, suppose cells D1 through D3 contain a table with the values 10,000, 20,000, and 40,000, and cells F1 through F3 contain the values 5%, 6%, and 7%. If you used the function LOOKUP(250000,D1:F3) it would return 6%. The LOOKUP function is identical to that of other worksheet programs.

The HLOOKUP and VLOOKUP functions contain a third argument, which is slightly different from that of other worksheet programs. HLOOKUP defines how far to move into the column, and VLOOKUP defines how far to move in the row. For example, using the look-up table described above, the function VLOOKUP(25000,D1:F3,3) returns 6%, and the function VLOOKUP(25000,D1:F3,1) returns 25000.

Summary

In this chapter, you have learned how to create two types of tables: what-if tables (using the Table command) and look-up tables (using the LOOKUP functions). What-if tables are used to apply a series of input values to one or more cells to create a series of output values. Look-up tables are used as substitutes for formulas for certain types of worksheet calculations.

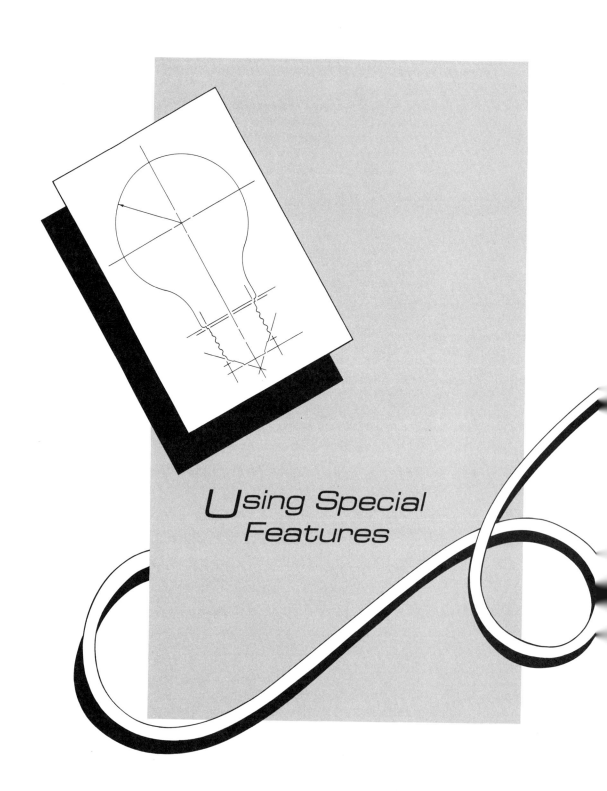

Using Special Features

6

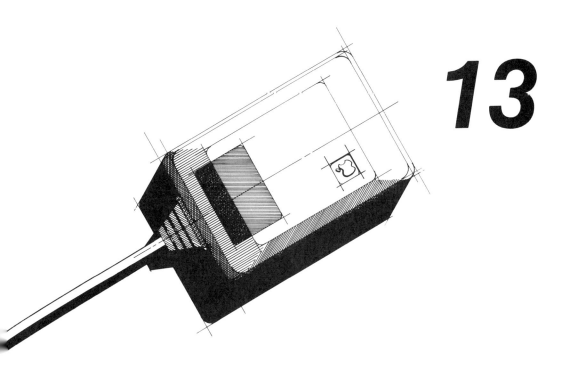

13

Although you have successfully created several worksheets by now, you have mainly used the standard features that are necessary for working with most worksheets—you've been moving, copying, using functions, and formatting.

In this chapter, you will be introduced to some of Excel's special features that make it even easier to create your worksheets. These include copying and clearing only specific information, entering a series of values, controlling when calculations are done, protecting cells, and using iterations. You will also explore some special printing features.

Excel has some additional special features that are covered in later chapters. These include linking worksheets, using arrays, and creating and executing macros.

$\mathcal{S}$elective Clearing and Copying

Excel stores two types of data for each cell: the value or formula and the format. Excel's Clear and Paste Special commands allow you to selectively work with only the values, formulas, or formats of the selected cells.

Special Clearing

The Clear command on the Edit menu can be used to delete only the formulas or formats of the selected cells, as well as to delete all the data. As Figure 13.1 shows, Excel's default selection in the Clear dialog box is All, which clears the values, formulas, and formats in the selected cells. If you click Formats, the selected cells will revert to the General template format. If you click Formulas, the formulas and values of the selected cells will be cleared, but the formatting information will remain. If you enter new values or formulas, they will be displayed in the previous format.

As an example, open your Sales Projections database and select a few target values in column C. Pull down the Edit menu, click Clear, click Format, and then click OK. The format of the cells that you cleared return to the General template format—the dollar signs and commas are gone. Reformat the cells to their previous format before you continue.

Special Copying

The Paste Special command on the Edit menu lets you control what you copy into another cell. You can copy just values, formulas, or

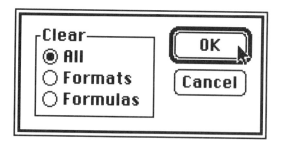

Figure 13.1: *The Clear dialog box.*

formats, instead of copying all the data from one cell or cell range to another.

As with the Clear dialog box, Excel's default selection in the Paste Special dialog box, shown in Figure 13.2, is All. The Operation part of the dialog box permits you to perform operations between cells as part of the copy process.

The Operation options are particularly useful for combining data from several worksheets into a single summary worksheet. For example, a sales manager may receive worksheets from several sales areas. He could use the Add option in the Operation part of the Paste Special dialog box to combine the totals when he copies them into a summary worksheet.

Let's see how the Paste Special command works. First, add a name to the end of your Sales Projections database. Notice that the value for TARGET is not formatted correctly. You could use the Format command to reformat the entry, but an easier method is to use the Paste Special command to copy only the format. Follow these steps:

1. Add two blank rows after row 9 (with the West total) so that the last database name is on row 28. Select row 10, pull down the Edit menu, click Insert, and then repeat this operation.

2. Enter the values for the new salesperson in row 29, as shown in Figure 13.3.

3. Click cell C28 to select the cell format to copy.

4. Pull down the Edit menu and click Copy.

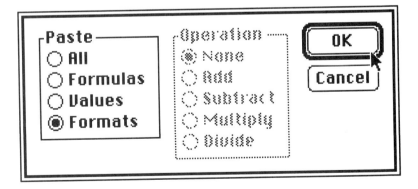

Figure 13.2: *The Paste Special dialog box.*

5. Click cell C29, which is the destination cell.

6. Pull down the Edit menu and click Paste Special.

7. When the Paste Special dialog box appears (Figure 13.2), click Formats, then click OK.

The new entry in cell C29 in now formatted correctly, as shown in Figure 13.4.

To see how an Operation option works, repeat steps 3 through 6 above. Then, when the Paste Special dialog box appears, leave All selected and click Add in the Operation box. The contents of cell C28 are added to the contents of cell C29 in the copy process, and your worksheet should have the result shown in Figure 13.5.

Tip:

Use the Copy and Paste commands whenever possible to enter data into new columns and rows in a worksheet. This saves entry time and helps prevent mistakes.

File   Edit   Formula   Format   Data   Options   Macro   Window

E32		

Sales Projections3

	A	B	C	D	E	F
26	Parker	Greg	$196,000	South		
27	Peterson	Tom	$98,000	Midwest		
28	Stevens	Carla	$110,000	East		
29	Abertson	George	100000	South		
30						
31						
32						
33						
34						
35						
36						
37						
38						
39						
40						
41						
42						
43						
44						

Figure 13.3: *Adding a new salesperson.*

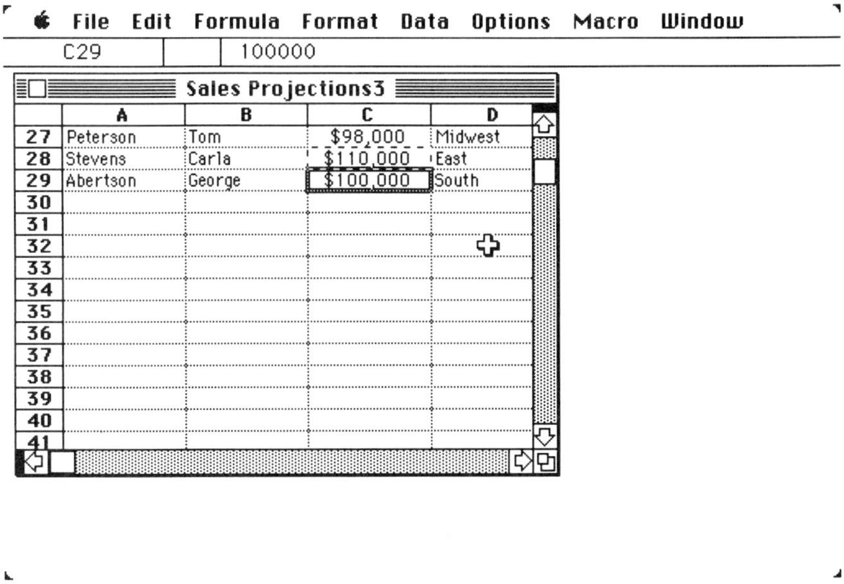

File   Edit   Formula   Format   Data   Options   Macro   Window

| C29 | | 100000 | |

Sales Projections3

	A	B	C	D
27	Peterson	Tom	$98,000	Midwest
28	Stevens	Carla	$110,000	East
29	Abertson	George	$100,000	South
30				
31				
32				
33				
34				
35				
36				
37				
38				
39				
40				
41				

Figure 13.4: *The result of using the Paste Special command.*

File   Edit   Formula   Format   Data   Options   Macro   Window

| C29 | | 210000 | |

Sales Projections3

	A	B	C	D
28	Stevens	Carla	$110,000	East
29	Albertson	George	$210,000	South
30				
31				
32				
33				
34				
35				
36				
37				
38				
39				
40				
41				
42				

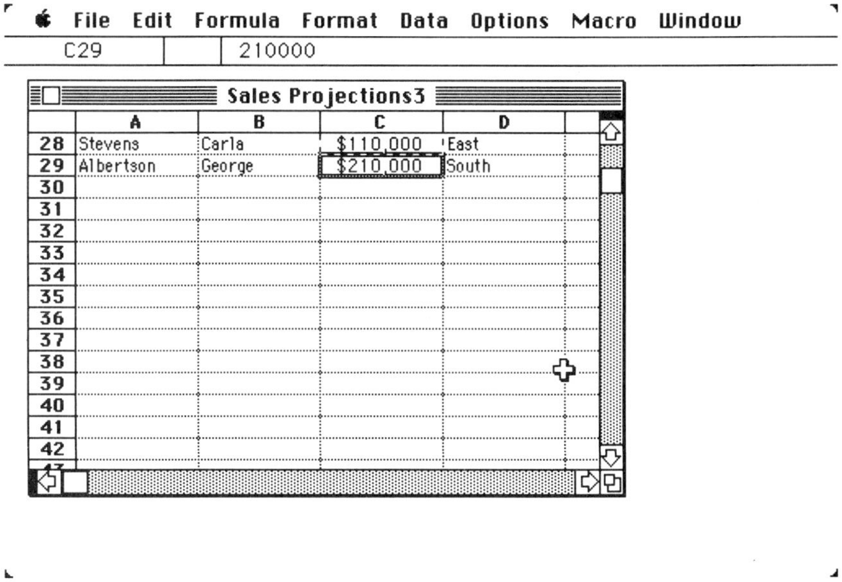

Figure 13.5: *Using the Paste Special command with an Operation option.*

Changing Formulas to Values

There may be times when you want the value of a cell that was calculated by a formula to remain at a particular value; that is, you want to change a formula value to a constant value. You can do this by using the Values option in the Paste Special dialog box (see Figure 13.2).

For example, you might want to employ this option after you've used the NOW function to date a worksheet. By using this function and the desired template, you can put the date and time on a worksheet, as you did earlier in your Amortization worksheet (see Figure 13.6). The problem is that each time that you load the worksheet, the NOW function immediately recalculates and stores the new date and time in the cell, making it impossible for you to see the original date and time of the saved worksheet. To resolve this problem, just before you save the worksheet, change the cells containing the date and time from formulas to values.

To change formulas to values, use the following procedure:

Edit	
Undo Copy	⌘Z
Cut	⌘H
Copy	⌘C
Paste	⌘U
Clear...	⌘B
Paste Special...	
Delete...	⌘K
Insert...	⌘I
Fill Right	⌘R
Fill Down	⌘D

1. Select the cell or cell range that contains the calculated values that you wish to change to constant values. Click copy.

2. Pull down the Edit menu and click Paste Special.

3. Click Values in the Paste Special dialog box (see Figure 13.2), then click OK.

Creating a Series of Values

Excel's Series command gives you a quick and easy way to enter sequential numbers into columns or rows. For example, the Series command would have been quite useful when you created the Amortization worksheet in Chapter 8. That worksheet contained a column with a series of numbers, as shown in Figure 13.6. At that time, you may have entered each number into column A sequentially, a laborious job since there were 60 payments in the example.

To use the Series command, you simply enter the starting value into the first cell of the row or column, select the cell range for the series (including the starting cell), pull down the Data menu, and click Series. When you see the Series dialog box shown in Figure 13.7, select whether you want the series in a row or column and

File Edit Formula Format Data Options Macro Window

E9

	A	B	C	D	E	
			Amortization			
	A	B	C	D	E	
1			AMORTIZATION SCHEDULE BY MONTH			
2			*Amortization Payment Schedule by Month*			
3						
4	************	**********	************	**		
5	Data Entry Area			*	7/29/85	
6	Principle	$8,000.00		*	14:12:54	
7	Interest	9.00%		*		
8	Term	48	Months	*		
9	************	**********	**********	**		
10	Payment:	$199.08				
11	Total Paid	$9,555.86				
12						
13	Month	Beginning	Ending	Payment	Total Paid	Tot.
14		Balance	Balance			
15	1	$8,000.00	$7,860.92	$199.08	$199.08	
16	2	$7,860.92	$7,720.80	$199.08	$398.16	
17	3	$7,720.80	$7,579.62	$199.08	$597.24	
18	4	$7,579.62	$7,437.39	$199.08	$796.32	
19	5	$7,437.39	$7,294.09	$199.08	$995.40	

Figure 13.6: *The Amortization worksheet.*

choose the series type (as explained below). Then, enter a step value for each increment of the series (the default value is 1). After you've made your selections, click OK, and Excel will automatically enter the Series values.

As Figure 13.7 shows, you have a choice of three types of series:

- A linear series, in which each entry is increased by a constant amount.

- A growth series, in which each entry is multiplied by the step value. For example, a linear series with a starting value of 1 and a step value of 2 would increase 1, 3, 5, and so on. A growth series with the same starting value and step value would increase 1, 2, 4, 8, 16, and so on. This type of series is useful for calculating compounded interest or growth rates.

- A date series, in which the date is increased by the unit (day, weekday, month, or year) that you select in the Date unit box in the Series dialog box. For example, to create columnar headings for the months of the year, enter the first month, select the row for the column titles, click Date, and then click Month.

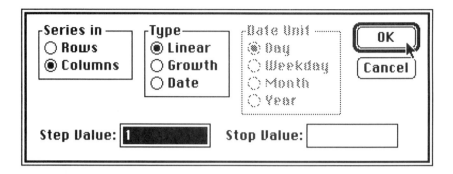

Figure 13.7: *The Series dialog box.*

You can also choose a stop value for a series. For example, if you did not know how many rows or columns your series would require, you could select a larger range than you needed and enter a specific stop value in the Series dialog box. The series would then terminate at that specified value.

Now, you can try the easy way of entering the data into column A of your Amortization worksheet. After you clear column A from row 15 down, follow these steps:

1. Enter the starting value of **1** into cell A15.

2. Select the range of cells A15 through A74.

3. Pull down the Data menu and click Series.

4. When the Series dialog box (Figure 13.7) appears, leave the default Columns and Linear options selected and click OK.

With just a few clicks, the series is now entered into column A.

Changing Reference Styles and Types

Excel gives you the flexibility to change both the style of cell referencing (from column letter and row number to numbers for both columns and rows) and the type of cell referencing (from absolute to relative and vice versa).

Changing Reference Styles

Some worksheet programs designate rows and columns in a different style than Excel uses. They reference a cell's location in R1C1 style—with an R followed by the row number and a C followed by the column number—rather than using Excel's column letter and row number (A1) style. For example, Figure 13.8 shows the formula for cell C15 of the Amortization worksheet in Excel's reference style. Figure 13.9 shows the same formula in R1C1 style. Notice the difference in both absolute and relative addressing.

If you are more familiar with the R1C1 style and would rather have Excel use it, you can change to that style by using the R1C1 command on the Options menu. The worksheet's column letters will change into numbers, so that both the rows and columns are referenced by numbers, as shown in Figure 13.10.

To change the worksheet back to Excel's normal referencing style, pull down the Options menu and click A1.

**   File   Edit   Formula   Format   Data   Options   Macro   Window**

| C15 | | =-PV($B$7/12,(B$8-A15),$B$10) |

Amortization

	A	B	C	D	E	
1			AMORTIZATION SCHEDULE BY MONTH			
2			*Amortization Payment Schedule by Month*			
3						
4	************	**********	************	**		
5	Data Entry Area			*	7/29/85	
6	Principle	$8,000.00		*	2:29 PM	
7	Interest	9.00%		*		
8	Term	48	Months	*		
9	************	**********	************	**		
10	Payment:	$199.08				
11	Total Paid	$9,555.86				
12						
13	Month	Beginning	Ending	Payment	Total Paid	Tot.
14		Balance	Balance			F
15	1	$8,000.00	$7,860.92	$199.08	$199.08	
16	2	$7,860.92	$7,720.80	$199.08	$398.16	
17	3	$7,720.80	$7,579.62	$199.08	$597.24	
18	4	$7,579.62	$7,437.39	$199.08	$796.32	
19	5	$7,437.39	$7,294.09	$199.08	$995.40	

Figure 13.8: *A formula in Excel's reference style.*

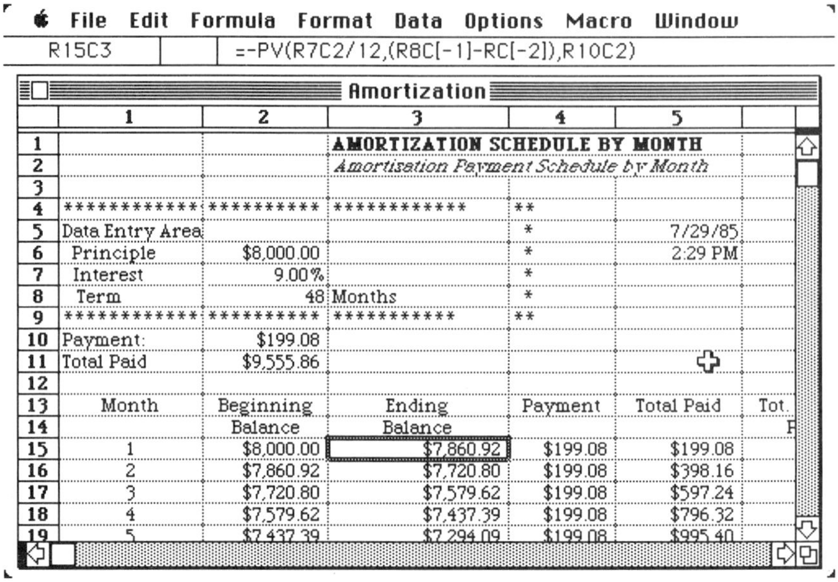

```
 ✿  File  Edit  Formula  Format  Data  Options  Macro  Window
    R15C3            =-PV(R7C2/12,(R8C[-1]-RC[-2]),R10C2)
```

	1	2	3	4	5	
1			**AMORTIZATION SCHEDULE BY MONTH**			
2			*Amortization Payment Schedule by Month*			
3						
4	***********	**********	***********	**		
5	Data Entry Area			*	7/29/85	
6	Principle	$8,000.00		*	2:29 PM	
7	Interest	9.00%		*		
8	Term	48	Months	*		
9	***********	**********	***********	**		
10	Payment:	$199.08				
11	Total Paid	$9,555.86			⊹	
12						
13	Month	Beginning	Ending	Payment	Total Paid	Tot.
14		Balance	Balance			P
15	1	$8,000.00	$7,860.92	$199.08	$199.08	
16	2	$7,860.92	$7,720.80	$199.08	$398.16	
17	3	$7,720.80	$7,579.62	$199.08	$597.24	
18	4	$7,579.62	$7,437.39	$199.08	$796.32	
19	5	$7,437.39	$7,294.09	$199.08	$995.40	

Figure 13.9: *A formula in R1C1 style.*

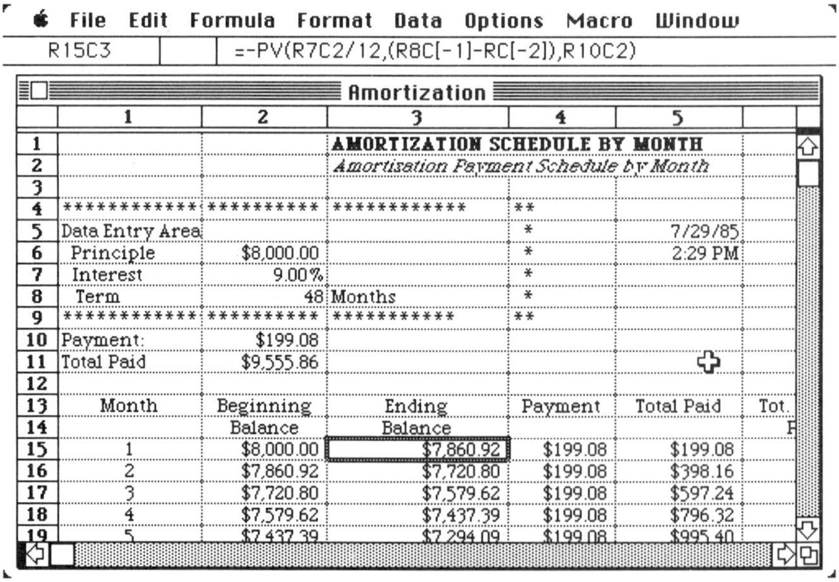

```
 ✿  File  Edit  Formula  Format  Data  Options  Macro  Window
    R15C3            =-PV(R7C2/12,(R8C[-1]-RC[-2]),R10C2)
```

	1	2	3	4	5	
1			**AMORTIZATION SCHEDULE BY MONTH**			
2			*Amortization Payment Schedule by Month*			
3						
4	***********	**********	***********	**		
5	Data Entry Area			*	7/29/85	
6	Principle	$8,000.00		*	2:29 PM	
7	Interest	9.00%		*		
8	Term	48	Months	*		
9	***********	**********	***********	**		
10	Payment:	$199.08				
11	Total Paid	$9,555.86			⊹	
12						
13	Month	Beginning	Ending	Payment	Total Paid	Tot.
14		Balance	Balance			P
15	1	$8,000.00	$7,860.92	$199.08	$199.08	
16	2	$7,860.92	$7,720.80	$199.08	$398.16	
17	3	$7,720.80	$7,579.62	$199.08	$597.24	
18	4	$7,579.62	$7,437.39	$199.08	$796.32	
19	5	$7,437.39	$7,294.09	$199.08	$995.40	

Figure 13.10: *The Amortization worksheet in R1C1 style.*

Changing the Referencing Type

There may be times when you need to change the type of cell reference in a formula. For example, when you click a referenced cell to enter it into a formula, it is automatically entered as a relative cell address. You can easily change the reference with a single mouse click: pull down the Formula menu and click Reference. This will change an absolute reference to relative or a relative reference to absolute.

There are only two points to note before you use the Reference command:

- The formula bar must be active (click the cursor in the formula bar).

- The command changes only the reference to the left of the insertion point in the formula bar, unless you have selected several references by dragging the cursor in the formula bar.

M oving to and Finding Cells

The Formula menu lists several commands that let you move quickly to particular cells and find cells that contain specific data.

Moving to Specific Cells

If you are using a large worksheet, you will occasionally need to move quickly to a particular cell on the worksheet. The Goto command on the Formula menu allows you to jump to any specified cell. When you use this command, you will see the dialog box shown in Figure 13.11. Simply enter the reference to the cell that you want to make active in the Reference box and click OK.

There is even an easier way to move to a particular cell. If there is a cell or cell range on your worksheet that you use often, assign it a name using the Define Name command on the Formula menu (see Chapter 11). Then, when you click Goto, you will see that name in the dialog box's list of active names. Double-click the name, and you'll move to that cell or cell range.

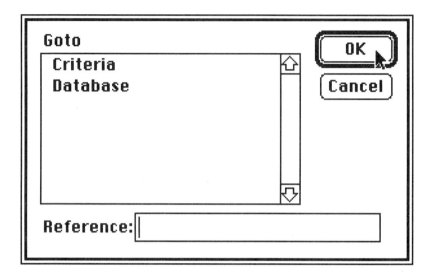

Figure 13.11: *The Goto dialog box.*

The Goto command actually has more uses than just getting you to a particular cell quickly—you can use it for range selection, formula entry, or viewing. Let's try a few simple experiments so that you can see for yourself.

First, open your Amortization worksheet and define a name for cell C18:

1. Select cell C18 (Be sure that you have Excel's normal A1 display).

2. Pull down the Formula menu and click Define Name.

3. Enter **Test** into the Define Name window, as shown in Figure 13.12, and click OK.

Now, use the Goto command to select a range:

1. Select cell C15.

2. Pull down the Formula menu and click Goto.

3. Hold down the Shift key and double-click Test in the Goto dialog box, as shown in Figure 13.13.

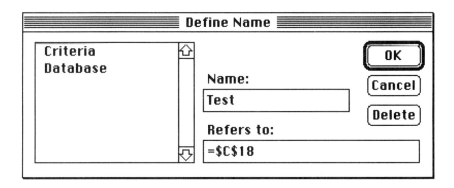

Figure 13.12: *The Define Name window.*

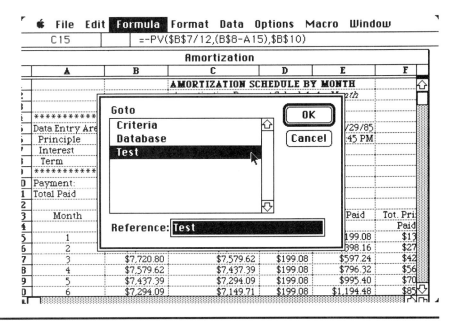

Figure 13.13: *The Goto dialog box with the name Test listed.*

You have now selected the entire cell range from C15 to C18. The result is shown in Figure 13.14. You can use both the Shift and Command keys to select a range for the Goto command, just as with any other type of cell range selection.

Note: As described in Chapter 4, pressing the Shift key while clicking allows you to select a range without dragging, and pressing the Command key while clicking permits you to select several discontinuous cells.

You can also use the Paste Name command on the Edit menu to paste a name into the Goto dialog box.

Tip: If there is a cell range that you use often, select the entire range and assign a name to it. You can then use the Goto command to quickly select that range.

Finding Specific Cells

There may be times when you need to find the specific cell that contains a particular value or formula. You can do this by using the Find command on the Formula menu.

When you select the Find command, you'll see the Find dialog box shown in Figure 13.15. Once you've entered what you want to

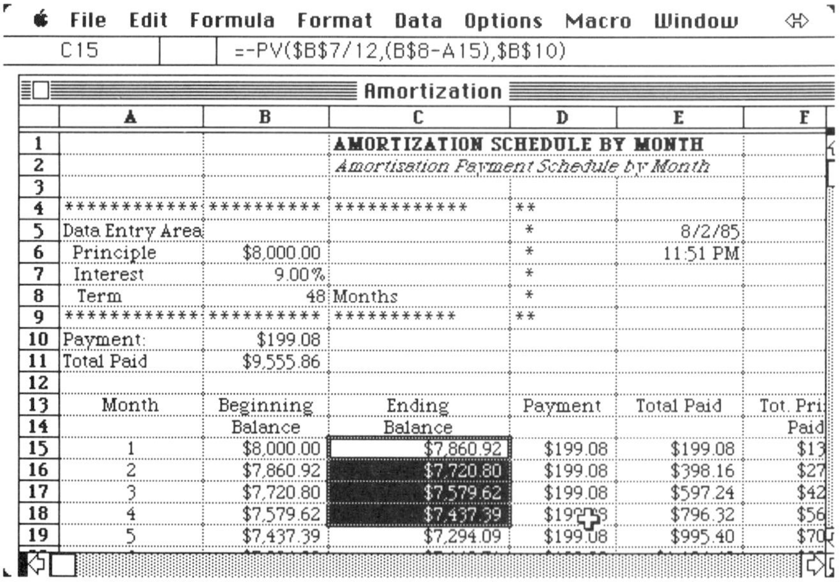

Figure 13.14: *Selecting a range with the Goto command.*

find in the Find What box, you can have Excel look in formulas or in values, look for the entry as a whole unit or as part of other entries, and look by columns or by rows.

Here are some other features of the Find command:

- If you have a single cell selected when you use the Find command, the entire worksheet will be searched. If you have a range selected, only the range will be searched.

- The search will stop when Excel finds the first occurrence. If you want to find the next occurrence, press both the Command and H keys. (This skips the dialog box.) To find the previous occurrence, press the Shift, Command, and H keys.

- In entering the search string into the Find What box, you can use the wild-card characters * and ?, where ? represents a single character and * represents a group of characters. You can also use any of the relational operators in specifying the search string (see Chapter 4).

- The Look By box is used to specify the direction of the search—either by rows or columns. If you know the approximate location of the cell on a large worksheet, specifying the correct direction here can speed up the search.

As an example, you can use the Find command to locate the cell on your Amortization worksheet that contains the final payment. Follow these steps:

1. Pull down the Formula menu and click Find.

2. When the dialog box is displayed (see Figure 13.15), enter **60.**

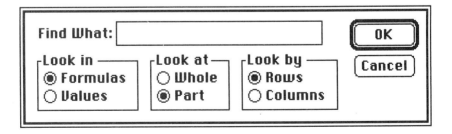

Figure 13.15: *The Find dialog box.*

3. Click Values to indicate that you wish to search in values instead of in formulas.

4. Click Whole to indicate that you want to skip cells (such as cell C14) in which the value is a part of the cell's contents.

5. Click OK.

The cursor should be on cell A62—the month cell in the last payment row.

Tip:

> When you've finished editing a worksheet, use the Find command to locate all unresolved references by searching for all #REF values.

Selecting the Last Cell

The Select Last Cell command on the Formula menu allows you to move quickly to the last cell of the worksheet. This cell is one of the most important cells in the worksheet because it determines the amount of memory needed for the worksheet. Occasionally, a cell in the remote regions of a worksheet can get "trashed" if you inadvertently select it and enter data. In other cases, you may simply wish to move quickly to the last cell, but you do not remember its location.

Displaying the Active Cell

You can use the Show Active Cell command on the Formula menu to quickly return to the worksheet's active cell. This is particularly useful when you select a cell or cell range, then scroll away to view something else on the worksheet.

Calculation Options

The Calculation command on the Options menu allows you to tell Excel when to recalculate values and when to use iteration.

Controlling Recalculations

Normally, each time that you change a value, formula, or name, Excel will automatically recalculate all cells that are dependent upon

the changed cells. The time required for Excel to recalculate a work-sheet depends upon the size of the worksheet and the number of open documents. If you are entering data on a large worksheet, recalculations can be quite time-consuming. You can speed up the process by using the Calculation command on the Options menu to turn off the calculations until you've entered all the data.

When you use the Calculation command, you will see the Calculation dialog box shown in Figure 13.16. Click Manual to turn off calculations, then click OK.

Tables are very time-consuming to recalculate, as the worksheet must be recalculated for each input value. For some worksheets, you may want Excel to automatically recalculate all values except for the tables. If you select this option on the Calculation dialog box, the tables will only be recalculated when you use the Table command on the Data menu.

The Iteration part of the Calculation dialog box controls iterations (see the next section). The Iteration option must be turned on if you plan to use iterations.

To calculate the worksheet after you have entered all the data, first be sure that the formula bar is not selected, then pull down the Options menu and click Calculate Now.

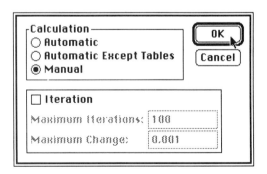

Figure 13.16: *The Calculation dialog box.*

If the formula bar is active when you select the Calculate Now command, Excel will evaluate the formula and enter the result (*not* the formula) into the active cell. You can also select part of a formula and use the Calculate Now command to evaluate only that part.

Remember, you only need to use the Calculate Now command when you have set Excel in the manual calculation mode. When it is in the automatic calculation mode, the Calculate Now command will do nothing, unless the formula bar is active, as described above.

Using Iterations

There may be times when your calculations require you to use formulas that depend upon each other in a circular manner. Excel allows you to perform these calculations by using *iterations.* Let's try an example so that you can get an idea of how this works.

Acme Manufacturing had a good year, and the Board decided to pay the employees a bonus. The amount allocated for the bonus payments was 5% of the net profit after the bonuses were subtracted from the gross profit. Create the worksheet shown in Figure 13.17 to help the Board calculate the bonus:

1. Enter the row titles **Gross Profit, Bonus,** and **Net Profit** in cells A3, A4, and A6, respectively, and enter **23500** as the value for Gross Profit.

2. Create the names by selecting rows 3 through 6 (entire rows), pulling down the Formula menu, and clicking Create Names. Click Left Column, then click OK, as shown in Figure 13.18.

3. Enter the formula for Net Profit as **Gross_Profit-Bonus.**

4. Enter the value of the Bonus as **Net_Profit∗5%.**

What happens? You will quickly get the error message shown in Figure 13.19: "Can't resolve circular references."

This message indicates that you have created formulas that depend upon each other in a circular manner. In this case, Net Profit is the Gross Profit minus the Bonus, but you need to know the Net Profit before the Bonus can be calculated. You need to use iterations in order to make your calculation.

Continue with the worksheet:

5. Pull down the Options menu and click Calculation.

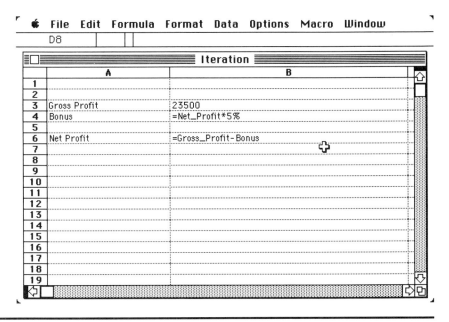

Figure 13.17: *The Iteration worksheet.*

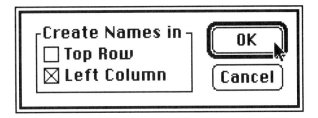

Figure 13.18: *The Create Names dialog box.*

6. When the Calculation dialog box appears, click Iteration, then click OK, as shown in Figure 13.20.

Excel will repeat the calculations until the Net Profit and Bonus change by 0.001 or less or a maximum of 100 iterations has occurred. As shown in Figure 13.20, these limits are set in the Calculation dialog box. The final Iteration worksheet is shown in Figure 13.21.

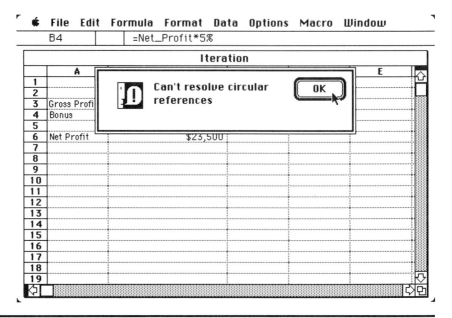

Figure 13.19: *The circular reference error message.*

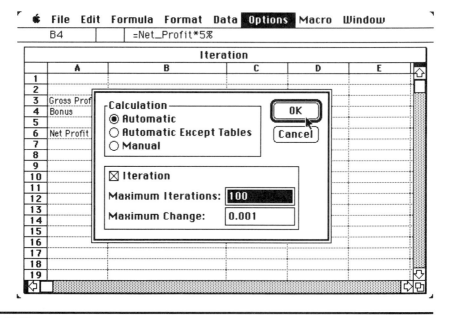

Figure 13.20: *The Calculation dialog box.*

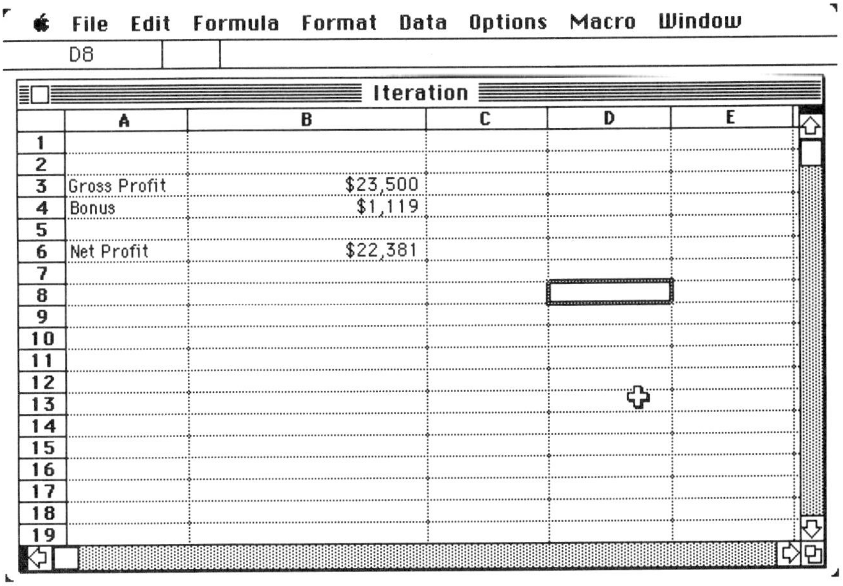

Figure 13.21: *The final Iteration worksheet.*

Note: In this case, the resulting values change less and less with each iteration. The iterations are said to converge to a solution. In some examples, the resulting values may change more and more with each iteration. In this case, the iterations diverge, and no real solution is possible. Both the design of the model and the starting values determine whether the solution converges or diverges.

Protecting and Hiding Cells

Excel allows you to protect cells on your worksheets so that their contents cannot be changed and to hide cells so that their formulas are not displayed in the formula bar.

Protecting Cells

The Cell Protection command on the Format menu and the Protect Document command on the Options menu together allow you to

protect cells on your worksheets. When you protect cells, you *lock* them so that no one can enter data into them or alter their contents. One example of the usefulness of cell protection is for a worksheet like the Amortization worksheet that you created in Chapter 8, in which only three cells were actually used for data entry. All of the remaining cells in the worksheet could be protected to prevent them from being altered.

When you use the Cell Protection command on the Format menu, unless you tell Excel otherwise, *all* the cells of the document are, by default, locked. So, the general procedure for protecting some of the cells on a worksheet is to first select the cells that should *not* be protected. Then, use the Cell Protection command on the Format menu to unlock these cells by clicking Locked in the Cell Protection dialog box. Protect the rest of the worksheet by selecting the Protect Document command on the Options menu.

When you use the Protect Document command, you must enter a password. If you forget this password, you will never be able to unlock the protected cells. For this reason *always check the password that you enter to be sure that it is what you intended before you click OK.* Keep a record of your passwords. The exact same word must be entered to unprotect the document.

When you need to unlock a protected cell, the procedure is just the reverse. First, use the Unprotect Document command on the Options menu. Then, select the cells that you want to unlock and use the Cell Protection command on the Format menu to unlock them.

When a document is protected, many commands are no longer available for use with that worksheet. The menus will change to reflect the loss of these commands—many commands are no longer highlighted. For example, all of the commands on the Format and Data menus, except the Find command, are inactive.

To see how cell protection works, try locking all but the data-entry cells on your Amortization worksheet. After you open that work-sheet, follow these steps:

1. Select cells B6 through B9 (the data-entry cells).

2. Pull down the Format menu and click Cell Protection.

3. When the Cell Protection dialog box shown in Figure 13.22 appears, click Locked to unlock the cells that you selected. (You will remove the X next to Locked to turn off this toggle option.) Then, click OK.

4. Pull down the Options menu and click Protect Document.

5. When the Protect Document dialog box shown in Figure 13.23 appears, enter the password **Secret,** then press Enter or click OK.

Figure 13.22: *The Cell Protection dialog box.*

Figure 13.23: *The Protect Document dialog box.*

Your Amortization worksheet is now protected. You can enter a new interest rate, principle, or term, but you cannot alter the contents of any other cells. Try to edit the other cells just to see what happens. Change the interest rate and watch what happens.

If it is ever necessary to alter the formulas or otherwise change the protected areas of your Amortization worksheet, follow the reverse procedure:

1. Pull down the Options menu and click Unprotect Document.

2. Enter **Secret** as the password in the Unprotect Document dialog box, as shown in Figure 13.24, then click OK.

3. Select the cells that you want to unlock.

4. Pull down the Formula menu and click Cell Protection.

5. Click Locked in the Cell Protection dialog box (Figure 13.22) to remove the X and unlock the selected cells.

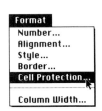
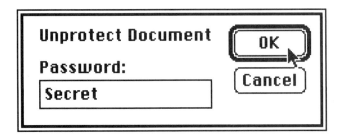

Figure 13.24: *Turning off the protection.*

If you forget which cells are protected, use the Display command on the Options menu to turn off the grid lines. The *unprotected* cells will be underlined, as shown in Figure 13.25.

Tip:

> Protect as many cells as possible in your document, leaving unprotected only the cells that depend upon input data. This prevents someone from accidentally changing a formula or constant data in a worksheet that may be the basis of important decisions.

Hiding Cells

You may wish to prevent a user from seeing the formula used in a particular calculation. You can do this by hiding a cell, using a procedure similar to the one that you use to protect cells. First, select the cell or cell range that you want to hide. Then, pull down the Format menu and click Cell Protection. When the Cell Protection dialog box appears (see Figure 13.22), click Hidden (the default mode is locked, not hidden). Then, click OK. Next, pull down the

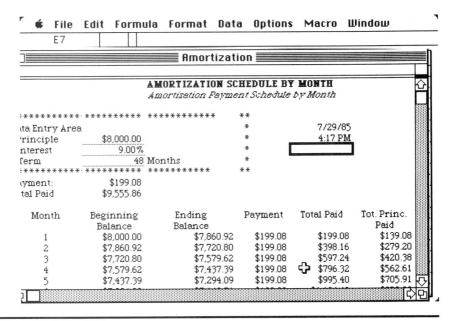

Figure 13.25: *Underlines indicate the unprotected cells on the Amortization worksheet.*

Options menu and click Protect Document. When the Protect Document dialog box (see Figure 13.23) appears, enter your password and click OK. Then, when the hidden cell is selected, its formula will not appear in the formula bar.

To recover hidden cells, use the Unprotect Document command on the Options menu. Enter your password in the Unprotect dialog box. As with protected cells, you must remember your password or you will never see the formulas again. Select the hidden cells that you want to recover and choose the Cell Protection command on the Formulas menu. Click Hidden in the Cell Protection dialog box, and the formulas will again appear in the formula bar when those cells are selected.

Note: Another way to hide a column of cells is to set the column width to zero. It is very easy, however, for any user to recover a column that was hidden by this method.

Controlling the Precision

Excel stores all the numbers that you enter into your worksheets with a full 14-digit precision. (*Precision* refers to the number of decimal places to which a value is carried when it is stored or displayed.) It performs all calculations with this full precision, without regard to how the number is displayed. In some cases, you may wish to switch this so that Excel stores the numbers and performs calculations only with the precision displayed. For example, you may want to switch the precision when the results of formulas do not seem to match the numbers used to calculate them. You can change the precision for all templates except the General template, which always stores numbers with full precision.

To switch from full precision to the displayed precision, pull down the Options menu and click Precision as Displayed. To switch back, pull down the Options menu and click Full Precision.

Printing Features

The advanced printing features include printing only part of a worksheet, printing selected titles, and printing the formulas.

Printing a Cell Range

Excel can print only a portion of a worksheet. To print a partial worksheet:

1. Select the cell range that you wish to print.

2. Pull down the Options menu and click Set Print Area.

3. Pull down the File menu and click Print.

4. When the Print dialog box appears, click OK.

Your printout will contain only the area of the worksheet that you selected. An example of this procedure is included in the Printing Formulas section later in this chapter.

Inserting Page Breaks

Excel normally calculates the best locations for page breaks based on the font size and type of print. If you want to insert a page break at a particular point, select the cell that you want to be the first cell on the next page. Then, pull down the Options menu and click Set Page Break. The printer will insert a page break above the selected cell if you are printing the document Tall or Tall Adjusted or to the left of the cell if you are printing Wide.

You can turn off any manual page break by selecting the cell that comes after the page break, pulling down the Options menu, and clicking Remove Page Break.

Setting Print Titles

You can use any text in a row or column on your worksheet as titles for the worksheet printout. First, select the row or column that contains the title, then pull down the Options menu and click Set Print Titles. Every page of the printout that contains cells in the same column or row as the title will have this title. You can select more than one row or column to be used as titles.

Printing Formulas

You can also print the formulas that were used for a worksheet. The basic procedure is simple: display the formulas, then print the worksheet. For an example, let's print the formulas for the two columns of your Cash-Flow Analysis worksheet. Open that worksheet and follow these steps:

1. Pull down the Options menu and click Display.

2. When the Display dialog box shown in Figure 13.26 appears, click Formulas, then click OK. The formulas are now displayed in each column. Notice that the columns are twice as wide as your regular column setting so that the formulas will fit.

3. Pull down the Options menu and click Font. Set the Font size to **9** so that three columns are displayed.

4. Pull down the File menu and click Page Setup. The Page Setup dialog box shown in Figure 13.27 appears. Be sure that the setup is Tall and not 50% reduced, then click OK.

5. Select columns A through C, pull down the Options menu, and click Set Print Area.

6. Pull down the File menu and click Print.

7. When the Print dialog box shown in Figure 13.28 is displayed, click OK.

You should now have a printout showing the formulas in the selected area. The final printout is shown in Figure 13.29.

Figure 13.26: *The Display dialog box.*

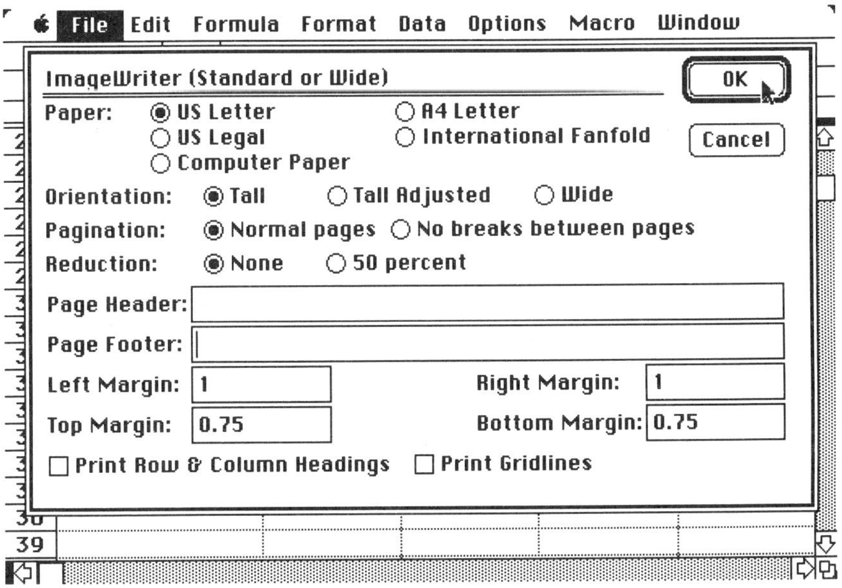

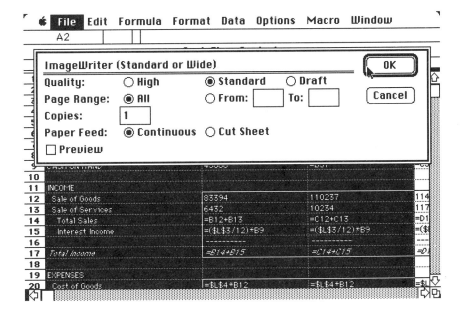

Figure 13.27: *The Page Setup dialog box.*

Figure 13.28: *The Print dialog box.*

	29586	29617
CASH ON HAND	43000	=B37
INCOME		
Sale of Goods	83394	110237
Sale of Services	6432	10234
Total Sales	=B12+B13	=C12+C13
Interest Income	=($L$3/12)*B9	=($L$3/12)*B9
	-----------	----------
Total Income	=B14+B15	=C14+C15
EXPENSES		
Cost of Goods	=$L$4*B12	=$L$4*B12
Rent	11543	8923
Salaries	19894	15234
Taxes	1204	1094
Supplies	2050	2050
Repairs	2873	2873
Advertising	=$L$5*B12	=$L$5*B14
Insurance	734	734
Utilties	2345	2345
Emp. Benefits	1234	1234
Dues, Subscriptions	254	254
Travel	1432	1432
Miscellaneous	500	500
	-----------	----------
Total Expenses	=SUM(B20:B32)	=SUM(C20:C32)
Net Income	=B17-B34	=C17-C34
Net Cash on Hand	=B9+B36	=C9+C36

Figure 13.29: *The printout with formulas.*

Linking Documents

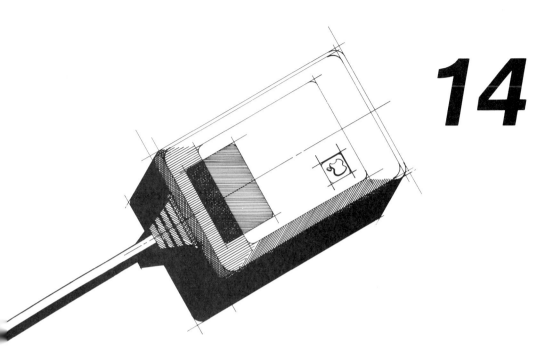

14

Linking documents creates a relationship in which a change in one document will automatically affect a cell or cells in the other. In Chapter 3, for example, you created a chart that was linked to a worksheet. Changes that you made in the worksheet were immediately reflected in the chart.

You can link cells or cell ranges in two or more documents. This allows you to set up a hierarchical structure of worksheets that will always reflect your most current data.

In this chapter, you will learn some of the basic concepts of linking documents. You will be guided through a simple example, then you will use this example to study the more complex aspects of linking documents.

L inking Worksheets

When you link cells in different worksheets, the values in one will change whenever you change the values in the other. This is an easy way to ensure that your associated worksheets are up to date without having to enter new data into each one. You can link individual cells of worksheets or whole cell ranges.

Linking Single Cells

Let's link two worksheets together to see how linking works. In the following example, you'll link one cell in the Sales Projections worksheet that you created in Chapter 9 to a cell in a new cash-flow analysis worksheet.

Assume that your Sales Projections worksheet was prepared by the Sales Department manager of a company, and he needs to copy the sales total for all the regions into a new worksheet that will be used by another department in the company for a cash-flow analysis. The projected sales total will change as the year progresses, and the company's managers want to have the cash-flow analysis worksheet updated automatically to reflect each change.

Note: | In this and the more complex examples in the next few chapters, I'll assume that you know the basic procedures. Although you'll be told what to do, I won't include all the steps on how to do it. If you need help, refer to the chapters in the first part of the book.

After you open your Sales Projections worksheet, follow the steps below to create two linked documents:

1. Be sure you have two blank rows after row 10. If necessary, insert two new rows after row 10. Make B11 the sum of cells B5 through B9, as shown in Figure 14.1. Add the hyphens in cell B10, then save this worksheet as Sales Projections3.

2. Use the New command on the File menu to open a new worksheet. Move and resize both worksheets so that you can see columns A and B in rows 5 through 11 and some of the first entries under TARGET in the database, as shown in Figure 14.2.

3. Enter the title **Acme Manufacturing** in cell B2 on the second worksheet and **Sales** and **Cost of Goods** in cells A6 and

 File   Edit   Formula   Format   Data   Options   Macro   Window

| C17 | | 500000 |

Sales Projections3

	A	B	C	D	E	F
5		$682,000				
6	East	$682,000			$682,000	
7	Midwest	$369,000				
8	South	$394,000				
9	West	$781,000				
10		- - - - - - - - - -				
11	Total	$2,226,000				
12						
13	LAST	FIRST	TARGET	REGION		
14	Adams	Chuck	$118,000	South		
15	Allen	Ellen	$90,000	East		
16	Atkins	Lee	$113,000	East		
17	Conners	Paul	$500,000	West		
18	Ellis	Nancy	$122,000	East		
19	Ford	Carl	$191,000	Midwest		
20	Glenn	John	$80,000	South		
21	Harris	Ken	$176,000	West		
22	Jackson	Robert	$112,000	East		
23	Keller	Janet	$105,000	West		

Figure 14.1: *Adding a total.*

 File   Edit   Formula   Format   Data   Options   Macro   Window

| C10 | | |

Sales ... Worksheet2

	A	B			A	B	C
5		$682,000		1			
6	East	$682,000		2		Acme Manufacturing	
7	Midwest	$369,000		3			
8	South	$394,000		4			
9	West	$781,000		5			
10		- - - - - - - - - -		6	Sales		
11	Total	$2,226,000		7	Cost of Goods		
12				8			
13	LAST	FIRST	TARGE	9			
14	Adams	Chuck	$118	10			
15	Allen	Ellen	$90	11			
16	Atkins	Lee	$113				
17	Conners	Paul	$500,000	West			
18	Ellis	Nancy	$122,000	East			
19	Ford	Carl	$191,000	Midwest			
20	Glenn	John	$80,000	South			
21	Harris	Ken	$176,000	West			
22	Jackson	Robert	$112,000	East			
23	Keller	Janet	$105,000	West			
24	Kennedy	Sandra	$135,000	East			

Figure 14.2: *Opening the second worksheet.*

A7, respectively, as the first two row headings, as shown in Figure 14.2.

4. Click cell B6 on the new worksheet to indicate that the sales total will be placed in this cell.

5. Enter an equal sign into the formula bar.

6. Click cell B11 in the Sales Projections3 worksheet twice. The first click will make this worksheet partially active, and the second click will enter the formula for cell B11 into cell B6 of the new worksheet.

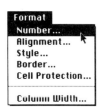

7. Click the enter box in the formula bar of the new worksheet to complete the entry.

8. The sales total from cell B6 of the Sales Projections3 worksheet is now in cell B6 of the new worksheet, as shown in Figure 14.3.

9. Format the total in the new worksheet by using the Number command on the Format menu.

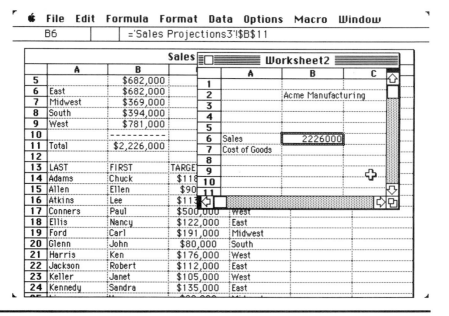

Figure 14.3: *The sales total on the second worksheet.*

Now, take a few minutes to examine your worksheets. Look at the formula for cell B6 in the new worksheet (see Figure 14.3). It consists of the linked worksheet's name in single quotation marks, an exclamation point, and an absolute reference to cell B11 of the linked worksheet. You could have entered the same formula from the keyboard.

Note:

The single quotation marks are necessary in this example because the worksheet name contains spaces. If there were no spaces in the worksheet name, the quotation marks would not have been necessary.

In summary, to link a cell in a worksheet to a cell in another worksheet, use the mouse or the keyboard to enter the name of the referenced worksheet, an exclamation point, and the cell references or names (as described later in this chapter) on the referenced worksheet.

Now, experiment with the linked worksheets to see what happens when you make changes. Change one of the target figures for a name in the Sales Projections database, and you will see the total in cell B11 change, as well as the total in cell B6 of the new worksheet.

Dependent and Supporting Documents

Whenever the values of targets in the Sales Projections3 worksheet change, the values in the new worksheet also will change. The new worksheet is called the *dependent document* because the value in at least one of its cells depends upon values in another worksheet. The Sales Projections worksheet, which contains the value for the dependent worksheet, is called the *supporting document*. The dependent worksheet contains an *external reference formula*—a formula that refers to a cell or cell range on the supporting document.

You can create complex and interlinked hierarchical documents that depend upon each other at several levels. You can also link several supporting documents to a single dependent document. For example, our theoretical company could have sales worksheets for several regions and use these as supporting documents for a single companywide Sales Projections worksheet.

Before leaving this section, continue to experiment with the link that you created. What happens, for example, if you save the dependent worksheet, change the values for a target in the supporting worksheet, and then open the dependent worksheet again? Have the values in the dependent worksheet been updated to reflect your change? The next few sections will explain some of the basic rules for linking documents and give you some tips on making the links effective.

Linking Cell Ranges

In the previous example, you linked a single cell in one worksheet to a single cell in another worksheet. You can also link a range of cells in one worksheet to a range of cells in another worksheet using the same basic procedure.

To link cell ranges, first select the range of cells on the dependent worksheet that you want to contain the formulas. Type in or copy the formula, referencing the appropriate cell range on the supporting worksheet. If you are copying a formula to a range of cells on a dependent worksheet, hold down the Command key while you press Enter or click the enter box.

Using Names

If you create linked worksheets and then use the Copy or Cut commands to move cells in the supporting worksheet, the relative cell addresses in the formulas will not be adjusted properly. To avoid this problem, use names instead of cell references for the linked cells.

Let's try an example to see how using names can help. With your linked Sales Projections3 and new worksheets open, follow these steps:

1. Select cell B11 on your Sales Projections3 worksheet.

2. Pull down the Edit menu and click Cut.

3. Select cell C11 on the Sales Projections3 worksheet.

4. Pull down the Edit menu and click Paste.

You'll see that the total on the dependent worksheet is now incorrect. In other words, the dependent worksheet has not been adjusted to refer to the new location of the sales total cell in the supporting worksheet. If you assign a name to that cell, the dependent worksheet will always be correct, even if you move the referenced cell on the supporting worksheet. Recover B11 and do this is now:

1. Select row 11 on the Sales Projections3 worksheet.

2. Pull down the Formula menu and click Create Names.

3. When the Create Names dialog box shown in Figure 14.4 appears, click Left Column, then click OK. You've given row 11 the name Total.

4. Click cell B6 on the dependent worksheet, type an equal sign, and click cell B11 on the Sales Projections3 worksheet once.

5. Pull down the Formula menu, click Paste Names, and click Total in the Paste Names dialog box.

6. Click the enter box.

Now, repeat the four steps at the beginning of this section. This time, the dependent worksheet will follow your changes in the supporting worksheet.

Tip: | When you create linked documents, use names as much as possible so that you can freely move and copy cells.

Saving Linked Documents

Saving linked documents is the same as saving documents that are not linked. Use the Save As command on the File menu to save each of the open documents.

Note: | Always save the supporting worksheet *before* saving the dependent worksheet. This insures that the name used to save the supporting worksheet is saved correctly with the dependent worksheet.

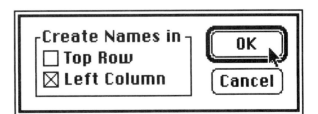

Figure 14.4: *Defining the name.*

Using Closed Dependent Documents

If the dependent and supporting documents are both open and either active or partially active, changes in the supporting document are always reflected in the dependent document. There may be times, however, when you have the supporting document closed (stored on the disk) while the dependent worksheet is open. To understand what happens in this case, you must distinguish between a simple external reference formula and a complex external reference formula.

A *simple* external reference formula references only one of the following:

- A cell or cell range

- A named cell or cell range

- A named constant value

In the previous examples, you used a cell reference and then a named cell, which are simple external references. The following are other examples of simple external references:

    Sales!East
    'Cash Flow Analysis'!$B$3

Any other type of reference is a *complex* external reference. For example:

    East!Total + West!Total + Midwest!Total + South!Total
    'Cash Flow Analysis'!SUM(A3:A5)

are complex external reference formulas.

Whenever you open or create a document that contains simple external references, Excel will try to calculate the formula. If the supporting worksheet is open, Excel can get the information from the computer memory, as in the last example. If the supporting worksheet is closed, Excel will search for the worksheet on the disk and try to find the values it needs. If Excel can't find the supporting worksheet on the disk, it will display a message and the dialog box shown in Figure 14.5. You can then switch to the disk that contains the supporting worksheet.

Unlike documents with simple external references, when you open a document with complex external reference formulas, the supporting worksheets *must be open*. Excel will not look for any

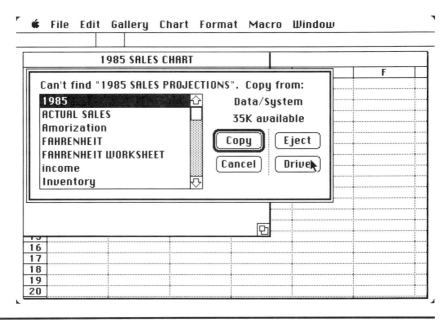

Figure 14.5: *Excel tries to find the supporting document.*

supporting data for complex external references that are not already in the computer memory. If you forget to open all your supporting worksheets, you will get the error message #REF! in the cells that cannot be calculated.

Note:

| If you want to open the dependent worksheet, but you don't want the dependent cells to be recalculated, use the Calculations command on the Options menu before you open the dependent worksheet. Click Manual in the Calculation dialog box (see Figure 14.6), then click OK. Then, when you open the dependent worksheet, the values will remain as they were when you last closed it.

L inking Charts

Whenever you create a chart, it is automatically linked to a supporting worksheet. Whenever the supporting worksheet is changed, the chart is updated to reflect the new values.

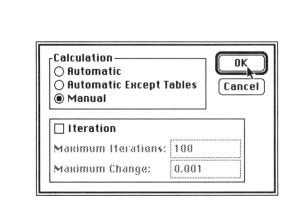

Figure 14.6: *Turning off the calculations.*

The procedure for linking charts follows the same rules as the one for linking worksheets:

- When you copy and paste a chart, Excel automatically creates the data-series formulas and external references.

- If you move supporting cells, Excel does not adjust external references to that cell. Use names to avoid this problem.

- You can block recalculation of a chart by choosing the Manual option in the Calculation dialog box.

- External references in a data-series formula must be absolute cell addresses or named references.

You can see how a chart and a supporting worksheet are linked by opening the Actual Sales database that you created in Chapter 12, the one with some actual sales figures. If you created a chart from these data, open that, too. If not, select cells A6 through C9 on the database and draw a chart (see Chapter 10). Then, click either of the columns on the chart. You will see the data-series formula, with the reference to the worksheet that created the chart, in the formula bar, as shown in Figure 14.7. The formula uses a simple external reference. This means that you can open the chart without opening the worksheet, and Excel will get the values it needs from the disk.

Viewing and Opening Links

Each time that you save a dependent document, Excel also saves the names of all the associated supporting worksheets. If you want to see a list of the names of all the worksheets used to support a currently active document, pull down the File menu and click Open Links. The Open Linked Documents dialog box shown in Figure 14.8 will appear. This dialog box list the names of all the supporting worksheets.

If you want to open any of these documents, select it and click Open. If you only need to view the list, click Cancel when you're done.

If you selected a worksheet and clicked Open, Excel will open it. You can select more than one worksheet by dragging or selecting the names while pressing the Command key. If Excel cannot find a

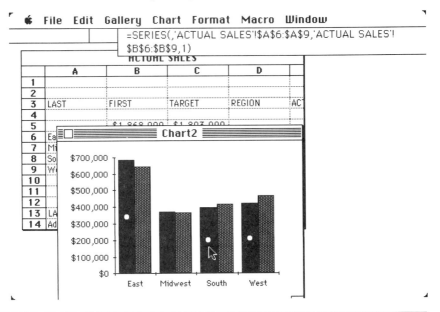

Figure 14.7: *The chart data-series formula showing the link.*

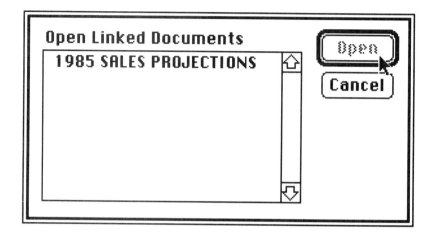

Figure 14.8: *Opening the links.*

supporting worksheet specified by the dependent document, it will permit you to change disks.

Removing Document Links

To remove the links in a dependent worksheet to any supporting document, you only need to remove the references to the supporting document. If you wish to scan a document and be sure that all the links are removed, use the Find command on the Formula menu (not the one on the Data menu) and search for the name of the supporting worksheet or for an exclamation point.

Summary

You have now had some experience in creating linked worksheets. You also have learned how Excel uses external references to create links between supporting and dependent worksheets and between a supporting worksheet and a chart.

Tip:

> Use linked worksheets instead of creating large worksheets, which are cumbersome to scroll and update.

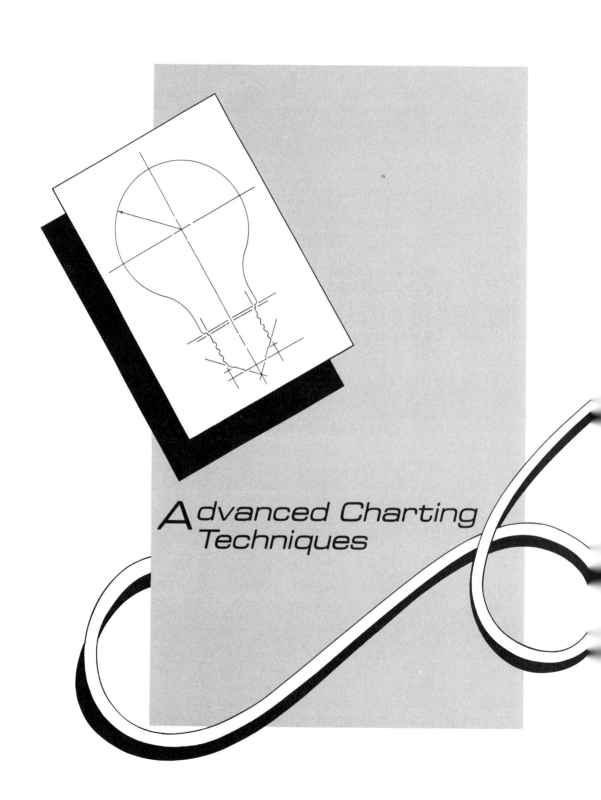

Advanced Charting Techniques

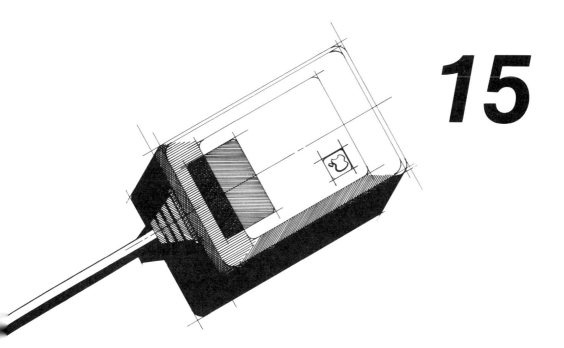

15

In Chapter 10, you were introduced to Excel's charting capabilities and you learned the basic concepts of charting. You may wish to quickly review Chapter 10 and the terms in that chapter before you continue.

This chapter explains how Excel treats the data series that you chart and how it uses the SERIES function to control what is graphed. You will also learn more about formatting the chart and the details of adding text, legends, and grid lines.

You will see that Excel's charting features are extremely flexible. Unlike the worksheet, you can control the font and style of every area of the chart. You can use overlays and copy and paste data series from one chart or worksheet to another chart. You can easily design presentation-quality charts that communicate quickly and effectively.

The Data Series

Charts are created from one or more data series. A data series is a collection of data points, each related to the other by some aspect. A data series could also be considered a series of values and a corresponding set of categories. In Figure 15.1, for example, the data series has four data points. The categories are the four regions, and the values for the categories are the sales projections.

A data series is always made up of numeric values. Categories can be either text or numeric values. If you do not specify the categories, Excel will assume that they are sequential numbers (1, 2, 3 . . .).

Charting a data series is very easy. You simply select the data series on the worksheet that you wish to chart, pull down the File menu, click New, and click Chart in the New dialog box.

Data-Series Assumptions

Understanding how Excel defines the data series is very important. Figure 15.2 shows some examples of how the data series, names,

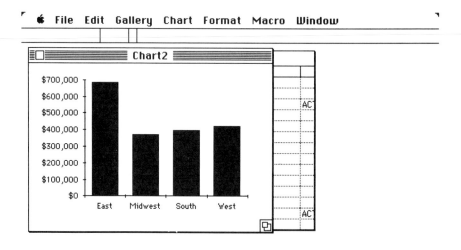

Figure 15.1: *The data series.*

and categories are defined. When you create a new chart or copy an existing one, Excel makes the following assumptions about the data series:

- If a data series is longer than it is wide, the text in the left column is used to define the categories, and each column after the first is used as a data series. The column heading, if selected, is used as the data-series name.

- If the data series is wider than it is long, the column headings are used to define the categories, and each row of values becomes a data series. The row heading is used as the data-series name.

- If the data series is square or the category headings are numeric, Excel does not define any categories for the chart, and each row of values is used as a data series.

Changing Data-Series Definitions

You can change the way that Excel defines the data series by using the Paste Special command on the Edit menu on the chart menu bar. When you click the Paste Special command, the dialog box shown in Figure 15.3 will appear. The options in this dialog box allow you to define a series of numeric values as your category

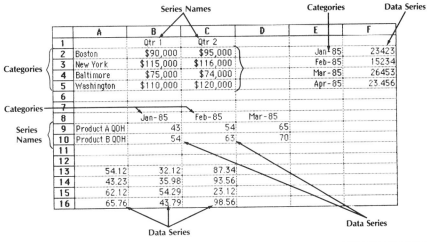

Figure 15.2: *Examples of data series, series names, and categories.*

headings or to switch Excel's normal definitions (see Figure 15.2) so that the chart has more data series than categories.

Adding a Data Series

After you've created a chart, you also can easily add another data series to it. First, select the values for the new data series on the worksheet. Pull down the Edit menu on the worksheet menu bar and click Copy. Click anywhere on the chart once to select it. Then, use either the Paste or Paste Special command (as described above) on the Edit menu of the chart menu bar to paste the data series onto the chart.

As an example, let's first create a chart from a single data series, then add another data series to the existing chart. Open the Actual Sales worksheet that you created in Chapter 12 (see Figure 15.4) and create the chart from the first data series:

1. Select cells A6 through A9.

2. Pull down the File menu and click New.

3. Double-click Chart. This should produce the chart shown in Figure 15.5.

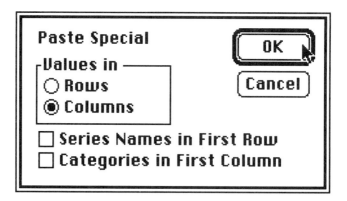

Figure 15.3: *Using the Paste Special command.*

```
 ⌐  🍎  File  Edit  Formula  Format  Data  Options  Macro  Window  ⌐
    D11
```

	A	B	C	D
	≡□≡≡≡≡≡≡≡≡ ACTUAL SALES ≡≡≡≡≡≡≡≡≡			
1				
2				
3	LAST	FIRST	TARGET	REGION
4				
5		$1,868,000	$1,893,000	
6	East	$682,000	$645,000	
7	Midwest	$369,000	$365,000	
8	South	$394,000	$418,000	
9	West	$423,000	$465,000	
10				
11				
12				
13	LAST	FIRST	TARGET	REGION

Figure 15.4: *The Actual Sales worksheet.*

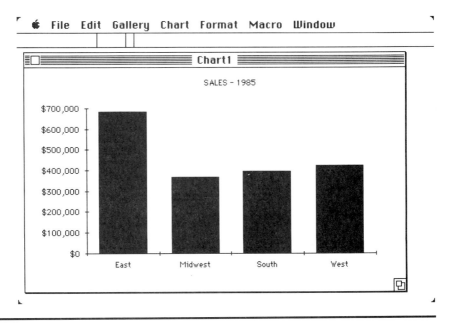

Figure 15.5: *Charting a single data series.*

Now, copy and paste the second data series onto this same chart:

Edit
Undo Copy ⌘Z
Cut   ⌘X
Copy   ⌘C
Copy Chart...
Paste   ⌘V
Clear...   ⌘B
Paste Special...

1. Select cells C6 through C9 on the Actual Sales worksheet.

2. Pull down the Edit menu and click Copy.

3. Select the chart.

4. Pull down the Edit menu and click Paste.

The final chart is shown in Figure 15.6.

Using this method, you can continue to copy and paste additional data series onto the chart. The new data series can be from the same worksheet or from another worksheet.

*T*he SERIES Function

Excel uses the SERIES function to create graphs. This function has four arguments:

1. The data-series title, if one exists, in quotation marks

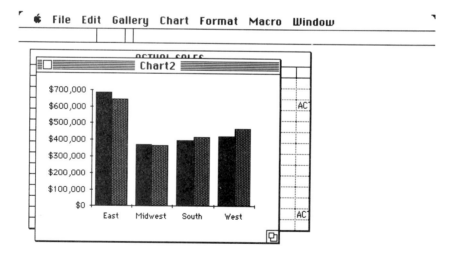

Figure 15.6: *The final chart.*

2. The category titles, which include the external reference to the linked worksheet

3. The data-series definition, which also includes a reference to the linked worksheet

4. The plot-order value

If you include a row or column title when you select the worksheet area to be graphed, Excel will automatically make that the data-series title argument. The category titles and data-series definition arguments are actually arrays, and they follow the rules for using arrays (see Chapter 16).

You can enter all of the SERIES arguments by pointing and clicking or by typing them in from the keyboard. The function can be edited in the formula bar, just like any other formula. For example, you can enter your own data-series title and then point and click to enter the next two arguments.

You can see an example of the SERIES function by clicking any one of the black columns on the graph that you just created (Figure 15.6). The formula bar will display the SERIES function used to create that graph, as shown in Figure 15.7. In this example, the first

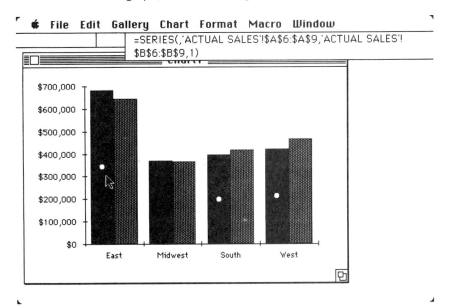

Figure 15.7: *The SERIES function for the first data series.*

argument is missing because a data-series title did not exist. The second argument defines the cells with the categories, and the third argument defines the cells with the values for the data series. The fourth argument defines the plot order, which is a value of 1 because this data series is the first one plotted on the graph.

Now, click any patterned column on the same graph, and the formula bar will display the function shown in Figure 15.8. The first argument, the data-series title, is omitted. The second argument defines the same categories used for the first plot, the third argument defines the cells with the values for the second data series, and the plot-order argument has a value of 2, indicating that this is the second plot on the graph.

Notice also how the chart is linked to the Actual Sales worksheet— the worksheet title and exclamation point are a part of the second and third arguments. This means that any time that the worksheet values change, the chart will also change to show a graph of the updated data series.

Now close the chart (without saving it) and create a new chart with the values of cells A5 through B9 on the Actual Sales worksheet. Click any column on the graph and examine the formula bar.

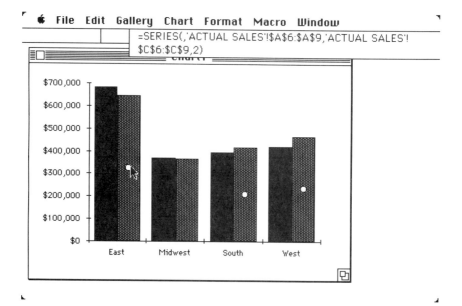

Figure 15.8: *The SERIES function for the second data series.*

This time, the first argument is the same as the column title on the worksheet ($1,868,000), and it becomes the title on the chart, as shown in Figure 15.9. In the function, the title is enclosed in quotation marks.

You can copy and paste the second data series from the worksheet onto the graph, but be sure to select only cells C6 through C9. If you copy and paste cells C5 through C9, the column title will be used in the first argument of the SERIES function as the data-series title, and it will be the chart title unless you change it using the Attach Text command on the Chart menu, as described below.

The next two sections explain how you can edit a graph's SERIES function to change the data-series titles, the legend titles, and the plot order.

*E*diting Titles and Legends

Excel automatically makes a graph's legend titles the same as the data-series titles in the first argument of the SERIES function. You can edit the legend by editing the data-series title in the formula bar.

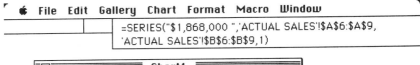

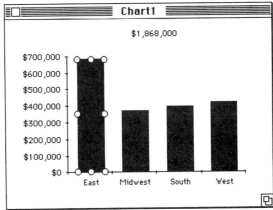

Figure 15.9: *Using the data-series title as a chart title.*

Now, let's create another chart from the Actual Sales worksheet. This time, you'll edit the data-series titles and add a legend. Follow these steps:

1. Create a new chart showing the projected sales values by selecting cells A5 through B9 and using the New command on the File menu. The chart will be created, but the title will be wrong.

2. Copy and paste the range of cells C6 through C9 onto this same chart to show the actual sales values.

3. Select one of the black columns on the chart and edit the formula bar so that the current title, "$1,868,000", becomes **"Projected Sales"**. To do this, pull down the Edit menu and use the Cut command to remove the current title. Then, type in the new title from the keyboard, as shown in Figure 15.10. Click the enter box when you're done.

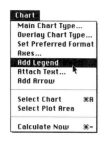

4. Click a patterned column. This data series has no title. Add the new title **"Actual Sales"** into the formula bar by typing it in from the keyboard, as shown in Figure 15.11.

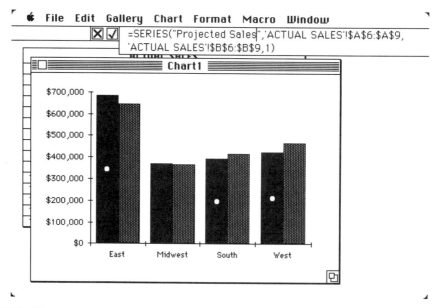

Figure 15.10: *Entering a title for the first data series.*

5. Pull down the Chart menu and click Add Legend.

The final chart should look like Figure 15.12. Save the chart (pull down the File menu and click Save As)—you will need it later.

Altering the Plot Order

Excel automatically plots the various data series in the order that you select them. You can alter the plot order by editing the fourth argument in the SERIES function, which is the one that controls the plot order. If you change the plot number to the number of another data series, the other series will be renumbered appropriately. For example, if you changed the plot-order value for the first plot in a three-plot graph to 2, Excel would automatically change the plot-order value of the current second plot to 1. If you omit the plot number when you enter a formula, the data series will be entered using the next available plot number. After you edit the function and click the enter box, Excel will redraw the chart and change the legend.

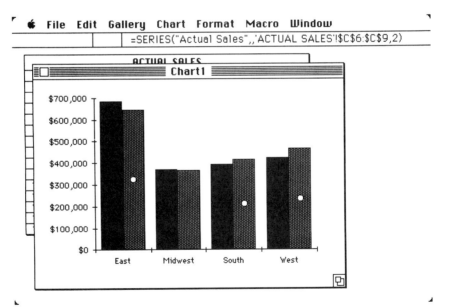

Figure 15.11: *Entering the second data-series title.*

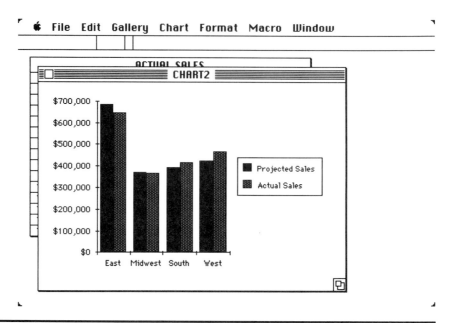

Figure 15.12: *The chart after adding the data-series titles and legend.*

Try changing the plot order on your example chart. Select the first data series and change the last argument of its formula to 2. Click the enter box, and Excel will redraw the chart. Click the second data series and notice it is now assigned a plot order of 1. Edit the formula for the first data series again so that it is the first series plotted.

Deleting a Data Series

If you wish to remove a data series from a chart, use the following procedure:

1. On the chart, click the data series that you want to delete. Its formula will appear in the formula bar.

2. Erase the formula by using the Backspace key or by using the Cut command on the Edit menu.

3. Press the Enter key or click the enter box.

The chart will be redrawn without that data series.

You can clear all the data series in a chart by using the following procedure:

1. Pull down the Chart menu and click Select Chart. Markers will appear to show that the entire chart is selected.

2. Pull down the Edit menu and click Clear.

3. When the Clear dialog box appears (see Figure 15.13), click Formulas, then click OK.

The entire chart will clear, but the formats (chart types) remain. If you copy and paste other data series into the chart, they will be in the format of the previous graphs.

*C*opying a Data Series

As with worksheets, you can easily copy data from one chart to another chart. To copy a data series and insert it on another chart, follow these steps:

1. Be sure that the source chart (the one with the data series that you are going to copy) is active.

2. Pull down the Chart menu and click Select Chart. The entire chart will be marked.

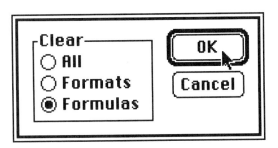

Figure 15.13: *The Clear dialog box.*

3. Pull down the Edit menu and click Copy. The chart will be marked with dotted lines, as with any other copy operation.

4. Make the destination chart active by clicking it, or pull down the File menu and click New to create a new chart.

5. Pull down the Edit menu and click Paste Special.

6. When the Paste Special dialog box (see Figure 15.14) appears, click Formulas, then click OK.

The data series will be copied to the second chart, but the format information (chart type) is not copied. This means that if you copy a data series that was displayed as a column graph into a line graph, the copied data series will also be plotted as a line graph.

Choosing the Chart Type

The Gallery menu can be used to quickly change from one chart type to another. The six basic chart types on the menu are area, column, bar, line, pie, and scatter. Each menu selection, in turn, displays a dialog box from which you can select a subset of the basic type. For example, the dialog box for the column chart type is shown in Figure 15.15.

Changing Chart Types

To change the type of a displayed chart, pull down the Gallery menu and click the new chart type. When the dialog box for that

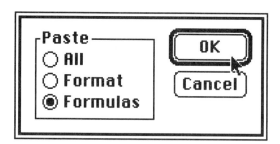

Figure 15.14: *The Paste Special dialog box.*

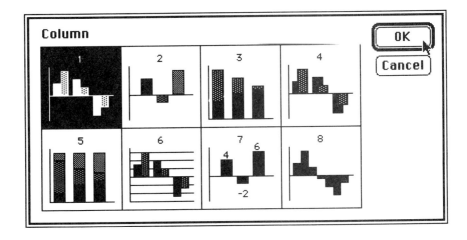

Figure 15.15: *Selecting the column chart type.*

type appears, click the format that you want to replace the existing type, then click OK. Excel will redraw the chart in the new type.

Another way to quickly change the graph type is to pull down the Chart menu and click Main Chart Type. When the dialog box shown in Figure 15.16 is displayed, click the desired type of chart.

Note: When you change the chart type using either of these methods, *all* the data series plotted on the chart will change to the new type. If you want to change the type of only one data series on the chart, use the overlay method described in the next section.

Setting a Preferred Type

You can also set a preferred chart type that will be used each time that you create a chart unless it is altered. In the default mode, Excel automatically draws a column chart. In all of our examples, the first graph defaulted to a column type. To change the preferred format type, first set the active chart to the desired preferred format. Then, pull down the Chart menu and click Set Preferred Format.

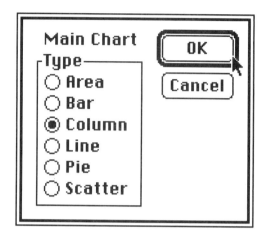

Figure 15.16: *The Main Chart Type dialog box.*

After you've selected a chart type as your preferred format, you can still select that type from the Gallery menu, just like any other type. You may find it useful to set a preferred format if you are going to alter your chart but you may want to switch back to the earlier format. Before you change the format, save the current format as the preferred format. Then, if you need to switch back, select the preferred format from the Gallery menu. This way, you won't have to remember which of the 42 chart formats was used for the original chart.

Moving Pie Wedges

A pie chart is different from other chart types in that is uses only a single data series. If you select more than one data series on a worksheet and try to create a pie chart, only the first series will be plotted. The legend lists categories instead of data-series titles.

When you "explode" a wedge in a pie chart, you separate it from the rest of the pie, as shown in Figure 15.17. To do this, simply select the wedge and drag it to the desired location.

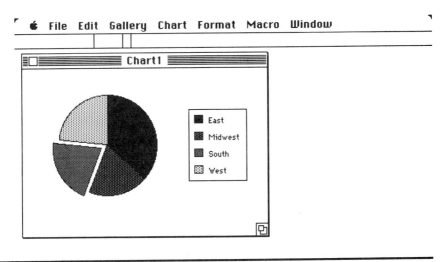

Figure 15.17: *A pie chart with an exploded wedge.*

Using Overlay Charts

You can plot two data series in different graph types by overlaying the charts. The overlays can even have different value axes.

As an example, let's use the Actual Sales worksheet values and plot the projected sales as a column graph and the actual sales as an overlay line graph. Follow these steps:

1. On the Actual Sales worksheet, select cells A6 through C9.

2. Open a new chart, plotting both data series as a column graph.

3. Pull down the Chart menu and click Overlay Chart Type.

4. When the Overlay Chart Type dialog box shown in Figure 15.18 appears, double-click Line.

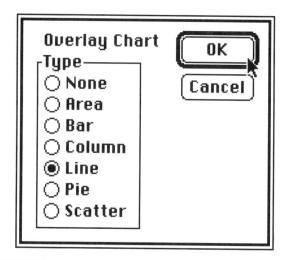

Figure 15.18: *The Overlay Chart Type dialog box.*

The chart will be redrawn with the actual sales values as an overlay, as shown in Figure 15.19. Notice that you did not select which data series was the overlay. Excel assumes that the first data series is the main chart type and the second data series is the overlay. You can alter this by editing the plot order in the SERIES function or by using the Overlay Chart command on the Format menu. If there are more than two data series, they will be divided equally between the main and overlay type. If there is an odd number of data series, the main chart will contain the extra data series.

To switch a chart with an overlay back to a single chart, pull down the Chart menu and click Overlay Chart Type. Double-click None in the dialog box, as shown in Figure 15.20.

*C*hart Presentation Features

Excel offers you many options that you can use to improve the appearance of your charts. You can add text at any point in the chart, control the font and size of the text and values, add arrows to empha-

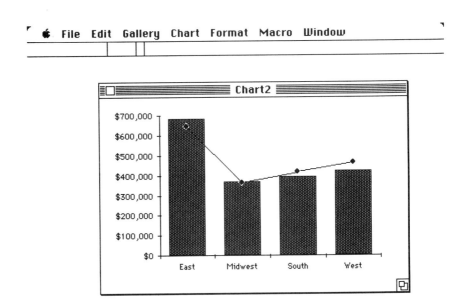

Figure 15.19: *Using an overlay chart.*

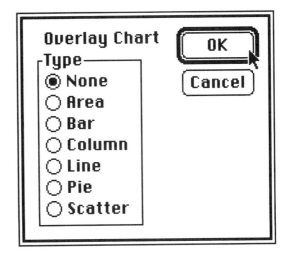

Figure 15.20: *Turning off the overlay.*

size parts of a chart, add titles to axes, change the legend position, or add grid lines. In this section, you'll practice using each of these features on the column chart showing the projected and actual sales values from the Actual Sales worksheet (see Figure 15.10).

Adding Text

You can add text to any part of the graph. If text is added to a pre-defined area of the graph (axis, data series, data point, or title) it is called *attached text,* as it is attached to that specific area. Text that is not associated with any particular part of the graph is called *un-attached text.*

Now, add a title to your chart as attached text:

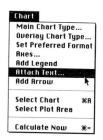

1. Pull down the Chart menu and click Attach Text.

2. When the Attach Text dialog box shown in Figure 15.21 appears, select the area to which the text is to be attached and click OK. There will now be a marker on the chart where the text will be entered.

3. Enter the text from the keyboard. It will be entered into the formula bar, and you can edit it just as you edit a formula. Enter **SALES ANALYSIS.**

4. Click the enter box or press the Enter key. The title will now be displayed on the chart, as shown in Figure 15.22.

Now, add a date to the chart as unattached text:

1. Type the date **7/31/85** on the keyboard. It appears in the formula bar and can be edited.

2. Press the Enter key or click the enter box. The date will be entered into approximately the center of the chart with little boxes around it, as shown in Figure 15.23.

3. Click the text and drag it to the upper right of the chart, below the title. The chart now looks like Figure 15.24.

To remove attached and unattached text, select the text and back-space over it to delete it.

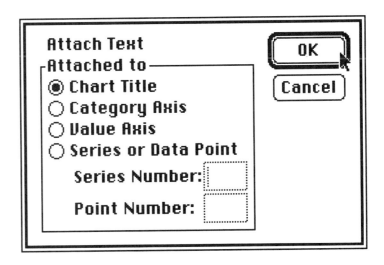

Figure 15.21: *Selecting the area to which the text is to be attached.*

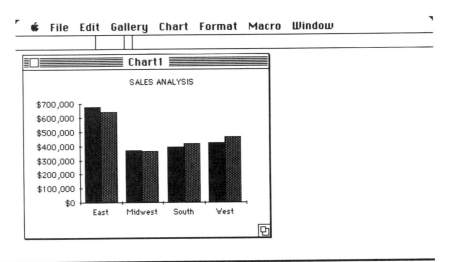

Figure 15.22: *Entering the title.*

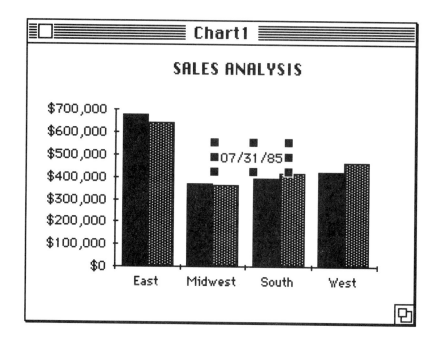

Figure 15.23: *Entering unattached text.*

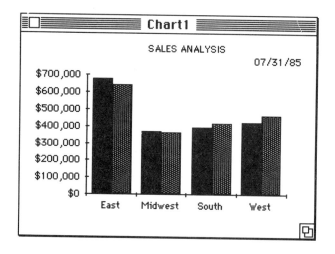

Figure 15.24: *Adding unattached text.*

Formatting Text

Excel lets you change the font, size, and style of any text on your chart. You can also change its orientation, making it vertical or horizontal.

To format both attached and unattached text, first enter the text and position it, then use the Text command on the Format menu. Follow these steps to boldface the title of your Sales Analysis chart:

1. Click the title, which is the text to be formatted.

2. Pull down the Format menu and click Text.

3. When the dialog box shown in Figure 15.25 is displayed, click Monaco, 12, and bold. Then click OK.

Your chart should now look like Figure 15.26.

You can use the same basic procedure to add a title to either or both axes, as you did in Chapter 10. Figure 10.15 in that chapter shows how axes titles appear on a graph. To add these titles, pull down the Chart menu and click Attach Text. When the dialog box

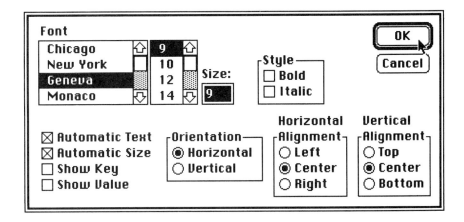

Figure 15.25: *The Text dialog box.*

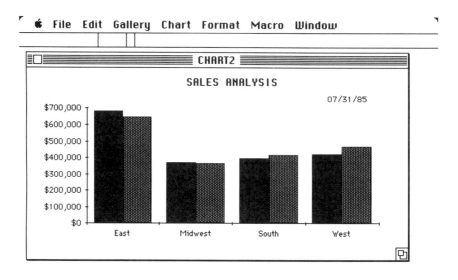

Figure 15.26: *Boldfacing the title.*

(see Figure 15.21) appears, select the axis that will be titled. Then, enter the title from the keyboard and click the enter box. To format the title, select the title and click the Text command on the Format menu. Select the font, size, and orientation in the Text dialog box (see Figure 15.25), and click OK.

Adding and Moving Legends

A legend is used to define the symbols and labels in the chart. On a pie chart, it defines the categories. On other charts, it defines the data series. Once you've added a legend to a chart, you can move it and reformat it.

To add a legend to a chart, simply pull down the Chart menu and click Add Legend. Excel will place the legend at the right of the plot area, and it will resize the graph to make room for the legend. You can readjust the window size if necessary. Add a legend to your Sales Analysis chart. It should look like Figure 15.27.

Note: Editing the legend titles was described earlier in this chapter. To add a legend title, edit the SERIES definition in the formula bar.

Now, let's move the legend to the bottom of the chart:

1. Pull down the Format menu and click Legend.

2. When the Legend dialog box shown in Figure 15.28 is displayed, click Bottom to move the legend to the bottom of the chart, then click OK.

The last thing you should do with your legend is format it:

1. Click the legend area on the chart.

2. Pull down the Format menu and click Text.

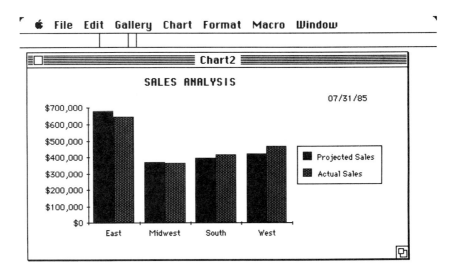

Figure 15.27: *Adding a legend.*

3. When the Text dialog box (see Figure 15.25) appears, select from the formatting options, then click OK.

Your chart should now look like Figure 15.29.

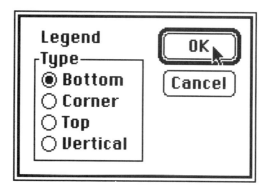

Figure 15.28: *Positioning the legend.*

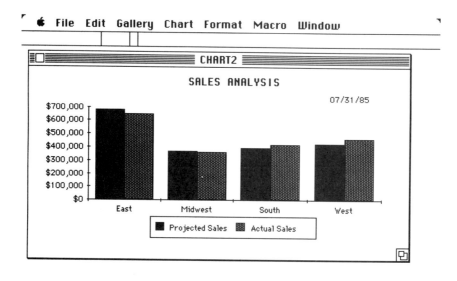

Figure 15.29: *Moving and formatting the legend.*

If you want to delete a displayed legend, pull down the Chart menu and click Delete Legend.

In the next few sections, experiment with your Sales Analysis chart to see how each of the features described affects it.

Formatting Grid lines

Grid lines appear on a chart as horizontal and vertical lines at regular intervals in the plot area. They help you to determine the value of a data point. You can add major (at tick marks) or minor (between tick marks) grid lines, or both, and make the lines heavier.

To add grid lines to a chart, follow these steps:

1. Pull down the Chart menu and click Axes.

2. When the Axes dialog box shown in Figure 15.30 is displayed, click the type of grid lines that you want, then click OK.

To control the weight of the lines, follow these steps:

1. Click a horizontal or vertical grid-line set.

2. Pull down the Format menu and click Patterns.

3. Select the line weight (in the Border Weight box) in the Pattern dialog box, shown in Figure 15.31, then click OK.

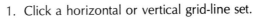

Figure 15.30: *Controlling the axes display.*

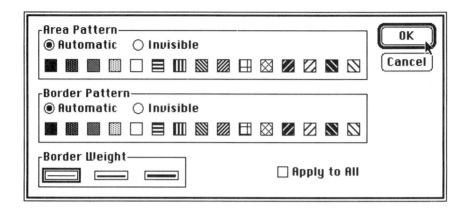

Figure 15.31: *Selecting the line weight and marker pattern.*

The weight selection in the Pattern dialog box applies to the grid lines, axis, or arrow selected before you used the Patterns command.

Formatting Axes

You can also control the formatting of either axis. The Axis command on the Format menu lets you control the tick marks, order of the categories, number of categories, scaling, and zero crossing of an axis. To use it, select the axis, pull down the Format menu, and click Axis. You will see the dialog box shown in Figure 15.32. See Appendix C for an explanation of the options in this dialog box.

You can also change the line weight of an axis. First, click the axis, then pull down the Format menu and click Patterns. When the Patterns dialog box (see Figure 15.31) appears, click the line weight that you want in the Border Weight box.

The Text command on the Format menu allows you to change the font, size, or style of the tick-mark labels on the axes. After you select the axis, pull down the Format menu and click Text. When the dialog box (see Figure 15.25) appears, select the desired format options, then click OK. To change the format of an axis label, click the label, then follow the same procedure.

 ⚹ **File   Edit   Gallery   Chart   Format   Macro   Window**

Value Axis   OK

Range   **Automatic**   Cancel

Minimum: ⬚0   ☒

Maximum: 1000000   ☒

Major Unit: 1000000   ☒

Minor Unit: 200000   ☒

**Category Axis   0   ☒
Crosses At:**

☐ **Logarithmic Scale**
☐ **Values in Reverse Order**

┌**Tick Label Position**────────────────────
○ **None**   ○ **Low**   ○ **High**   ⦿ **Next to Axis**

Figure 15.32: *Formatting the axis.*

To turn off the axis display (but leave the category and value head-ings) pull down the Chart menu and click Axes. When you see the Axes dialog box (Figure 15.30), click Axis under the appropriate heading (Category Axis or Value Axis) to remove it from the chart.

Formatting a Data Series

You can select a new pattern for a data series, stack two data series, and overlap bar and column charts.

To change the data-series marker pattern, select the data series, pull down the Format menu, and click Patterns. You'll see the dialog box shown in Figure 15.31, which gives you your choices for pat-terns. Select the new pattern and click OK.

To stack or overlap data series, pull down the Format menu and click Main chart or Overlay chart. The dialog box shown in Figure 15.33 appears. The options in this dialog box control the relation-ship of the main chart to the overlay chart, as described below:

- Stacked: The second data series is added as a stacked graph to the first data series.

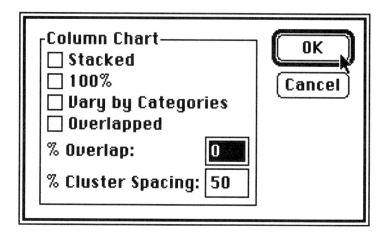

Figure 15.33: *Controlling data-series stacking and overlap.*

- 100%: The category values are normalized to 100%. The absolute values do not appear on the chart.

- Vary by Categories: The pattern for each data point is varied (for a single data series only).

- Drop lines: Lines extend from the highest value in each category to the axis.

- Hi-Lo Lines: Lines extend from the highest point in each category to the lowest.

- Overlapped: Bar and column charts are overlapped.

- % Overlap: Controls the amount of overlap.

- % Cluster Spacing: Controls spacing between bars.

- Angle of First Slice: Controls the angle of the first edge of the first slice from the vertical (for a pie chart).

A dding Arrows

Another one of Excel's presentation features is the capability to add arrows. If you want to add an arrow to emphasize any part of a chart, follow these steps:

1. Pull down the Chart menu and click Add Arrow. An arrow then appears on the chart, as shown in Figure 15.34.

2. Click the arrow and drag it where you want it to appear on the chart. You can move either end by dragging the black box at that end, as shown in Figure 15.35.

3. Use the Patterns command on the Format menu to change the width of the arrow line and the type of arrowhead.

You can repeat this procedure and add as many arrows as you want to any chart.

To delete an arrow, click the arrow, pull down the Chart menu, and click Delete Arrow.

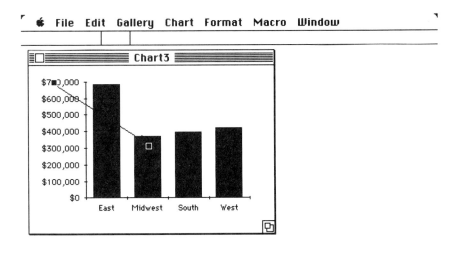

Figure 15.34: *Adding an arrow.*

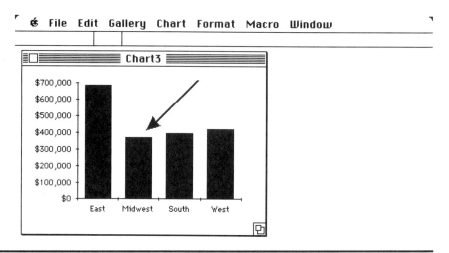

Figure 15.35: *Using an arrow for emphasis.*

Summary

This chapter has given you a complete overview of Excel's extensive charting capabilities. The chart is always drawn from one or more data series that you defined. After the basic chart is created, you can alter the type of chart, label the chart or axes, add a legend, arrows, or unattached text, and control the format of any part of the chart. You can use these charting features to create high-quality graphics, suitable for reports and presentations.

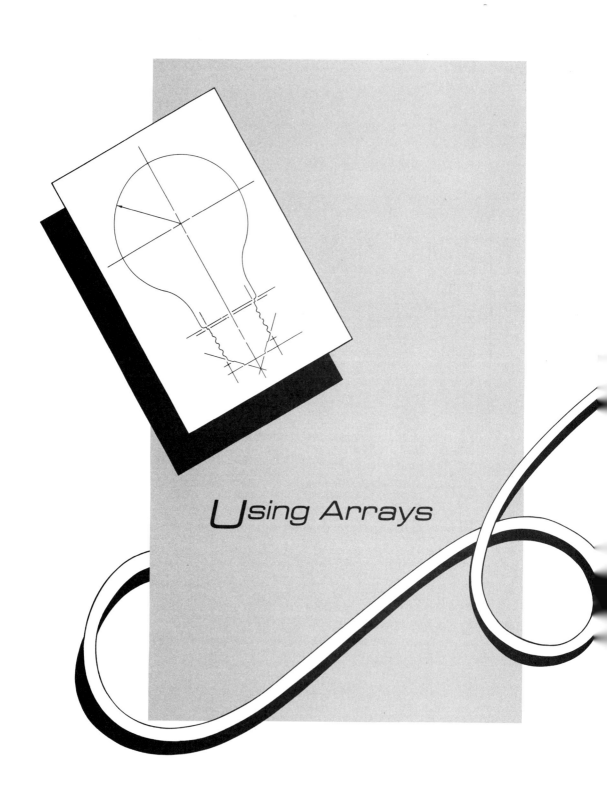

Using Arrays

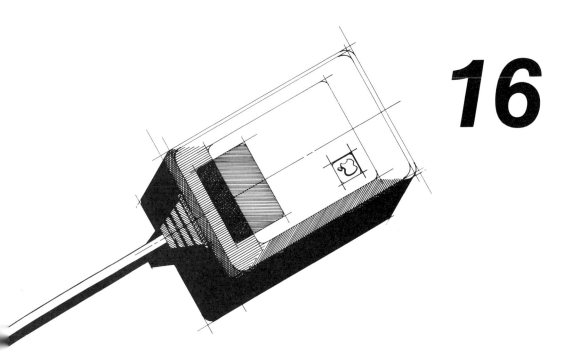

16

In some applications, you may want to use multiple values as an argument for a function, or you may want a function to produce multiple values. Such a list of multiple values is called an array. Excel is the first worksheet program that has the capability of using arrays as function arguments.

In all of the examples in the previous chapters, you have used only function arguments with a single value. In this chapter, you will learn about Excel's capability of using multiple-value arguments, or arrays. The basic concept of using arrays will be illustrated with a simple example. Then, you will work through a more complex example that clearly shows how arrays can make your worksheet calculations much easier.

*A*rray Uses

An *array*, as used in a function argument, is a list of values. In a
simple function, the arguments each refer to a single value—a single
cell or a single cell range. For example, the result of the formula
= SUM(A1:A11) is the sum of the values from cells A1 through
A11—a single cell range. But suppose that you wanted to use the
same function argument for several values. You could repeat the
function for each value, or you could use the easy method: you
could include an array as the function argument.

Entering an Array

The following exercise will give you an idea of how arrays work.
Suppose that you have an Inventory worksheet that lists four products and a quantity on hand and a cost for each one, as shown in
Figure 16.1. The extended cost for each product equals the quantity
on hand multiplied by the cost. The total inventory value, then, is
the sum of the extended costs for each product. Enter the data for the
inventory worksheet, using the formulas shown in Figure 16.2.

	A	B	C	D	E	F
1						
2			INVENTORY			
3						
4						
5		Product A	Product B	Product C	Product D	
6	Qty on Hand	125	215	165	34	
7	Cost	$64.95	$119.50	$91.25	$175.00	
8						
9	Ext. Cost	$8,118.75	$25,692.50	$15,056.25	$5,950.00	
10						
11						
12	Total	$54,817.50				

Figure 16.1: *The Inventory worksheet.*

Notice that you entered the same formula three times in the Ext. Cost row. There is an easier way to calculate the total value of the inventory. Instead, you can use arrays to obtain the total without the extended cost calculation. Clear the Ext. Cost row (row 9) and type in the following formula for the total in cell B14:

$$= SUM(B6:E6 * B7:E7)$$

After you have entered the formula from the keyboard, *hold down the Command key while you press Enter or click the enter box.* This will force Excel to accept the arguments as arrays. As shown in Figure 16.3, the displayed total in cell B14 is still the same, but the formula used to calculate that total is different.

Examine the formula. Notice that it is exactly as you entered it, except that it is enclosed in braces. The values for the cell ranges B6 through E6 and B7 through E7 are treated as an array, or list of values. The SUM function multiplied the corresponding values in each list and then summed the products to get the final total.

As you just learned, there is a simple technique for using arrays with Excel: After you enter a function with an array, hold down the Command key while you press the Enter key or click the enter box. Excel will add braces to indicate that the function contains an array.

Many of the functions listed in Chapter 8 *require* array arguments. With these functions, it is not necessary to use the Command key, as Excel assumes the argument is an array. Later in the chapter, you will use one of these functions.

Calculating Multiple Output Values

In the previous example, multiple values were used to obtain a single output value. In some cases, you may have multiple output values;

	A	B	C	D
1				
2			INVENTORY	
3				
4				
5		Product A	Product B	Product C
6	Qty on Hand	125	215	165
7	Cost	64.95	119.5	91.25
8				
9	Ext. Cost	=Qty_on_Hand*Cost	=Qty_on_Hand*Cost	=Qty_on_Hand*Cost
10				
11				
12	Total	=SUM(B9:E9)		

Figure 16.2: *The Inventory worksheet formulas.*

that is, the output of the function is an array. To understand how you could use multiple outputs, let's look at a linear-regression example.

Linear regression is often used to project a future trend from known data about the past. This technique is used by manufacturing operations to project data on future productivity based on changes in the number of employees, working conditions, and other factors. It can also be used by a sales department to plan warehousing, marketing, and sales representation.

Suppose, for example, that your company discovered there was a relationship between the disposable income per person in various areas and the sale of its product. You have information about the disposable income in future years, and you wish to project your sales for these future years so that you can plan how much warehouse space is needed, the number of sales representatives to employ, your marketing costs, and other factors. You'll use linear regression to make this projection. In the following example, you'll first do the linear regression using conventional worksheet techniques. Then, you'll do the same linear regression using arrays.

Figure 16.4 shows how the linear regression would be done without arrays. The formulas are shown in Figure 16.5, and the values

File   Edit   Formula   Format   Data   Options   Macro   Window

B14	{=SUM(B6:E6*B7:E7)}

Inventory

	A	B	C	D	E	F
1						
2			INVENTORY			
3						
4						
5		Product A	Product B	Product C	Product D	
6	Qty on Hand	125	215	165	34	
7	Cost	$64.95	$119.50	$91.25	$175.00	
8						
9	Ext. Cost	$8,118.75	$25,692.50	$15,056.25	$5,950.00	
10						
11						
12	Total	$54,817.50				
13						
14		54817.5				
15						
16						
17						

Figure 16.3: *Using arrays to calculate the total.*

are plotted in Figure 16.6 (the x axis is the disposable income, and the y axis is the sales). As the graph shows, there seems to be a correlation that could be used to plan future sales.

The data for the disposable income and sales are used to calculate the constants for the linear regression. This calculation is done in cells C16 and C17 using the following formula:

$$b = \frac{\Sigma xy - \bar{x}\Sigma y}{\Sigma x^2 - \bar{x}\Sigma^x}$$

$$a = \bar{y} - b\bar{x}$$

$$y_n = a + bx_n$$

LINEAR REGRESSION EXAMPLE

Year	Disposable Income ($K)	Projected Disp. Income ($K)	Sales ($)	Disp. Income X Sales	Sales Squared	Projected Sales
1975	$200		$2,350	470,000	40,000	
1976	$260		$2,500	650,000	67,600	
1977	$270		$2,400	648,000	72,900	
1978	$190		$2,390	454,100	36,100	
1979	$119		$2,360	280,840	14,161	
1980	$115		$2,260	259,900	13,225	
1981	$325		$2,575	836,875	105,625	
1982	$350		$2,550	892,500	122,500	
1983	$302		$2,503	755,906	91,204	
1984	$212		$2,475	524,700	44,944	
1985		$250				2,453.40
1986		$275				2,480.62
1987		$325				2,535.07
Sum	2,343.00		24,363.00	5,772,821	608,259	
Average	234.30		2,436.30	577,282	60,826	

Value of a= 1.08898019
Value of b= 2181.15194

Figure 16.4: *Doing a linear regression the hard way.*

	A	B	C	D	E	F	G
1							
2							
3			LINEAR REGRESSION EX				
4							
5							
6							
7	Year	Disposable Income ($K)	Projected Disp. Income ($K)	Sales ($)	Disp. Income X Sales	Sales Squared	Projected Sales
8							
9							
10							
11	1975	200		2250	=B11*D11	=D11*D11	
12	1976	260		2500	=B12*D12	=D12*D12	
13	1977	220		2400	=B13*D13	=D13*D13	
14	1978	190		2390	=B14*D14	=D14*D14	
15	1979	119		2360	=B15*D15	=D15*D15	
16	1980	115		2360	=B16*D16	=D16*D16	
17	1981	325		2350	=B17*D17	=D17*D17	
18	1982	380		2360	=B18*D18	=D18*D18	
19	1983	302		2303	=B19*D19	=D19*D19	
20	1984	212		2479	=B20*D20	=D20*D20	
21	1985		250				=C30+(C29*C21)
22	1986		275				=C30+(C29*C22)
23	1987		325				=C30+(C29*C23)
24							
25	Sum	=SUM(B11:B20)		=SUM(D11:D20)	=SUM(E11:E20)	=SUM(F11:F20)	
26							
27	Average	=B25/10		=D25/10	=E25/10	=F25/10	
28							
29		Value of b=	=((B25-(D27*D25))/(F25-(				
30		Value of b=	=(D27-(C29*B27))				

Figure 16.5: The formulas for the linear-regression example.

Enter the data for the entire worksheet, as shown in Figure 16.5. You can use the Fill Down command to enter much of the data, but you will still find it cumbersome to use this approach to obtain your projections.

Now try the same thing using arrays:

1. Copy the Projected Disp. Income values in column C into the Disposable Income column (column B) for a single Income array.

2. Combine the Sales and Projected Sales columns into a single column.

3. Delete all but the three columns that contain the data for the two input arrays, which are labeled Disp. Income and Sales. Sales will also be the output array. Your worksheet should now look like Figure 16.7.

4. You will need to use iteration for this calculation, as some of the input array values are missing in the beginning. Pull down the Options menu, click Calculation, and click Iteration in the dialog box, as shown in Figure 16.8. Then, click OK.

5. Enter the first array formula. You will need to use two functions: SUM and LINEST. The LINEST function has two arrays

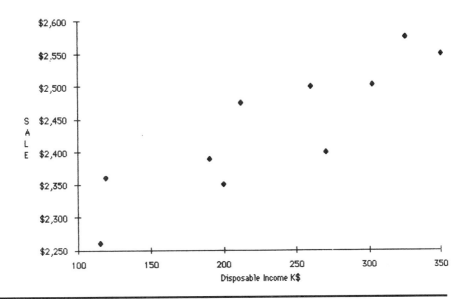

Figure 16.6: *The chart of the linear regression.*

for an input and one array for an output (see Chapter 8). Enter the following formula into cell C21:

= SUM(LINEST($C$11:$C$23,$B$11:$B$23) * {250,1})

In this case, you should also enter the braces from the keyboard.

6. Copy the formula in cell C21 into cells C22 and C23, then use the commands on the Edit menu to paste the proper sales

LINEAR REGRESSION EXAMPLE
Using Arrays

Year	Disposable Income ($K)	Projected Sales
1975	$200	$2,350
1976	$260	$2,500
1977	$270	$2,400
1978	$190	$2,390
1979	$119	$2,360
1980	$115	$2,260
1981	$325	$2,575
1982	$350	$2,550
1983	$302	$2,503
1984	$212	$2,475
1985	$250	$2,453 *
1986	$275	$2,481 *
1987	$325	$2,535 *

* Projected

Figure 16.7: *The linear-regression input data.*

value into each formula. Your final formulas should look like those shown in Figure 16.9.

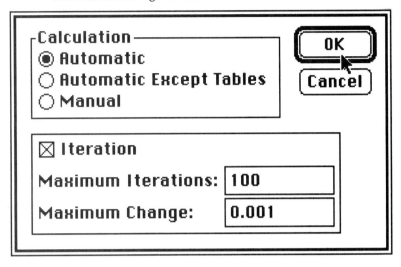

Figure 16.8: *Turning on the iteration.*

	A	B	C
1			
2			
3		LINEAR REGRESSI|	
4		*Using Arrays*	
5			
6			
7	Year	Disposable	Projected
8		Income	Sales
9		($K)	
10			
11	1975	200	2350
12	1976	260	2500
13	1977	270	2400
14	1978	190	2390
15	1979	119	2360
16	1980	115	2260
17	1981	325	2575
18	1982	350	2550
19	1983	302	2503
20	1984	212	2475
21	1985	250	=SUM(LINEST($C$11:$C$23,$B$11:$B$23)*{250,1})
22	1986	275	=SUM(LINEST($C$11:$C$23,$B$11:$B$23)*{275,1})
23	1987	325	=SUM(LINEST($C$11:$C$23,$B$11:$B$23)*{325,1})
24			
25		* Projected	

Figure 16.9: *The final linear-regression formulas using arrays.*

7. Format the worksheet as shown in Figure 16.10, then print it out.

The final projected values are the same as those that you obtained the hard way, but your work is much, much less.

Let's review the array formula that you just used. The LINEST function will return an array of two values: the slope (m) and the intercept (b) of the line of regression, represented by y=b+mx. These are the same constants that you calculated earlier using multiple columns,

LINEAR REGRESSION EXAMPLE
Using Arrays

Year	Disposable Income ($K)	Projected Sales
1975	$200	$2,350
1976	$260	$2,500
1977	$270	$2,400
1978	$190	$2,390
1979	$119	$2,360
1980	$115	$2,260
1981	$325	$2,575
1982	$350	$2,550
1983	$302	$2,503
1984	$212	$2,475
1985	$250	
1986	$275	
1987	$325	

* Projected

Figure 16.10: *The final printout using arrays.*

squares, sums, and averages. Excel does it all with a single function that uses array inputs to calculate an array output. The rest of the formula multiplies the first argument of the LINEST function (the slope) by an X value (250) and adds the second part of the LINEST function (the y intercept) multiplied by 1.

You could also try an exponential regression using the LOGEST function. The other functions that require arrays are GROWTH, TREND, COLUMNS, ROWS, and TRANSPOSE. The LOOKUP functions and others (such as MIRR) also can use arrays. Even functions that normally use single-value arguments, such as SUM, can also work with array arguments.

Array Constants

In Chapter 7, you created a Cash-Flow Analysis worksheet that had a parameter file with several constants. These constants could then serve as inputs for formulas used elsewhere in the worksheet. In the same way, you could store an array as a single constant and use it in formulas, just as you would an array.

To enter an array of values into any cell, type in the values separated by commas and enclose the array in braces. Do not use the Command key. For example, if you enter {**1,2,3**} into a cell, the cell will contain a 1 by 3 array with the values 1, 2, and 3. You can enter arrays with multiple rows by separating the rows with semicolons. For example, the array {2,4,5;1,2,6} represents an array of five columns and two rows.

Rules for Using Arrays

Here are some general rules for using arrays:

- The values of an array must be constant values and not formulas. An array can contain numeric, text, logical, or error values (such as #VALUE!). Text values must be enclosed in quotation marks.

- When an array is used with a function, the type of values must be consistent with what is required by the function.

- When an array formula is entered into a range of cells, the formulas should produce an array that is the same size as the selected cell range.

- Relative cell addresses in an array are considered relative to the cell in the upper-left corner of the range.

- You cannot enter arrays that have a mixed number of columns in the rows. For example, {4,9,1;3,4} is an illegal array.

- If an array is used as an argument in a function, all other arguments in the same function should be arrays of the same size. For example, SUM(A7:C7 + A8:C8) is normal. If you use SUM(A7:C7 + B8:C8), Excel will expand the second array to the same size.

Editing an Array Formula

Edit	
Undo Paste	⌘Z
Cut	⌘H
Copy	⌘C
Paste	⌘U
Clear...	⌘B
Paste Special...	
Delete...	⌘K
Insert...	⌘I
Fill Right	⌘R
Fill Down	⌘D

You can edit an array formula by using the commands on the Edit menu. If you click the cursor on any point in the formula bar, whatever you type will be entered at the cursor location. You can also drag the cursor in the formula bar to mark a range of characters, then use the Cut command to delete the marked characters. Once you have finished editing the formula, clicking the enter box or pressing the Enter key will complete the entry.

You can enter an array formula into a range of cells in the same way that you enter any formula into a range of cells: hold down the Command key while you press the Enter key. There is a difference, however, when you are editing a formula that has been entered into a range of cells. After an array formula is entered into a range, you cannot edit or clear an individual cell or delete rows or columns within that range. The entire cell range must be treated as a single unit. You must select and edit or clear the entire range.

Linking Worksheets with Arrays

A worksheet that uses array formulas and references can be linked to another worksheet by using external references, just like any other linked formulas. A cell on a dependent worksheet can reference a cell on a supporting worksheet by using the worksheet name, an exclamation point, and the worksheet cell reference.

Remember that if cells on the supporting worksheet are moved, corresponding references on the dependent worksheet will not follow the move. For this reason, you should use names to define cells or cell ranges. You can assign a name to a cell range within a row or column and use the name as an array on a dependent worksheet. When you use a name as an array, the only additional step that you need to take is to hold down the Command key while you click the enter box or press Enter to complete the formula entry. To see how this works, let's link a cell in a new worksheet to the cell that contains the total value in the Inventory worksheet that you created at the beginning of this chapter. Follow these steps:

1. Open the Inventory worksheet that you just created and define the row titles on it as names (see Chapter 11).

2. Open up a new worksheet window and display both windows on the screen, as shown in Figure 16.11.

3. Enter the title **Inventory Summary** in cell B1 of the new worksheet.

4. Select cell B3 as the cell for the total, pull down the Formula menu, and click Paste Function. You'll see the Paste Function

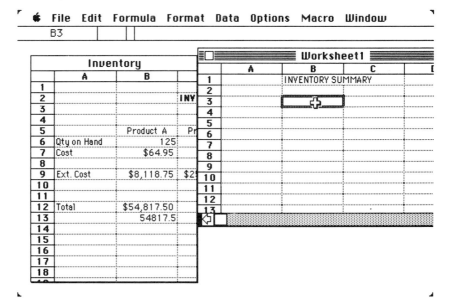

Figure 16.11: *Pasting an array name into a linked document.*

dialog box shown in Figure 16.12. Scroll to SUM and double-click it.

5. Click anywhere in the Inventory worksheet to partially select the window, pull down the Formula menu, and click Paste Name. You'll see the Paste Name dialog box shown in Figure 16.13. Double-click Qty_on_Hand.

6. Enter * from the keyboard.

7. Pull down the Formula menu, click Paste Name, and double-click Cost in the Paste Name dialog box.

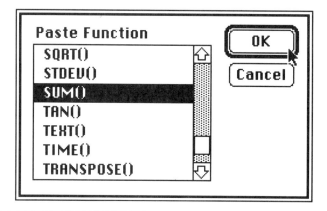

Figure 16.12: *Pasting a function name.*

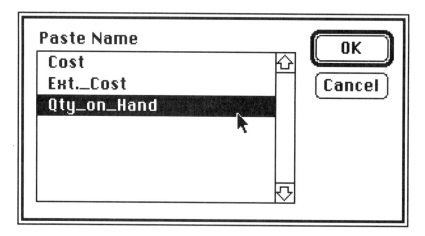

Figure 16.13: *Pasting a name.*

Now note this difference:

8. Hold down the Command key and click the enter box or press Enter.

The correct total is now in cell B3 on the new worksheet, and the formula is in its formula bar, as shown in Figure 16.14.

Using Arrays with Charts

Excel uses the SERIES function to create charts (see Chapter 15). Two of the arguments of this function—categories and values—are always arrays. You can edit any chart's SERIES function to convert the array references to constants. For more details, refer to Chapter 15.

File	Edit	Formula	Format	Data	Options	Macro	Window

B3	{=SUM(Inventory!Qty_on_Hand*Inventory!Cost)}

Inventory

	A	B	
1			
2			INY
3			
4			
5		Product A	Pr
6	Qty on Hand	125	
7	Cost	$64.95	
8			
9	Ext. Cost	$8,118.75	$2
10			
11			
12	Total	$54,817.50	
13		54817.5	
14			
15			
16			
17			
18			

Worksheet1

	A	B	C	
1		INVENTORY SUMMARY		
2				
3		54817.5		
4				
5				
6				
7				
8				
9				
10				
11				
12				
13				

Figure 16.14: *The final worksheets.*

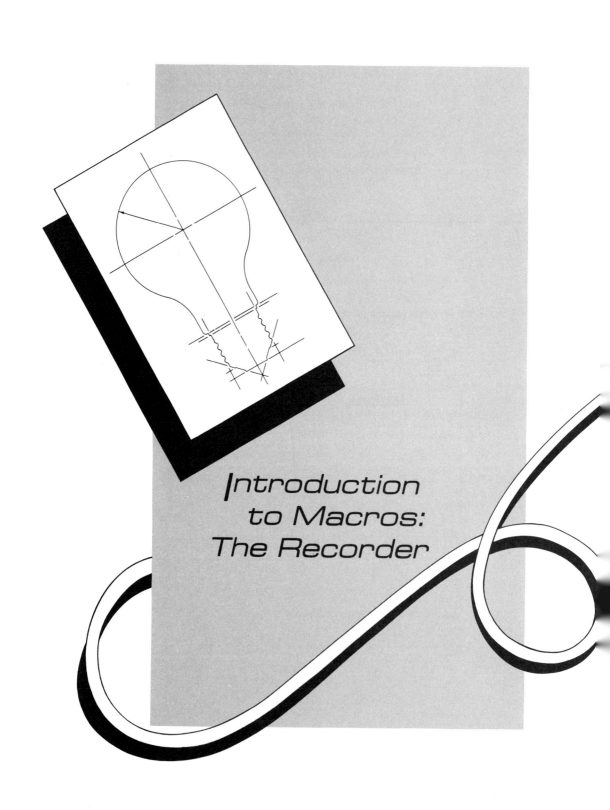

Introduction
to Macros:
The Recorder

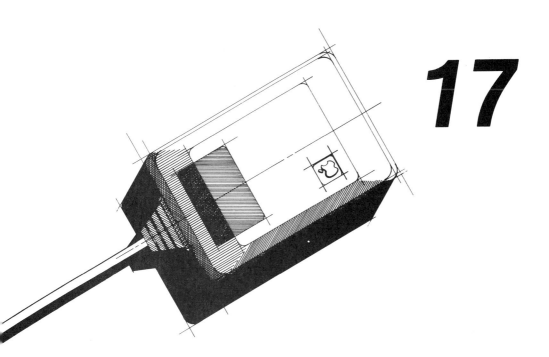

17

A macro is a program that represents a series of actions. In effect, macros permit you to write and name your own application programs using worksheet commands and functions. You can execute these programs as many times as you wish. For this reason, macros are generally considered one of the most important features of any worksheet software package.

Although macros are a part of many worksheet products, Excel's macros have three major distinctions: they are easy to use, they don't take up worksheet room (they're saved on separate macro sheets), and they utilize a special macro language that you can use to write your own macros.

With Excel, you can create both function and command macros. In this chapter, you will learn how to use Excel's recorder to create a simple command macro and how to work with macro documents. Chapter 18 describes function macros, and Chapter 19 provides details on the more advanced techniques for using command macros.

Command Macro Uses

A command macro is a series of commands that accomplish a desired action. The commands are stored as a single program, which can be executed as many times as necessary.

Command macros are primarily used in two applications: whenever it is necessary to repeat a series of steps two or more times and whenever a complex series of steps must be performed. The latter application is particularly useful when the program will be executed by an inexperienced user. For example, suppose that a series of annual reports must be prepared from data that will not be available until a few days before an annual meeting. Weeks before the annual meeting, macros could be created to produce the final report from dummy data. Once the actual data are available, the same macros could be used by almost anyone to create the final reports in a very short time.

Creating a Command Macro

There are essentially three steps to creating a command macro:

1. Opening the macro sheet and setting the range

2. Recording the program

3. Naming the macro

Now, suppose that you are one of the managers of Acme Manufacturing who creates a number of quarterly reports that all use the same heading, which is shown in Figure 17.1. You've decided to take advantage of Excel's macro feature and create a macro that will add this heading to any worksheet. The following sections describe how to create this command macro.

Opening the Macro Sheet and Setting the Range

The steps that you will take are recorded on a separate macro sheet, which is much like any Excel worksheet. First, open a regular worksheet. Then, follow these steps to open the macro sheet and set the range for the macro:

1. Pull down the File menu and click New.

2. When the New dialog box shown in Figure 17.2 appears, click Macro Sheet, then click OK.

3. A new document titled Macro1 will open on the screen. The menu bar has not changed.

4. Click the column A designator on the macro sheet to indicate that you will record your macro in this column.

5. Pull down the Macro menu and click Set Recorder.

6. Size the macro sheet slightly smaller and click your original worksheet again to make it active, as shown in Figure 17.3.

Recording the Program

With your worksheet active, you must turn on the recorder and then actually perform the task that you want the macro to accomplish.

Figure 17.1: *The worksheet heading.*

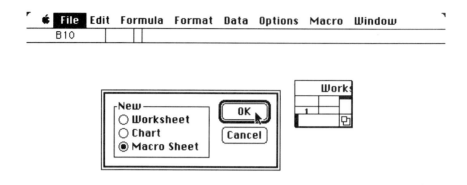

Figure 17.2: *The New dialog box.*

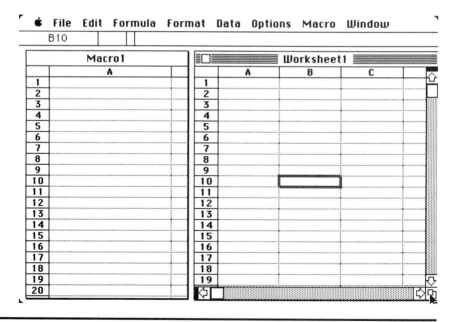

Figure 17.3: *The macro and worksheet windows.*

Follow these steps:

1. Pull down the Macro menu and click Start Recorder. Nothing on the macro sheet or worksheet will change.

2. Carry out the steps that you want the macro to execute:

   a. Select cell C1.

   b. Enter the title **ACME MANUFACTURING.**

   c. Widen column A. Select column A, pull down the Format menu, and click Column Width. When the dialog box appears, change the width of column A to 20 characters and click OK, as shown in Figure 17.4.

   d. Enter the column titles. Select cell B3 and drag to cell E3. Enter the column titles shown in Figure 17.1.

   e. Center the titles. Select rows 1 through 3, pull down the Format menu, click Alignment, and double-click Center or click Center and click OK, as shown in Figure 17.5.

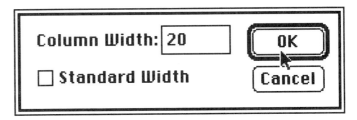

Figure 17.4: *Setting the column width.*

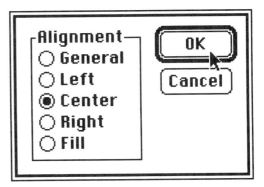

Figure 17.5: *Setting the alignment.*

f. Put the title in boldface print. Select cell C1, pull down the Format menu, and click Style. When the dialog box appears, click Bold and click OK, as shown in Figure 17.6.

3. Pull down the Macro menu and click Stop Recorder.

Your macro sheet should now look like Figure 17.7. Notice that your commands have been stored in column A using a special language.

Naming the Macro

The macro has now been recorded, but it must be assigned a name before you can use it. You also can assign the macro a keystroke sequence that you could use to execute the program.

Follow these steps to name your macro:

1. Select the macro sheet.

2. Select the first cell in the macro sheet.

3. Pull down the Formula menu and click Define Name. You will see the window shown in Figure 17.8. Notice that the familiar window now has some new options that apply only to macros and that the Refers To box references $A$1, which is the first cell of the macro commands. The cursor is in the Name box.

4. Enter the name **HEADING** in the Name box. Do not click OK yet.

5. In the Macro box, click Command to indicate that you are creating a command macro.

6. Click the Option-Command key box and enter an uppercase **X.** (You can use uppercase or lowercase letters to define your keystroke sequence.)

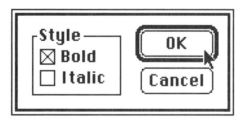

Figure 17.6: *Selecting the style.*

7. Click OK.

You have now named your command macro and defined a key-stroke sequence that you can use to execute this macro.

*E*xecuting Your Command Macro

You can use either of two methods to execute your HEADING macro:

- Choose the Run command on the Macro menu
- Press the keyboard sequence

Macro1		
	A	
1	=SELECT("R1C3")	
2	=FORMULA("ACME MANUFACT	
3	=SELECT("C1")	
4	=COLUMN.WIDTH(20)	
5	=SELECT("R3C2:R3C5")	
6	=FORMULA("Qtr 1")	
7	=SELECT("R3C2:R3C5","R3C	
8	=FORMULA("Qtr 2")	
9	=SELECT("R3C2:R3C5","R3C	
10	=FORMULA("Qtr 3")	
11	=SELECT("R3C2:R3C5","R3C	
12	=FORMULA("Qtr 4")	
13	=SELECT("R3C2:R3C5")	
14	=HSCROLL(0%)	
15	=SELECT("R1:R3")	
16	=ALIGNMENT(3)	
17	=SELECT("R1C3")	
18	=STYLE(TRUE,FALSE)	
19	=RETURN()	
20		

Figure 17.7: *The macro worksheet after the command entry.*

However, before you use either method, the macro sheet that contains the macro must be open.

Before you start, clear your worksheet by selecting the entire worksheet, pulling down the Edit menu, and clicking Clear. When the dialog box shown in Figure 17.9 appears, click All, then click OK.

To execute your command macro using the Macro menu, follow these steps:

1. Be sure that the worksheet is clear and selected.

2. Pull down the Macro menu and click Run.

3. When the dialog box shown in Figure 17.10 is displayed, double-click the macro name HEADING.

Excel will execute the macro, and the heading will be entered onto the worksheet. Your worksheet should look like Figure 17.1.

To execute a command macro from the keyboard, first clear the worksheet area, then hold down the Command key, press the Option key, and press the key that you assigned to the macro (an uppercase X in our example). The macro will be executed to create the worksheet heading shown in Figure 17.1.

Saving the Macro

Macros are not associated with any worksheet or chart document; they are stored as separate macro documents. You must save the

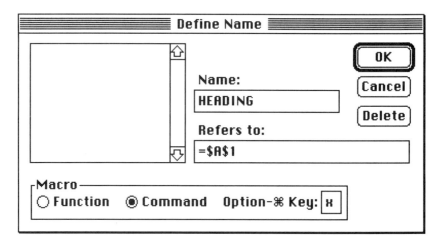

Figure 17.8: *The Define Name window for macros.*

macro sheet after it is created if you want to use the macro that it contains.

Follow these steps to save your command macro:

1. Select the macro sheet.

2. Pull down the File menu and click Save As.

3. When the dialog box shown in Figure 17.11 appears, enter the name **HEADING,** then click OK.

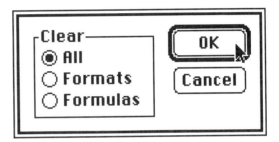

Figure 17.9: *Clearing the worksheet.*

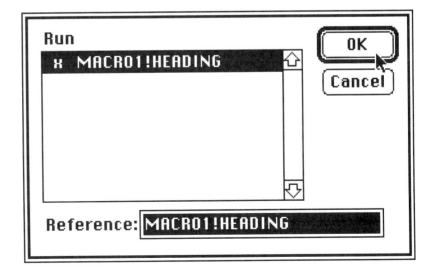

Figure 17.10: *The Run dialog box.*

You can store many macros on the same document. Then, when you open that one document, all the command macros stored on it will be available for your use.

Opening a Macro Document

The macro document must be open before any macros stored on the document can be used. To open a macro document, pull down the File menu and click Open. The dialog box shown in Figure 17.12 will appear. Select the name of the macro document, then click OK.

The Macro Language

Open the macro sheet that you just created and examine that document carefully. It should look like Figure 17.7. Column A consists of a series of formulas that are much like the formulas that you use on your worksheets. The formulas contain functions from the Excel macro language. Like any functions, these have arguments. The SELECT function selects the cell or cells specified in the argument, and the FORMULA function is used to enter data into a specified cell or cell range. Compare each function in the column with what you remember as your actions when you set up the worksheet heading. In Chapter 19, you will learn more about how to use Excel's macro language.

Save Macro Sheet as: Excel Disk
                                        33K available
HEADING

● Normal   ○ SYLK   [Save]   [Eject]
○ Text   ○ WKS   [Cancel] [Drive]

Figure 17.11: *Saving the macro document.*

Editing a Macro

You can edit the macro sheet, just like any other Excel document. You can change arguments, delete or insert rows, or even create the entire macro by manually entering it from the keyboard.

You can experiment by making the following changes in your macro sheet:

1. Change the column width of column A to 25 characters.

2. Put the title in italics instead of boldface.

Now, execute your command macro again using the new macro.

You can also edit the macro name. To change the name or keystroke sequence, follow these steps:

1. Select the macro sheet.

2. Select the first cell of the macro.

3. Pull down the Formula menu and click Define Name.

4. When the dialog box shown in Figure 17.13 appears, click the macro's name.

5. Edit the name in the Name box or the keyboard code in the Macro box.

6. Click OK.

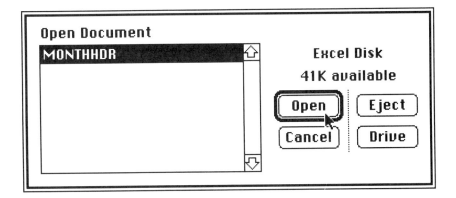

Figure 17.12: *Opening a macro document.*

Using Command Macros

This chapter is intended as only a brief introduction to command macros. Here are some basic rules for using command macros:

- Be sure that you think through what you are trying to accomplish before you enter the commands after starting the recorder. You may wish to do a dummy run to test the sequence before you record it. In this way, you can avoid entering errors or unnecessary extra steps into the macro sheet.

- Generally, the first step in recording a macro is to position your cursor at the desired point on the worksheet. Don't forget to start the recorder, *then* position the cursor.

- Don't be bashful about using macros. Anytime that you find yourself planning to repeat a command sequence, save it as a command macro.

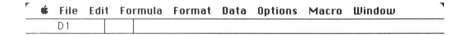

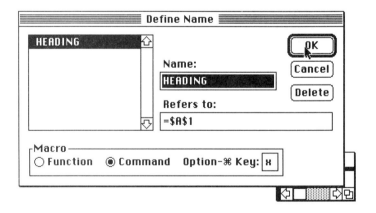

Figure 17.13: *Editing a macro name.*

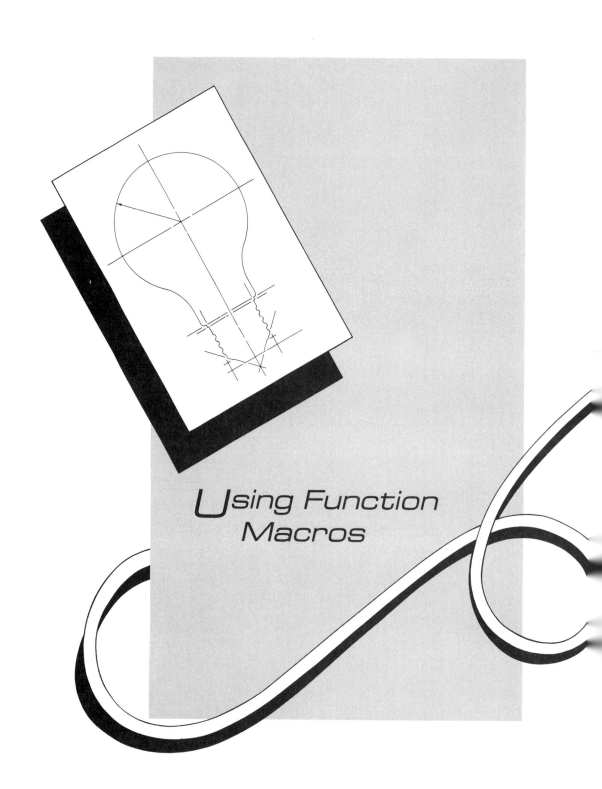

Using Function Macros

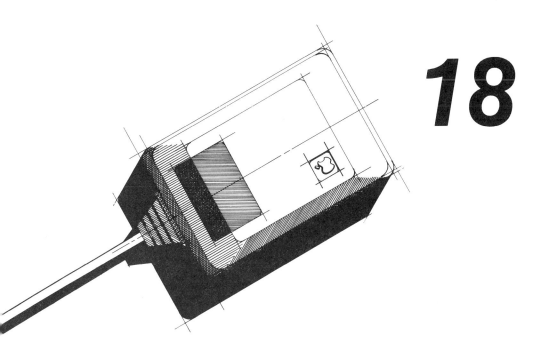

18

Excel's function macro capability permits you to create your own functions. You can decide what arguments are needed in the function and what results are to be returned in the worksheet cell. Once you create a function macro, you can include it in formulas, just as you would use any other Excel function.

For most standard applications, Excel's extensive built-in functions can be used. However, you may need to define your own functions for special applications, such as civil engineering and financial analyses, in which lengthy, specialized formulas are used frequently.

In this chapter, you will learn how to create function macros and how to use some of Excel's macro language functions.

Function Macro Uses

A function macro is essentially a user-defined function. As explained in Chapter 8, a function is an abbreviation for a formula. A function can also be defined as an operator, similar to a symbol operator such as + or −. It contains one or more arguments that are used as input to calculate a result. When you create a function macro, you define the arguments, results, and formulas to calculate the results. You should create function macros whenever you need to use special formulas many times in several worksheets. When you use function macros, you no longer need to remember the formulas to get a specific result. You only have to remember the name of the function and the type and order of the arguments.

Creating a Function Macro

Now, let's create a simple function macro that can be used to convert a temperature from centigrade to Fahrenheit. There are three steps to creating a function macro:

1. Defining the formulas and arguments

2. Entering the function

3. Defining the name

Defining Formulas and Arguments

The formula for the temperature-conversion function is $b = (9/5) * a + 32$, where b equals the temperature in Fahrenheit and a equals the temperature in centigrade. The function will have the name FAHRENHEIT and contain one input argument for the temperature in centigrade.

Entering the Function Macro

To create the function macro, first open a macro sheet by pulling down the File menu, clicking New, and double-clicking Macro Sheet on the New dialog box (see Figure 18.1). This will open a blank macro sheet. Function macros must be entered manually—you cannot use the recorder.

Now, follow these steps to enter the FAHRENHEIT function macro:

1. Click the column A designator to select the range on the macro sheet. Pull down the Macro menu and click <u>Set Recorder</u>.

2. Enter the function macro title **FAHRENHEIT** into cell A1, as shown in Figure 18.2.

3. In cell A2, define the input argument for the function using the ARGUMENT macro language function. Enter **=ARGUMENT-("Centigrade")**, including the quotation marks with the argument name.

4. In cell A3, define your formula: **= (9/5)*Centigrade + 32.**

5. In cell A4, use the RETURN macro language function with the reference to the cell on the macro sheet that contains the result: **RETURN(A3).**

These are the rules that you followed when you entered the FAHRENHEIT function macro:

- Excel's macro language functions are preceded by an equal sign, like any other function.

- In the macro language functions, the names of the input arguments are enclosed in quotation marks.

- In the formulas, the names of the input arguments are not enclosed in quotation marks.

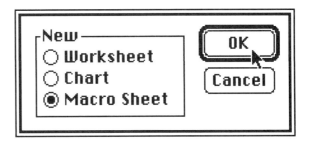

Figure 18.1: *The New dialog box.*

> *Tip:* Comment on your function macros. If the macro is entered to column A, use column B to comment on your macro. Specify the arguments, results, and the calculations.

Naming the Function Macro

The last step is to assign a name to the function macro. Use the following procedure:

1. Be sure that the first cell of the macro sheet is selected.

2. Pull down the Formula menu and click Define Name.

3. When the Define Name window appears, the name FAHREN-HEIT from the first cell is displayed in the Name box, as shown in Figure 18.3. Click Function in the Macro box, then click OK.

Saving the Function

Before you use this function macro, save the macro sheet by following these steps:

1. Select the macro sheet.

2. Pull down the File menu and click Save As.

3. When the dialog box shown in Figure 18.4 appears, enter the name **FAHRENHEIT.**

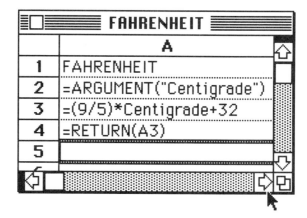

Figure 18.2: *Entering the function macro.*

Using Function Macros

Once you've defined a function macro, you can use it in formulas on a worksheet just as you would use any other function. Let's use the FAHRENHEIT macro to see how a function macro works:

1. Create the simple worksheet shown in Figure 18.5. Enter the row titles **Centigrade** and **Fahrenheit** in cells A2 and A3.

2. Enter the formula:

   a. Select cell B3.

   b. Pull down the Formula menu and click Paste Function.

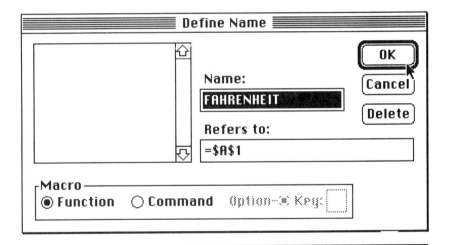

Figure 18.3: *The Define Name window.*

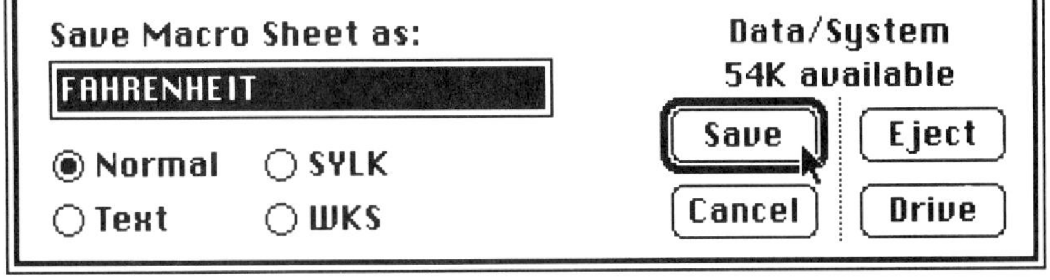

Figure 18.4: *Saving the function macro.*

c. Scroll to the end of the list on the dialog box and click the name of your new function, as shown in Figure 18.6. The formula for cell B3 should now appear in the formula far, as shown in Figure 18.7.

d. Click cell B2 on the worksheet. This completes the formula entry, as shown in Figure 18.8.

e. Click the enter box or press Enter. The result 176 is displayed in cell B3.

Experiment with your new worksheet—enter a few values into cell B2 and watch the results change in cell B3. Use these values to check your function:

Centigrade	−30	0	28	100
Fahrenheit	−22	32	82.4	212

Here is the procedure for using your FAHRENHEIT macro to create a table:

1. Create two columns, A and B, for the temperatures. In row 5, label the first column **Centigrade** and the second column **Fahrenheit,** as shown in Figure 18.9.

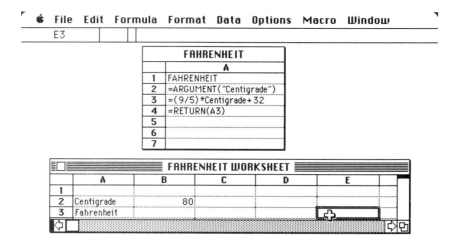

Figure 18.5: *The Fahrenheit worksheet.*

2. In cell A7, enter the first centigrade temperature to be used: **0.**

3. Use the Series command on the Data menu to fill in the rest of column A to at least 100 degrees. Use a step value of 5.

4. Put your formula in cell B6. Select cell B6, pull down the Formula menu, and click Paste Function. When the Paste Function dialog box (Figure 18.6) appears, click your new FAHRENHEIT function, then click OK. Next, click cell C6 to indicate that it is the input cell for the argument, then click the enter box.

5. Select the range for the table. Click cell A6 and drag to the end of column B.

6. Set up the table. Pull down the Data menu and click Table. When the Table window appears, click Column Input Cell, click cell C6, and then click OK.

Excel will then apply each input centigrade temperature to cell C6, use this as an input to the FAHRENHEIT formula in cell B6, and

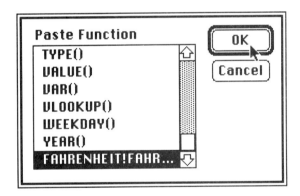

Figure 18.6: *The Paste Function dialog box.*

 File   Edit   Formula   Format   Data   Options   Macro   Window

B3   ☒ ☑   =FAHRENHEIT!FAHRENHEIT()

Figure 18.7: *Starting the formula.*

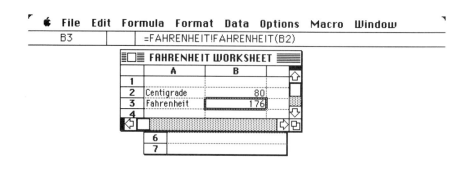

⌘ File   Edit   Formula   Format   Data   Options   Macro   Window

| B3 | | =FAHRENHEIT!FAHRENHEIT(B2) |

▤□≣ FAHRENHEIT WORKSHEET ≣

	A	B	
1			
2	Centigrade	80	
3	Fahrenheit	176	
4			
6			
7			

Figure 18.8: *Completing the formula.*

⌘ File   Edit   Formula   Format   Data   Options   Macro   Window

| A1 | | FAHRENHEIT |

FAHRENHEIT WORKSHEET

	A	B	
5	Centigrade	Fahrenheit	
6			
7	0		
8	5		
9	10		
10	15		
11	20		
12	25		
13	30		
14	35		
15	40		
16	45		
17	50		
18	55		
19	60		
20	65		
21	70		
22	75		
23	80		
24	85		
25	90		

▤□≣ FAHRENHEIT ≣

	A
1	FAHRENHEIT
2	=ARGUMENT("Centigrade"
3	=(9/5)*Centigrade+32
4	=RETURN(A3)
5	
6	

Figure 18.9: *Using a function macro in a table.*

then put the results in column B. Figure 18.10 shows the worksheet with the calculated values.

The ARGUMENT and RESULT Functions

Excel's macro language ARGUMENT and RESULT functions can be used to control the types of input and output values calculated by your function macros.

The ARGUMENT Function

The ARGUMENT function is used to pass values from the worksheet to the function. In the previous example, the ARGUMENT function contained a single argument. You can also use an additional argument to control the type of value passed. This optional second argument is primarily used to ensure that the proper type of argument is included in a function macro. Another purpose of the second argument is to permit the use of arrays as input arguments.

File Edit Formula Format Data Options Macro Window

B6 | =FAHRENHEIT!FAHRENHEIT(C6)

FAHRENHEIT WORKSHEET

	A	B
1		
2	Centigrade	80
3	Fahrenheit	176
4		
5	Centigrade	Fahrenheit
6		32
7	0	32
8	5	41
9	10	50
10	15	59
11	20	68
12	25	77
13	30	86
14	35	95
15	40	104
16	45	113
17	50	122
18	55	131
19	60	140
20	65	149

FAHRENHEIT

	A
1	FAHRENHEIT
2	=ARGUMENT("Centigrade")
3	=(9/5)*Centigrade+32
4	=RETURN(A3)
5	
6	
7	

Figure 18.10: *The worksheet after the table calculation.*

The form of the function with the second argument is = ARGU-MENT(*name,type*), where *type* is one of the following numbers:

Type Value	Required Argument
1	Numeric
2	Text
4	Logical
8	Reference
16	Error
64	Array

If the input value for the function is not of the proper type, Excel will try to convert it. If the value cannot be converted, Excel will return the error value #VALUE! without executing the function. The *type* argument values can be combined to permit the entry of several data types. If the argument is omitted, Excel uses 7 as a default value, which permits the entry of numeric, text, and logical values.

There is also a third form of the ARGUMENT function: = ARGU-MENT(*name,type,ref*). In this case, *ref* is used to refer to a specific cell on the macro sheet. You can then use formulas on the macro sheet to refer to the input value by a name or by a cell reference. For example, on your FAHRENHEIT macro sheet, you could change cell A2 to the value:

= ARGUMENT("Centigrade",1,A5)

and the formula for cell A3 to:

= (9/5) * A5 + 32

and the formula would still work correctly. The third argument, A5, refers to a cell on the macro sheet. Try this, and you'll see that the centigrade value from the worksheet is entered into cell A5 on the macro sheet, which is used as the input cell for the formula.

When you are defining a function, you can include several arguments. Each is specified in a separate cell of the macro sheet, using the ARGUMENT function. The Excel documentation includes examples that show how to use several arguments. It is also possible that a function may not use any input arguments.

The RESULT Function

You can use the RESULT function to indicate the type of returned value, in the same way that you use the ARGUMENT function to control the input value. The function takes the form = RESULT(*ref,type*).

The numeric values for *type* are the same as those for the ARGU-MENT function. If the result of the function calculation is of a different type, Excel will try to convert it. If Excel cannot do this, it will return the error value #VALUE!.

Note: | The RESULT function is not the same as the RETURN function. RESULT should be used as the first formula on the macro sheet in your function macro.

As with the ARGUMENT function, you can use the second argument of the RESULT function to have an array as the output result. Just be sure that you use the proper *type* value for an array. You can also combine values so that your output could be several types of data. For example, a value of 71 would permit numeric, text, or logical values or arrays.

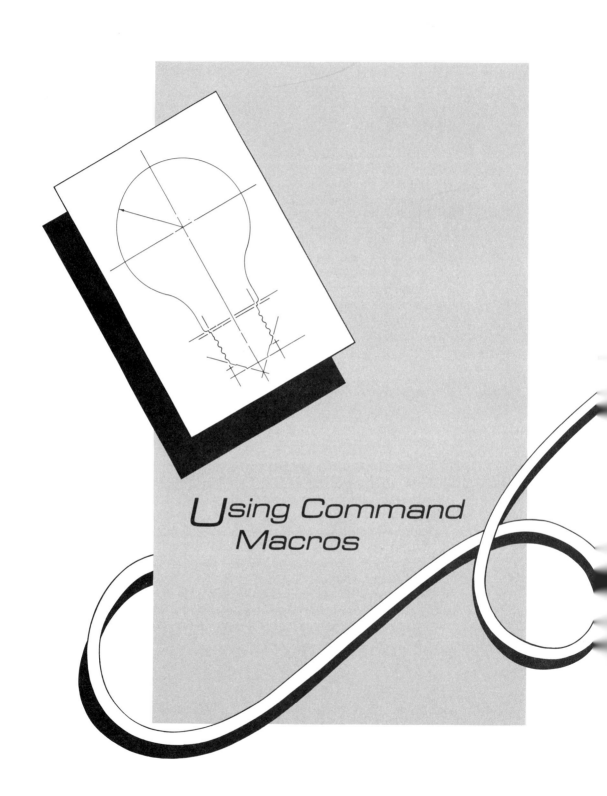

Using Command
Macros

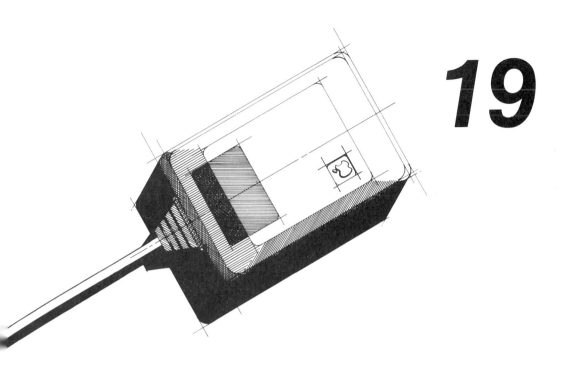

19

Even someone with very little experience can easily create Excel command macros by doing nothing more than turning on the recorder. However, you cannot create very complex macros with the recorder. If you need more advanced command macros, you can use Excel's macro language to write your own programs.

This chapter describes how to use Excel's macro language to create interactive macros and macros with decision structures and loops. You will also learn more about using both relative and absolute cell addressing in macro sheets, how to interrupt an executing macro, and how to organize your macro sheets. Before beginning this chapter, be sure that you have already used the recorder to create a few command macros.

Recording Cell References

Your more complex command macros may require both relative and absolute cell references. Excel's recorder can handle both types of cell addressing. In the default mode, the cell references entered in a macro are relative to the cell that was active when you started the recorder.

To switch to absolute cell addressing, pull down the Macro menu. Absolute Record should be displayed as one of your choices. This means that the current reference mode is relative. If you click Absolute Record, the references that you record will use absolute cell addressing. The next time that you pull down the Macro menu, Relative Record will be displayed instead of Absolute Record. Click it to switch back to relative cell addressing.

You can switch from relative to absolute cell addressing and back at any time while you are recording, and the final macro could be a mixture of both types. However, once the macro is recorded, the references cannot be switched by using a command on the Macro menu. You would then have to edit the macro sheet to change the reference types.

As an exercise, record a simple command macro that enters the title ACME MANUFACTURING into cell C1 and the value of Test two rows below the title cell, as shown in Figure 19.1. It will be recorded using the default relative cell addressing. Then, repeat the exercise, but this time, pull down the Macro menu and select Absolute Record. When you're done recording, run each macro, starting with the cursor on a cell other than C1.

Recorder Messages

Occasionally, while you're creating a macro, the recorder may stop, and Excel will display the error message "Recorder area full," as shown in Figure 19.2. This means that you did not choose a large enough macro sheet range when you started recording the macro. If there is room on the macro sheet, select a new macro range that includes the old range and continue. If there is not enough room on the macro sheet, replace the RETURN function on the old macro sheet with a GOTO function that references a cell on a new macro sheet and continue on the new sheet. For example:

GOTO (LIBRARY!A1)

would have the macro continue in the first cell of a macro sheet titled LIBRARY.

Writing Macro Programs

You may need to create a command macro with some special features that cannot be added using the recorder. Typical examples include interactive macros and macros that contain branching and loops. To include these features, you will need to write your own macro sheet or alter an existing one. In this section, you will learn more about these programming techniques.

Tip:

> When you create your own macros, in many cases it is better to record a simple version of the macro first, then insert the extra steps without the recorder.

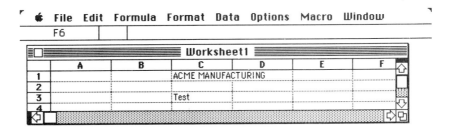

Figure 19.1: *Testing relative and absolute cell addressing in macros.*

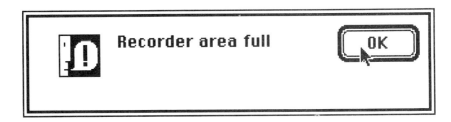

Figure 19.2: *Recorder error message.*

Creating Interactive Macros

There may be times when you want your command macro to stop during execution and obtain an input value from the user, then continue.

Interactive macros can be used for very simple tasks, as well as for complex programs, such as one that creates advanced macro sheets automatically, with the user entering only the data needed at the proper steps. Remember, however, that the development of complex macros takes quite a bit of programming development time.

Note:
> The first release of Excel does not have a menu capability that allows you to create menu programs. This feature will be added in later releases.

There are three ways to make an Excel macro interactive:

- Using the INPUT function
- Using the question mark form of a command
- Using an ALERT command

Let's take an example and try each of these methods.

In the example, you will create a simple macro that will insert a worksheet heading. The heading will contain the months, but you need to make the macro interactive because you want to specify the starting and ending months. You also want the macro to stop and display a message and wait for you to tell it to continue.

To start, create a macro that will generate the worksheet shown in Figure 19.3. Follow these steps (refer to Chapter 17 if you need help):

1. Clear the worksheet, open a macro sheet, set the recorder, and select the worksheet.

2. Start the recorder.

3. Select cell C1, enter the title, and put it in boldface print.

4. Expand column A to 20 characters by using the Column Width command on the Format menu.

5. Enter **Jan-85** in cell B3.

6. Use the Series command on the Data menu to enter the remaining months. Select column B through column M of row 3. Then,

select Month in the Date Unit box in the Series dialog box (see Figure 19.4).

7. Center the data in the first three rows.

8. Stop the recorder.

The final macro sheet should look like Figure 19.5. Run the macro to be sure that it works.

Note: | If your macro sheet does not look exactly like the figure, it will probably still be usable in the following exercises. You'll just need to locate the proper step referred to in the exercise.

You will now modify this macro sheet to make the command macro interactive in three different ways.

The INPUT Function   You can replace any of the macro sheet's existing function arguments with the INPUT function. Then, when the macro reaches that function, it will stop and ask for the input value. The

File   Edit   Formula   Format   Data   Options   Macro   Window

E18

Worksheet1

	A	B	C	D	E
1		ACME MANUFACTURING			
2					
3		Jan-85	Feb-85	Mar-85	Apr-85
4					
5					
6					
7					
8					
9					
10					
11					
12					
13					
14					
15					
16					
17					
18					
19					

Figure 19.3: *The worksheet for the interactive command macro.*

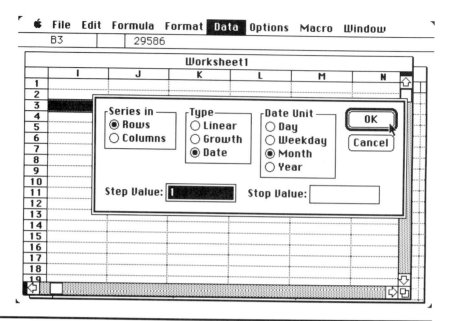

Figure 19.4: *The Series dialog box.*

```
 File  Edit  Formula  Format  Data  Options  Macro  Window
       A1              =SELECT("R1C3")
                            Worksheet1
  [ Macro1 ]
              A                       C        D        E
                              E MANUFACTURING
  1  =SELECT("R1C3")
  2  =FORMULA("ACME MANUFACT          Feb-85   Mar-85   Apr-85
  3  =STYLE(TRUE,FALSE)
  4  =SELECT("C1")
  5  =COLUMN.WIDTH(20)
  6  =SELECT("R3C2")
  7  =FORMULA("Jan-85")
  8  =SELECT("R3C2:R3C13")
  9  =DATA.SERIES(1,3,3,1,)
 10  =HSCROLL(0%)
 11  =SELECT("R1:R3")
 12  =ALIGNMENT(3)
 13  =RETURN()
 14
 15
 16
 20
```

Figure 19.5: *The macro sheet.*

form of the input function is INPUT(*prompt,type,title*). Its arguments represent the following:

- *prompt* is the message to be displayed to the user in the window.

- *type* is an integer that represents the type (or types) of input numbers that can be accepted (see Chapter 18).

- *title* is the name of the window. If *title* is omitted, it is assumed to be Input.

Now, edit cell A7 on the macro sheet so that it reads:

= FORMULA(INPUT("Enter the starting date ",1))

Repeat the macro execution. The program will stop and display the Input window shown in Figure 19.6. Enter the starting date **Nov-85** and click OK. Column B on the worksheet is now headed Nov-85, and the remaining headings automatically increment from that date, as shown in Figure 19.7. Repeat this exercise again, entering letters that aren't a valid month abbreviation, such as **Apl.** What happens?

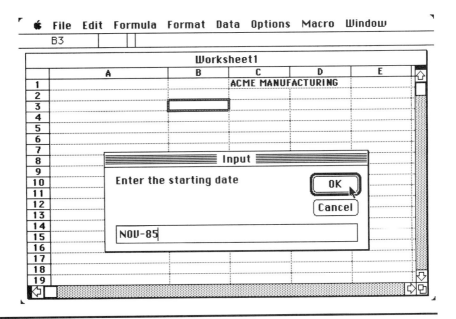

Figure 19.6: *The Input window.*

The Question Mark Command Form   Another method for obtaining input is to use the *question mark form* of the command. Most macro language commands that produce a dialog box have a question mark form. If you want your macro to stop and display the command's dialog box, replace the command with its question mark form.

To specify the ending month in the heading that your macro creates, and thus control the number of columns printed when the macro is executed, you need to use the Series dialog box. Cell A9 on the macro sheet contains the DATA SERIES command. Replace this command with:

= DATA.SERIES?( )

Now, execute your macro again. After you have filled in the Input window, you will see the Series dialog box, as shown in Figure 19.8. Click Month, enter a stop value of **Jan-86,** and click OK. Your worksheet will be printed with only three columns.

Alert Boxes   A third way to obtain input during a macro execution is through the use of an alert box. The form of the ALERT function is = ALERT

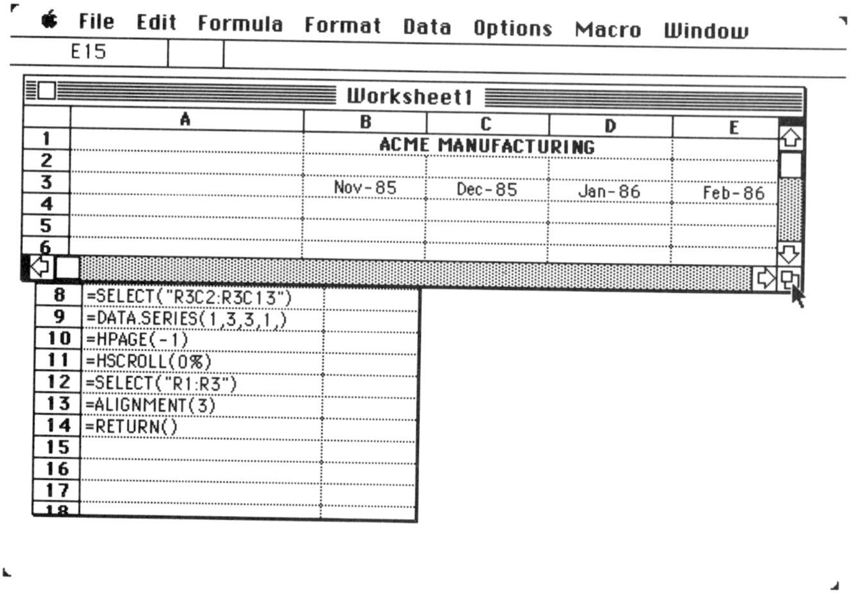

Figure 19.7: *The worksheet after entering a date in the Input window.*

(text,type), where *type* is a value for the type of icon and buttons to display, and *text* is the prompt to display in the box. The values available for *type* are:

Type	Icon	Buttons
1	? (means caution)	OK, Cancel
2	* (means note)	OK
3	! (means stop)	OK

After the DATA.SERIES? command in cell A9 of your macro sheet, insert a new line (select the row, pull down the Edit menu, and click Insert). On this line, add the following command:

= ALERT("Are you having fun? ",1)

Now, execute your macro one last time. The program will stop and display an alert box, as shown in Figure 19.9. Click OK, and the macro will continue.

Branching: Making Decisions

You can use the IF and GOTO functions in your macros to create program branches, loops, and other controls.

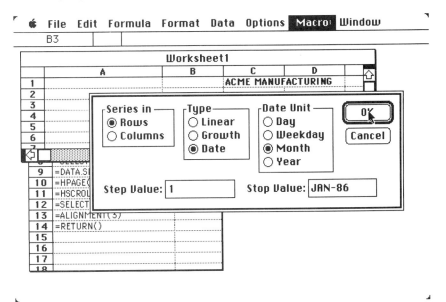

Figure 19.8: *Using the question mark form of the command.*

Using the IF Function   You can use the IF function in a macro so that it makes decisions based on a certain value. For example, you could use the ROWS function in cell A1 of the macro sheet to return the number of rows in a range selection. It would have the following form:

= ROWS(SELECTION( ))

Later in the program, the macro could examine this value and make a decision based on the number of rows. For example, the command

= ALIGNMENT(IF(A2 = 1,3,2))

would adjust the alignment according to the number of rows. If there is one row, the ALIGNMENT function will use 3, and the display will be centered. If not, the alignment will be 2, and the display will be left-justified. The first value applies if the IF function is true, the second if the function is false.

You can combine the IF function with the GOTO function to control the direction of the program execution with the IF statement. For example, the command:

= IF(A2 = 1,GOTO(A13))

would have the program go to cell A13 if the value in cell A2 was 1.

You can also use Boolean operators (AND, OR, etc.) to combine conditions before a decision. For example, the command:

= IF(AND(A2 = 1,A3 = 1),GOTO(A13))

would have the program go to cell A13 only if both cells A2 and A3 had a value of 1.

The GOTO function can even be used to branch to another macro and, when that macro is completed, return to the calling macro to continue.

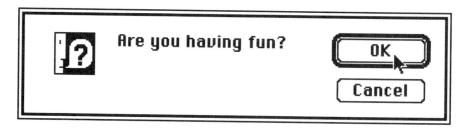

Figure 19.9: *Using an alert box.*

Looping   You can also use the IF function to control looping in a macro. To use loops, you must first set a variable in a cell to an initial value using the SET.VALUE function. For example, the command

= SET.VALUE(A25,1)

in cell A2 would put the value of 1 in cell A25 on the macro sheet. In cell A25, the following would be entered:

= A25 + 1

When the macro is executed, each time that cell A25 is encountered, the value of that cell would be incremented by 1. You could then have the macro test the condition after cell A25 is incremented and determine if it should remain in the loop by using the following command:

= IF(A25 < = 25,GOTO(A3))

Be sure that you loop back *after* the SET.VALUE function.

Other Control Structures   Using the IF and GOTO functions, you can set up a wide variety of control structures, such as IF-THEN-ELSE and WHILE-DO commands. The techniques are the same as with other languages, and examples are provided in the Excel documentation.

Calculation Order

When Excel calculates a worksheet, it does the entire worksheet without regard to the order of the cells. Each time that you edit a cell, all cells that depend upon the edited cell are recalculated. However, the calculation order for a macro sheet is quite different. The macro sheet represents a procedural program, and the order of the cells determines the order of the execution. Calculation begins at the first cell of the macro and proceeds down the column until a RETURN or HALT function is encountered. The only way to change the order of the cell execution is by using the GOTO function.

Interrupting a Macro Execution

You can interrupt the execution of a macro, just as you would interrupt a printing, by pressing the Command key and a period. The dialog box

shown in Figure 19.10 is then displayed. This box shows the current
cell to be calculated on the macro sheet and has three buttons: Halt,
Continue, and Step. The Halt button terminates the macro execution,
the Continue button continues the execution, and the Step button displays the Single-Step window shown in Figure 19.11. You can use this
window to go through the macro one step at a time, which is useful for
checking macros created without the recorder.

Using Macro Sheets

With many competing products, a macro is stored on the actual worksheet with which it is used, and the macro can only be run with that
worksheet unless you copy it into another worksheet. Because macros
are entered into a remote area of the worksheet, the worksheet is

Figure 19.10: *The dialog box displayed when you interrupt a macro.*

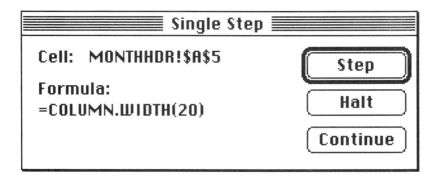

Figure 19.11: *The Single-Step window.*

much larger and requires more computer memory. Excel's macros are stored in separate sheets, and they can be used with any worksheet. You should, however, be careful in creating links and using names as external references on macro sheets, since these features are always identified with specific worksheets. If you use an exclamation point without a worksheet name in a formula, the reference always refers to the active worksheet.

Commenting and Labeling Macros

If you enter a constant into a cell on a macro sheet, it will be ignored during the execution of the macro. You can use this feature to add comments, create program labels, or to title the program. It is a good idea to use comments and labels liberally to document your macros. Include in the comments the definition of each argument, the type of each argument, and the definition and type of result expected. Put the name of the macro in the first cell on the macro sheet.

On the macro sheet, you can use the column next to the macro for comments on the various steps. For example, if the macro is stored in column A, use column B for comments.

To add labels, put the label in any cell, then use the Define Name command to label the cell with the name. You can then use the name with the GOTO function.

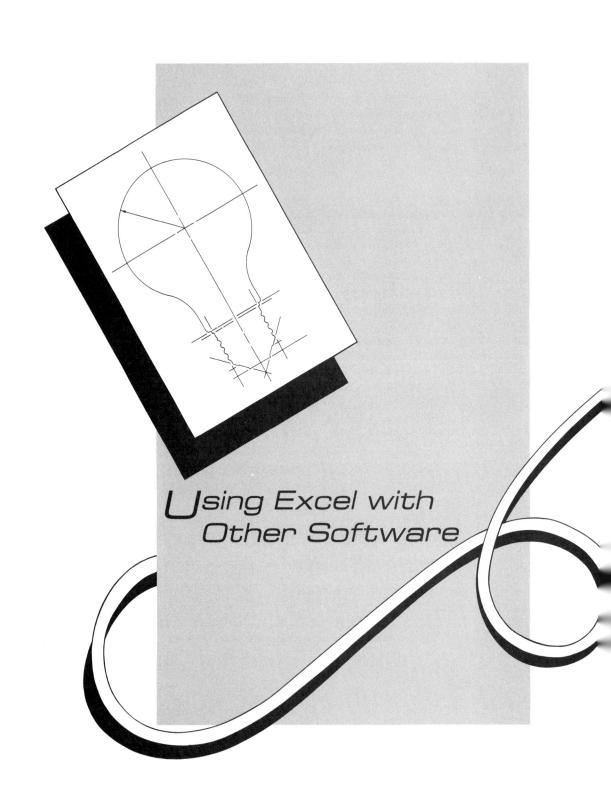

Using Excel with
Other Software

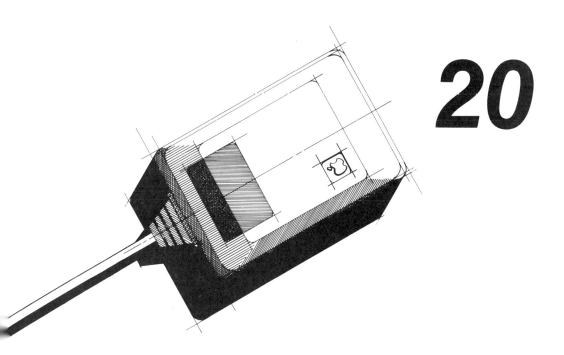

20

Now that you've mastered Excel, you may want to use it with other software products, such as spreadsheet programs, word processors, and database managers. You can transfer data from most of these programs to Excel, and you can also transfer Excel data to most of these programs. Here are some typical reasons for using Excel with other software:

- You want to insert a worksheet or chart that was created with Excel into a word-processor document created with MacWrite or Microsoft Word.

- You have several worksheets that were created on an IBM-PC with Lotus 1-2-3, and you wish to transfer them to your Macintosh and print them using Excel's presentation features.

- You have a database file that was created with Microsoft File, and you want to use it on an Excel worksheet to do some special analyses.

- You created an Excel worksheet at home on your Macintosh, and you need to transfer it to Lotus 1-2-3, which you are using at work on an IBM-PC.

You can also use the Switcher with Excel and your word-processor (Microsoft Word or MacWrite). The Switcher permits you to keep both your word-processor program and Excel in the Macintosh memory at the same time and copy and paste data quickly between the two. This, in effect, gives you an integrated program capability.

In this chapter, you will learn the techniques for transferring data between Excel and other programs, including how to use the Switcher with Excel and a word processor.

Excel with MacWrite or Microsoft Word

There is two-way transfer capability between Excel and MacWrite and Microsoft Word—you can transfer data from Excel to these programs or from them to Excel. If you plan to transfer much data between Excel and a word processor, you should use the Switcher, as described in the following section. Otherwise, you can use one of the methods described in this section.

Transferring Data to a Word Processor

If you need to copy a worksheet or chart from Excel into a word-processor document, there are two methods you can use. The first is generally the preferable method.

The Copy Picture and Copy Chart Commands

Edit	
Undo Copy Picture	⌘Z
Cut	⌘X
Copy	⌘C
Copy Chart...	
Paste	⌘U
Clear...	⌘B
Paste Special...	

Edit	
Can't Undo	⌘Z
Cut	⌘H
Copy Picture	⌘C
Paste	⌘U
Clear...	⌘B
Paste Special...	
Delete...	⌘K
Insert...	⌘I
Fill Right	⌘R
Fill Down	⌘D

The easiest way to transfer Excel worksheet data to a word processor is by using a special form of the Copy command on the Edit menu. First, select the cells or cell range that you wish to copy. Then, hold down the Shift key, pull down the Edit menu, and click Copy Picture. (When you hold down the Shift key, the Copy command on the Edit menu changes to Copy Picture if a worksheet is active.)

To copy a chart, first select the chart, then click Copy Chart on the Chart menu (it is not necessary to use the Shift key). When you choose the Copy Chart command, the dialog box shown in Figure 20.1 will be displayed. This dialog box is used to select whether you wish the copy to be like the screen display or like the printed version.

The above procedure will copy the selected range into the Clipboard (you can use the Show Clipboard command on the Window menu to see it). Next, exit Excel and start the word processor. Open your word-processor document and select the area for the copied worksheet or chart. Use the Paste command on the word processor's Edit menu to paste the Clipboard contents into the document.

Note: | To use the Clipboard, keep a system/data disk in your internal drive. Start with the Excel disk in the external drive. When you exit Excel, you will be able to eject the Excel disk and insert the word-processor disk in the external drive. Except for this manual change, the Macintosh will prompt you for any other necessary actions.

Transferring from Text Form   The second method for transferring data from Excel to a word processor is to save the worksheet data in text form and then use this text form in your word-processor document. You would follow these steps:

1. Use the Save As command on the File menu. When the dialog box appears, click Text to save your document in text form, as shown in Figure 20.2.

2. Click Save in the dialog box.

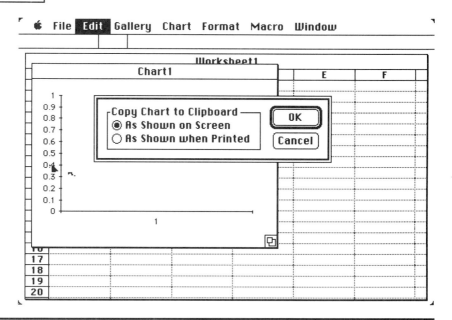

Figure 20.1: *The Copy Chart dialog box.*

When the worksheet is saved in text form, each row becomes a line with the columns separated by tabs. There will be no formatting—no dollar signs, borders, or commas.

Transferring Data from a Word Processor

Before you transfer data from a word processor to Excel, it must be in the correct format: each line should end with a carriage return and columns should be separated by tabs. Save the word-processor data as text, using the Text Only option.

Then, start Excel. Use the Open command on the File menu to load the document. Each tab-separated value will be in a separate cell in the row, and each carriage return will start a new row.

Using the Switcher

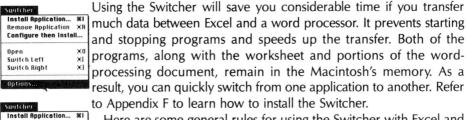

Using the Switcher will save you considerable time if you transfer much data between Excel and a word processor. It prevents starting and stopping programs and speeds up the transfer. Both of the programs, along with the worksheet and portions of the word-processing document, remain in the Macintosh's memory. As a result, you can quickly switch from one application to another. Refer to Appendix F to learn how to install the Switcher.

Here are some general rules for using the Switcher with Excel and MacWrite or Microsoft Word:

1. Use the Options command on the Switcher's Switcher menu to set up a common Clipboard for Excel and the word processor.

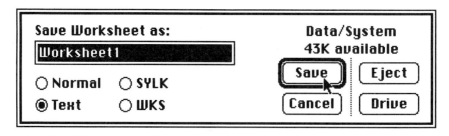

Figure 20.2: *Saving the worksheet in text form.*

2. Initially install Excel with 256K of RAM and Microsoft Word (or MacWrite) with 128K of RAM. The amount of memory required by Excel will depend upon the size of the worksheet. The amount of memory required by Microsoft Word does not depend on the size of the document, since only a portion of the document is kept in the computer memory.

3. Keep a system/data disk with the Switcher program in the internal drive. Install either the word processor's or Excel's program disk in the external drive. The Switcher program will then prompt you, while it's executing the transfer, for the proper disk to insert in the external drive.

Using the Scrapbook

If you need to move many items from one application to another, it is often quicker to use the Scrapbook. You would begin by following these steps to move the selected data to the Scrapbook:

1. Move the data to the Clipboard using the Copy command on the Edit menu. Do not use Copy Picture (with the Shift key).

2. Pull down the Apple menu and click Scrapbook.

3. Pull down the Edit menu and click Paste.

The Clipboard will show only the size of the copied area (such as 4R × 1C), but the Scrapbook shows the actual worksheet text.

Repeat the above procedure for each item that you want to transfer. Then, use the following procedure to copy the Excel data from the Scrapbook into the second application:

1. Start the application. Open the document that will receive the copy of the first item.

2. Pull down the Apple menu and click Scrapbook.

3. Scroll through the Scrapbook until you find the item that you need.

4. Select the item and use the Cut or Copy command to move the item from the Scrapbook to the Clipboard.

5. Select an insertion point in your document and use the Paste command to move the item from the Clipboard into your document.

6. Repeat steps 1 through 5 for each item that you want to transfer.

Note: Be sure that the Scrapbook file is on the same disk as your destination application.

Using Excel with Lotus 1-2-3

If you already have Lotus 1-2-3 on an IBM-PC, you can move worksheets from Lotus 1-2-3 to Excel or from Excel to Lotus 1-2-3.

To transfer data in either direction, you will need some type of communications software. This is considered a binary-file transfer, so both computers will need communications software that has binary-file transfer capability and that uses the same protocol. For example, Peter Mackie's PC to Mac and Back (Seaquest Software, 4200 N.W. Columbia Ave., Portland, OR 97229) is an inexpensive and easy-to-use communications program. It permits the Macintosh to be hooked directly to the IBM-PC, and the transfer is made at very fast speeds (9,600 baud). Follow the directions with your communications software to transfer the files between the computers.

When you transfer in either direction, the cell properties of your worksheet, including values, formulas, format, and protection, and any names that you assigned are converted. However, window properties (such as panes) are not converted. Although the function arguments and their order in Excel are often different from those in Lotus 1-2-3, when you transfer files, Excel automatically converts them. For example, you can take the Amortization worksheet that you created in Chapter 8, which has the PMT and PV functions; transfer it to Lotus 1-2-3, which uses different arguments; and the Lotus 1-2-3 worksheet will be correctly calculated using the proper formulas.

Excel has many functions and features (such as arrays) that are not a part of Lotus 1-2-3. These, of course, cannot be converted correctly. If you plan to do many transfers from Excel to Lotus 1-2-3, avoid using arrays and Excel's other special functions. Appendix E provides more details on how to transfer data between Excel and Lotus 1-2-3.

Transferring from Excel to Lotus 1-2-3

To transfer an Excel document to Lotus 1-2-3, first save the document as a WKS document. Do this by pulling down the File menu and clicking Save As. When the dialog box appears, enter the document name, using the extension .WKS; for example, TEST.WKS would be a valid name. Then, click WKS and click Save, as shown in Figure 20.3. Use your communications programs to transfer the WKS document to the IBM-PC. The document can then be loaded and used with Lotus 1-2-3.

Note: | Be sure to use the WKS extension with the transferred document's name, or Lotus 1-2-3 won't load it.

Transferring from Lotus 1-2-3 to Excel

Transferring Lotus 1-2-3 worksheets to Excel is very easy. Use your communications programs to transfer the document to Excel. Then, simply start Excel and open the document using the Open command on the File menu. The Open Document dialog box, shown in Figure 20.4, will include the name of the Lotus 1-2-3 document. No special options are needed.

Excel and Other Software

Excel can also be used with Microsoft File for database-management applications, with Microsoft Chart, and with Multiplan.

Figure 20.3: *Saving a document that will be transferred to Lotus 1-2-3.*

To move Excel records to Microsoft File, save the records as text from Excel. Before loading the data, create the database structure. The fields of the database must match your Excel database fields. Charts can be moved to Microsoft File to use as picture fields. To move a chart to a picture field, use the Copy Chart command on the Edit menu.

You can use Microsoft Chart to do more extensive chart formatting. The file format for Microsoft Chart is identical to that of Excel's chart file. You can use the same files with either program. The Gallery and Format menus are also identical in both programs.

As when you use Excel with Lotus 1-2-3, when you transfer data between Excel and Multiplan, data, formulas, formats, and names are converted. Window properties (such as panes) are not transferred. Any Excel documents that you want to transfer should be saved in the SYLK file format (see Figure 20.3). Multiplan files are not in the same format as Excel files, but if you use the Open command on Excel's File menu, the Multiplan file will be recognized and converted properly, just as a Lotus 1-2-3 WKS file is converted. If a worksheet is saved in SYLK format, formulas are not converted and some may not be read correctly by Multiplan. Excel also has many functions and features that are not a part of Multiplan and cannot be converted.

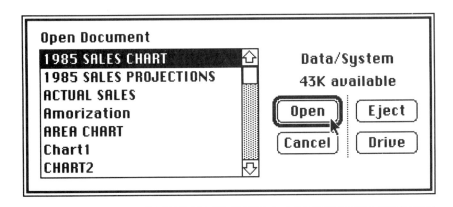

Figure 20.4: *Opening a Lotus 1-2-3 document that was transferred to Excel.*

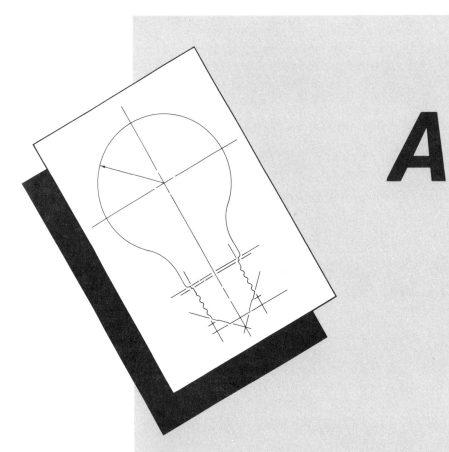

A

Glossary

Term	Definition
A1 format	A type of worksheet cell designation in which the columns are represented by letters and the rows by numbers. For example, in A1 format, C4 represents the cell at the intersection of the third column and the fourth row.
absolute cell reference	A reference to a specific cell or group of cells on a worksheet. An absolute cell reference does not change with moving or copying. In Excel's format (A1), an absolute reference is designated with a dollar sign before the column and row (for example, $A$5).
active cell	The cell in which any current keyboard entry is stored. The active cell is always marked by a heavy border. The formula bar shows the contents of the active cell.
active window	The window that is currently selected.
alert box	A type of interrupt dialog box that can be created with Excel's macro language to give the user the option of cancelling the program or continuing.
alignment	The position of text or a value in a cell. Alignment can be left, right, or centered.
argument	Values used as input for a function to calculate its output value.
array	A two-dimensional collection of values, normally arranged in rows and columns.
attached text	Text that is attached to a specific object on a chart, such as the chart title, axes labels, and legend. It is created with the Attach Text command on the Chart menu.
axes	The straight lines used on the graph for measurement and reference. A pie chart has no real axis, other types have two.

Term	Definition
border	The line around an area on a worksheet or chart.
cancel box	The small box in the formula bar that contains an X. Clicking this box discards any changes you have made in the formula bar.
category	A name associated with a numeric value in a data series. Each data point in a series has a category name and a value.
cell	The intersection of a row and column. It is the basic unit of the worksheet used for storing values, formulas, and text.
chart	One or more graphs displayed in a single document.
chart format	The basic information that defines how a data series is plotted. Excel has 42 chart formats.
chart object	Any part of the chart: axes, markers, lines, legend, plot area, chart, etc.
chart style	The basic type of chart used in a document. Excel has six chart types: area, bar, column, line, pie, and scatter.
circular references	Two or more formulas that depend upon each other for results.
click	To point to a command with the mouse, press, and then release the mouse button.
close box	The small square box in the upper left of each window that can be clicked to close the window. Clicking the box releases the document from the computer's memory and, optionally, saves it to the disk.
cluster	On a chart, a group of bars or columns in the same category.
column	On a worksheet, a vertical range of cells.

Term	Definition
command macro	A series of actions to accomplish a desired result, which is stored as a single program for execution one or more times.
complex external reference	Any reference to a cell on another worksheet that is not a simple external reference (see external reference and simple reference).
constant value	Anything entered into a cell that is not a formula.
criteria	A test used to find, extract, or delete records in a database.
criteria area	The cells on the worksheet that are used to define which records Excel finds, extracts, or deletes in the database. The area is defined with the Set Criteria command on the Data menu.
criteria name row	The cells in the criteria area that contain the criteria names. It is always the first row in the criteria area.
data point	A category with a corresponding numeric value.
data series	A collection of data points, each related to the other by some aspect.
database	An organized collection of data about one or more items. Each item is represented by a row in the database, and each piece of data about the item is stored as a field in the record. In an Excel database, the records are represented by rows and the fields by columns.
database area	The worksheet cells that contain the field names and the records on which the Find, Delete, and Extract commands operate. The area is defined with the Set Database command on the Data menu.

Term	Definition
dependent document	Any document in which one or more cells have a formula that contains a reference to another worksheet.
designators	The indicators at the top and left of the display area that designate the rows and columns. At the left of the worksheet are the row designators, and at the top are the column designators.
document	Any worksheet, chart, or macro sheet either active or saved to the disk.
double-click	To point at a command or cell with the mouse, press, and release the mouse button twice in quick succession.
drag	To hold the mouse button down while moving the mouse. Used to select a range of cells.
enter box	The small box in the formula bar that contains a check mark. Clicking this box completes a formula bar entry or edit.
Excel macro language	A special group of functions that can be used to write Excel command macros.
external reference	A reference to a specific cell or group of cells, normally on another worksheet. The reference consists of the worksheet name, an exclamation point, and the cell reference. You can also refer to the currently active worksheet as an external reference by using an exclamation point and the cell reference. This is useful in macros that must refer to cells in several worksheets generically.
extract	To copy records from a database that meet specific criteria.
field	Each piece of data stored about an item in a database. Each cell in a database is one

Term	Definition
	field. Fields are represented as columns in a database, and records are represented as rows.
font	The specific design for the characters used to represent text. You can change the font of an entire worksheet, and, in a chart, you can change the font of individual objects. You can add fonts to Excel by using the Font Mover program external to Excel.
footer	A line of text that appears at the bottom of each printed page of a worksheet or chart; for example, the page number is a footer.
format	Information that controls how the contents of the cell will be displayed. It consists of a template, style, alignment, font, and font size.
formula	One or more values, cell references, names, functions, and operators that are stored in a cell to produce a value.
formula bar	An area below the menu bar that is used for displaying and editing the contents of the active cell.
function	An abbreviation of a formula. A function produces an output value (or values) from a specified input. (Some functions, such as NOW, do not require an input value.)
function macro	A user-defined function. The user defines the arguments, results, and formulas to calculate the results.
graph	A visual representation of one or more data series. It includes the plotted area, labels, legends, and comments.
grid lines	The grid lines on a worksheet are the

Term	Definition
	dotted horizontal and vertical lines between adjacent cells. Grid lines on a chart are the horizontal and vertical lines that extend from the axis across the plot area. Major grid lines extend from the tick marks; minor grid lines extend from the axes between the tick marks.
header	A line of text that appears at the top of each printed page of a worksheet or chart.
input cell	The cell used with a table to hold each of a series of input values.
insertion point	A blinking vertical line that determines the entry point for text typed in from the keyboard. It can be created by clicking in the formula bar or in a text-entry area of a dialog box.
key	A row or column that contains the values that control a sort. To sort rows, the key must be a column. To sort columns, the key must be a row.
label	Text in a chart used to identify that part of the chart.
legend	The symbols with labels used to identify the different types of data on the chart.
link	A defined relationship between two documents caused by formulas in a dependent document referencing cells in a supporting document.
lock	To protect a cell so that its contents cannot be altered.
look-up table	A table that can be used, like a function, to produce an output value from one or more input values.
macro	A collection of functions that can be

Term	**Definition**
	executed as a procedure to produce some specified result.
macro recording	An Excel mode in which actions taken by the user are recorded on a separate sheet as a program. The program can then be executed again at a later time to repeat the procedure.
macro sheet	A worksheet used to store macros.
main chart	The primary graph on a chart.
marker	A type of indicator used on a graph to indicate the data. For example, in a column chart, each column is a marker.
menu bar	The bar at the top of the screen that contains the available menus. The mouse is used to pull the menus down from the menu bar.
mixed cell reference	A reference that consists of both absolute and relative cell addresses (for example, $A5).
overlay chart	A second graph that is plotted in the chart window, which is identical in size and position to the main chart.
pane	A subdivision of a worksheet window.
plot area	The area bounded by the axes, or, in the case of the pie chart, the area within the circle.
point	To move the mouse pointer to an area of the screen.
pointer	The small cursor on the screen that tracks the movement of the mouse.
precision	The number of decimal places with which a value is stored or used in calculations.
print area	That part of the worksheet that will be printed with a Print command.

Term	Definition
protect	To make active the protection that has been defined. One or more cells or cell ranges are unlocked or hidden with the Cell Protection command on the Format menu, then the Protect Document command on the Options menu is used to activate the protection for the entire worksheet.
R1C1 format	A type of worksheet cell designation in which the columns and rows are designated by numbers. For example, in R1C1 format, R4C3 represents the cell at the intersection of the fourth row and the third column.
range	One or more cells that have been designated to be acted upon by a command.
record	Any row within a database range. A record consists of one or more fields.
row	A horizontal line of cells.
scale	The range of values covered by the y axis on the chart.
select	To specify a worksheet or chart area or a command.
simple external reference	A reference to a cell or cell range on another worksheet that is absolute and refers only to a single cell or cell range or a named cell or cell range. Linked dependent documents with only simple external references will be updated automatically, even if the supporting document is not open. (See external reference.)
split bar	The small black rectangle at the top of the vertical scroll bar and at the left of the horizontal scroll bar. It is used to separate the window into panes.

Term	Definition
style	The appearance of the font on the worksheet. Excel has four styles: normal, boldface, italics, and boldface-italics.
supporting worksheet	Any worksheet containing a cell referenced by a dependent worksheet.
Switcher	A program that permits two application programs to reside in the Macintosh memory simultaneously. The user can move from one program to the other quickly, without having to reload the program and data from the disk.
table	A range of cells containing the results of applying a series of values to an input cell.
template	One or more characters used to identify how a value is to be displayed. For a number, the template controls the number of digits to be displayed to the right of the decimal and whether a dollar sign or commas are displayed.
tick-mark label	Labels identifying the tick marks on a chart.
tick marks	The axes divisions. Used to indicate categories or scale. The marks are short lines perpendicular to the axes at regular intervals.
toggle	To switch between one of two modes. For example, in the Display dialog box, you can toggle on or off the display of formulas, row and column designators, and grid lines.
unattached text	Text on a chart that is not attached to any object and can be moved.
wild card	Special characters used to stand for any other characters in text. A question mark (?) is used to represent any single character; an asterisk (*) represents a group of characters.

Term	Definition
window	An area on the screen that displays a portion of a worksheet or chart.
worksheet	A grid of cells 256 columns wide by 16,384 cells long into which you can enter formulas and values.
x axis	The horizontal (or category) chart axis.
y axis	The vertical (or value) chart axis.

update

1. Initialized HD

 w/ Apple HD SC setup on
   either S.T. #1 or M. #1

2. Create start-up on HD
   w/ Installer on
   S.T. #1
   ~~And~~ S.T. #2

---

utilities

1. copy ST #1 & #2 to HD
   by dragging

2. ~~Use it #2 to add~~
   use Font/DA mover it #2
   to add Deskacc.

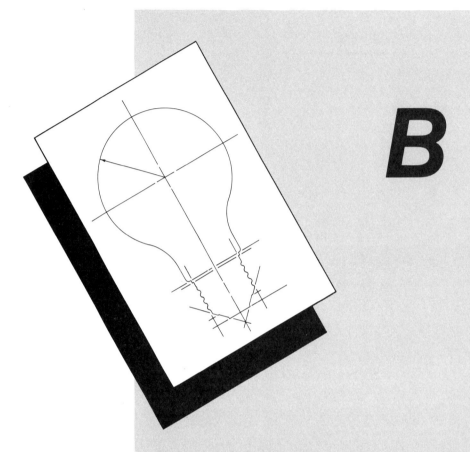

B

*T*he Worksheet
Commands

Excel has nine worksheet and database menus: Apple, File, Edit, Formula, Format, Data, Options, Macro, and Window. This appendix describes the functions available with each of these menus.

The Apple Menu

This menu is similar to the Apple menu in other applications, except that it includes an About Microsoft Excel command. This command displays a window (Figure B.1) that describes memory usage and lists help topics. To get help on any topic, click the topic, then click the Help button. The information is then displayed. When you have finished reading about the topic, select your next alternative from the four buttons displayed:

- **Topics** means go back to list of help topics.

- **Next** means go to the next help topic.

- **Previous** means go to the previous help topic.

- **Cancel** means cancel the About Microsoft Excel command.

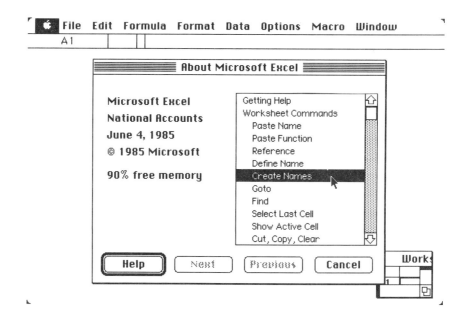

Figure B.1: *The About Microsoft Excel window.*

The File Menu

The File menu is used to manage documents. The commands on this menu allow you to open, close, delete, or print a document. This menu is also used to end an Excel session.

New

The New command creates an empty worksheet or macro sheet or creates a chart from a displayed document. When the dialog box (Figure B.2) is displayed, select the desired alternative:

- **Worksheet** creates an empty worksheet.

- **Chart** plots a chart from an active worksheet.

- **Macro Sheet** creates an empty macro sheet.

Open

The Open command opens a document that is already on the disk and displays it as a window. When the command is selected, a

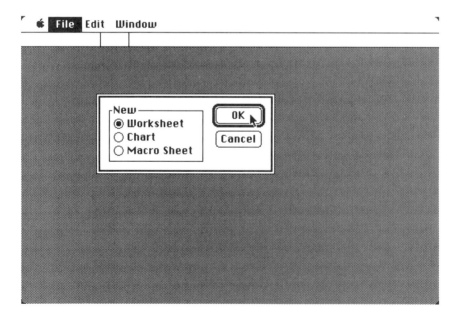

Figure B.2: *The New dialog box.*

dialog box (Figure B.3) that lists the documents on the disk is displayed. Click the desired document name and then click Open. The following options are available:

- **Open** opens the selected document.

- **Eject** ejects the indicated disk. You can then insert another disk, and the contents of that disk will be displayed.

- **Drive** selects the alternative drive.

- **Cancel** cancels the command.

Excel can open a document in the following formats: Excel, WKS, SYLK, Text, or Multiplan. The format is automatically recognized, and the document is opened.

Open Links

The Open Links command is used to open documents that are linked to the currently active document. If a dependent document is active and you wish to load one or more of the supporting

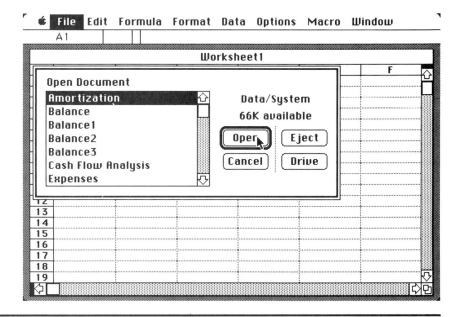

Figure B.3: *The Open dialog box.*

worksheets, use the Open Links command. The currently linked documents will be displayed in a dialog box (Figure B.4). Click the supporting documents that you want to open. You can make more than one document active at a time by dragging across several names in a range while pressing the Shift key or by pressing the Command key while clicking to add documents to a selected group (just as you select cells on a worksheet).

Close All

The Close All command closes all active windows on the screen. For each window that contains a document with unsaved changes, a dialog box (Figure B.5) will be displayed, asking if you want to save the current changes. Click **Yes** to save changes, **No** to omit changes, or **Cancel** to stop the Close All command. You can also close single windows by clicking their close boxes.

Save

The Save command is used to save a document under the name with which it was opened or assigned when you last used the Save As command. The Save command can only be used with worksheets

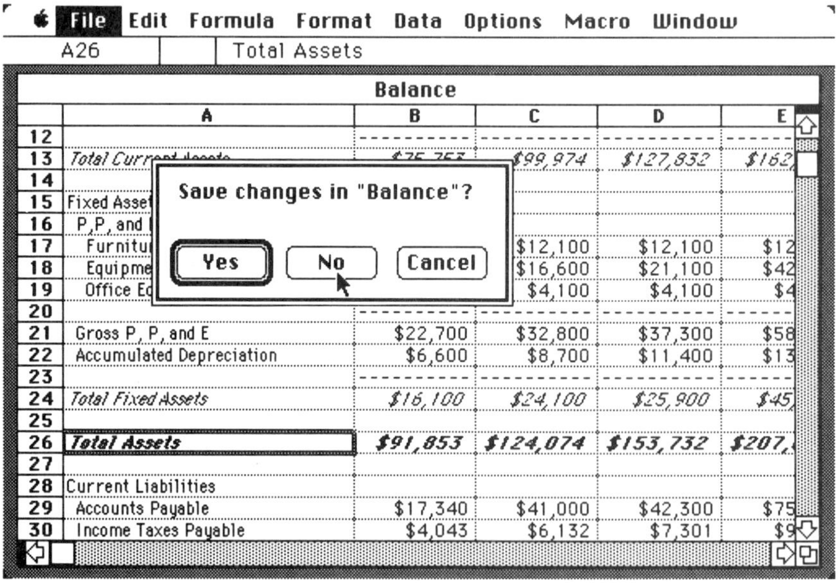

Figure B.4: *The Open Links dialog box.*

opened in normal Excel format or SYLK format. No backup copy is created. The document remains on the screen for further editing.

As you create or edit a document, it is a good idea to save it with this command periodically. The first time that the document is saved, use the Save As command and specify the new name of the document. Successive saves can be done using the Save command.

Save As

The Save As command is used to save a document under a name that you assign in a format that you define. When the command is selected, the dialog box (Figure B.6) suggests the name of the currently active document and displays the name of the disk on which the document will be saved. To save the document under this name in normal Excel format on the specified disk, click the Save button. If you will overwrite an existing file with the same name, Excel will prompt you with this information and permit you to abort the save. The following buttons are available in the Save As dialog box:

- **Drive** changes the drive on which the document will be saved.

- **Eject** ejects the disk with the displayed disk name. You can then insert another disk on which the document can be stored.

	A	B	C	D	E	F
		Jan-85	Feb-85	Mar-85	Apr-85	May-85
15	Interest Income	$323	$323	$262	$481	$6
16						
17	*Total Income*	*$90,149*	*$120,794*	*$126,609*	*$193,843*	*$134,4*
18						
19	EXPENSES					
20	Cost of Goods	$45,867	$45,867	$60,630	$63,010	$64,4
21	Rent	$11,543	$8,923	$8,923	$8,923	$8,9
22	Salaries	$19,894	$15,234	$15,234	$15,234	$15,2
23	Taxes	$1,204	$1,094	$1,094	$1,094	$1,0
24	Supplies	$2,050	$2,050	$2,050	$2,050	$2,0
25	Repairs	$2,873	$2,873	$2,873	$2,873	$2,8
26	Advertising	$8,339	$8,983	$12,047	$12,635	$19,3
27	Insurance	$734	$734	$734	$734	$7
28	Utilities	$2,345	$2,345	$2,345	$2,345	$2,3
29	Emp. Benefits	$1,234	$1,234	$1,234	$1,234	$1,2
30	Dues, Subscriptions	$254	$254	$254	$254	$2
31	Travel	$1,432	$1,432	$1,432	$1,432	$1,4
32	Miscellaneous	$500	$500	$500	$500	$5

(Menu bar: File Edit Formula Format Data Options Macro Window — Cell B7: 29586 — Window title: Cash Flow Analysis)

Figure B.5: *Closing a document.*

- **Cancel** terminates the command without saving the document.

- **Save** saves the document under the specified name on the specified disk.

You can use this same command to save the document in any of four formats. Unless specified, the document is saved in normal Excel format. The following formats are available for selection:

- **Normal** is the normal format for a saved Excel document. Use it if worksheets are to be linked or used with other Microsoft worksheet programs on the Macintosh computer.

- **SYLK** is the format to select if you plan to use the document on another type of computer with other Microsoft products that support this format.

- **Text** is the format to use to save the worksheet in a text format, with columns separated by tabs and rows delimited by carriage returns. Formatting information is lost.

- **WKS** is the format to select if you plan to use the document with Lotus 1-2-3 on the IBM-PC.

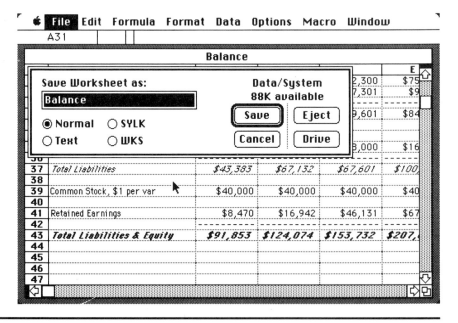

Figure B.6: *The Save As dialog box.*

Delete

The Delete command is used to delete a document on the currently selected disk. When the command is selected, the Delete dialog box (Figure B.7) is displayed. Select the document that you want to delete (you may have to scroll) and click the Delete button. More than one document can be deleted during a single use of the command. To return to the worksheet, click Cancel. The following buttons are available in the dialog box:

- **Drive** changes the drive from which the document will be deleted.

- **Eject** ejects the disk with the displayed disk name. You can then insert another disk on which the document can be deleted.

- **Cancel** terminates the command without further deleting.

- **Delete** deletes the document under the specified name on the specified disk.

Note: | You cannot undo a Delete command. Check your entry carefully before clicking Delete.

Page Setup

The Page Setup command controls the appearance of the printed document. Each time that you save a document, the current values of the Page Setup command are saved with the document. Two different dialog boxes are available. The one that will be displayed

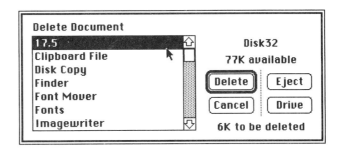

Figure B.7: *The Delete dialog box.*

depends upon the type of printer selected with the Printer Setup command. Figure B.8 shows the dialog box for the Macintosh ImageWriter printer. The following options are available:

- **Paper** controls the paper setting. US Letter is the normal paper setting. You can also select Legal, Computer (15-inch Image-Writer), A4 (European letter size), or International Fanfold.

- **Orientation** controls the orientation of the document. Tall is normal vertical orientation. Tall Adjusted adjusts pictures for proportion. Wide is a horizontal orientation.

- **Pagination** controls whether perforations between pages are printed over.

- **Reduction** controls the amount of reduction.

- **Page Header** controls the header on the page (see Chapter 6).

- **Page Footer** controls the footer on the page (see Chapter 6).

- **Left Margin** controls the size of the left margin.

- **Top Margin** controls the size of the top margin.

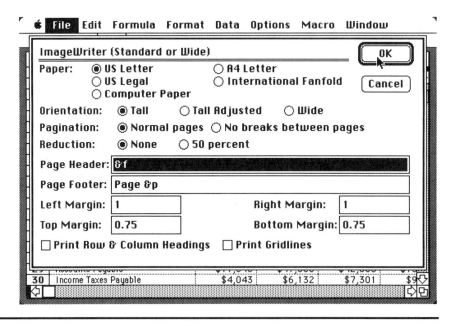

Figure B.8: *The Page Setup dialog box.*

- **Print Row & Column Headings** controls whether the designators are printed.

- **Print Gridlines** controls whether the grid lines are printed.

Print

The Print command prints all or part of the active worksheet. If no area of the worksheet is selected with the Set Print Area command on the Options menu, the entire worksheet is printed. The form of the printout is determined by the Page Setup command. As with the Page Setup command, there are two dialog boxes, and the one displayed depends upon the printer selected with the Printer Setup command. The dialog box for the ImageWriter is shown in Figure B.9. With a normal printout (no 50% reduction) all of the following options are available:

- **Quality** selects the resolution of the printout (high, standard, or draft).

- **Page Range** selects the pages of the worksheet to print.

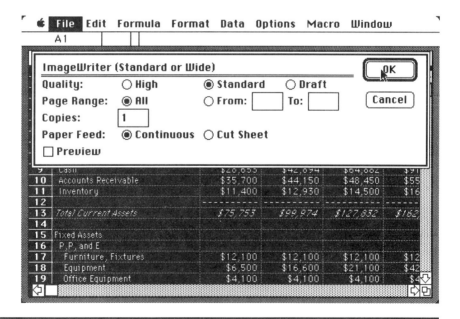

Figure B.9: *The ImageWriter printer dialog box.*

- **Copies** determines the number of copies to print.

- **Paper Feed** selects continuous or single-sheet (cut sheet) printing.

- **Preview** displays the document on the screen as it will be printed.

In the preview mode, the cursor changes to a magnifying glass. You can click any part of the page to see it full size. The Option key changes the pointer to a hand, which can drag the document. To cancel, click the Cancel button.

Printer Setup

The Printer Setup command is used to define the type of printer or modem that you are using. When the command is selected, the dialog box shown in Figure B.10 appears. Click the options for how you wish to direct the printer output:

- **Printer Setup** selects the driver to be used with your printer. Normally, select the driver that is the same type as your printer.

- **Port** selects the output connector to which the output will be directed.

- **Baud** selects the speed of the output.

Note: | Port and Baud can only be selected if the TTY printer option is used. The default setting is the ImageWriter printer.

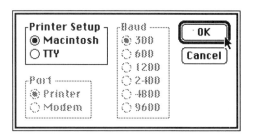

Figure B.10: *The Printer Setup dialog box.*

Quit

The Quit command is used to terminate an Excel session. All files are closed and the current status (size and position of the windows) is saved in a Resume Status document. If you have saved information on the Clipboard, it is also saved.

Note: The current worksheet cannot be displayed or edited again using the Resume Status icon. Only the arrangement of the windows is saved.

Whenever you quit Excel, the program will prompt you for each document that has not been saved with the latest changes and permit you to save the document (see Figure B.5).

The Edit Menu

The Edit menu is used to edit a worksheet, and it contains commands that are similar to Macintosh editing commands in other application programs.

Undo

The Undo command is used to undo Edit menu commands. Any Edit menu command can be undone until another command is selected. The menu displays the type of undo available. You can also undo formula-bar entries.

Note: You cannot undo a Delete command on the File menu or a Sort command on the Data menu.

Cut

The Cut command is used to move information on a worksheet or to move information from one worksheet to another. You can also use the Cut and Paste commands in the formula bar to move a part of the formula to another place in the formula bar. Moves are done with the Cut and Paste commands. Copies are done with the Copy and Paste commands.

When the Cut command is used, the contents of the selected area are moved from the worksheet to the Clipboard. The destination area is then selected. The Paste command is used to move the data from the Clipboard to the destination area, and the source area is then cleared. With the Cut and Paste commands, the Clipboard area is cleared—to use the Paste command again, you must select another area to cut.

Copy

The Copy command is used with the Paste command to copy a cell's contents from one cell to another cell on the same worksheet or another worksheet. You can also use the Copy and Paste commands to copy a portion of a formula in the formula bar into another place in the formula bar. Unlike with the Cut and Paste commands, the original cell contents are not cleared. The Clipboard also is not cleared after pasting, so multiple pastings can be done from one copy into the Clipboard.

To copy a cell's contents, select the cells or cell range and then click the Copy command. Select the destination cell or cell range and click the Paste command. The selected source range must be a single, continuous, rectangular area. After the Copy command is selected, the specified range will be marked. In defining the destination range, it is only necessary to specify the starting cell. The Paste command will paste the contents in the cells following the order of the source cells.

When the Copy command is normally used, the Clipboard will show only the size of the cells that were transferred. A special copy command—Copy Picture—is required when the Clipboard is used to transfer worksheet data to external programs. To use this command, pull down the Edit menu, *hold down the Shift key,* and the Copy command becomes Copy Picture. Click it to transfer the display image of the worksheet to the Clipboard.

Paste

The Paste command is used with the Cut or Copy commands to move or copy data from one cell into another or from one part of the formula bar into another. The Paste command is not active until a cut or copy selection is made. Multiple pastes can be made with a single Copy command, but only one paste can be made with a Cut command. All cell properties of the source cell are moved or copied, including values, formulas, and format. If you need to copy only a portion of these, use the Paste Special command.

In a cut-and-paste operation, the source and destination cell ranges must be of the same size. With a copy-and-paste operation, one of the following applies:

- If the source range is larger than the destination range, the entire source will be copied anyway, starting with the specified cell or cell range. This means that only the starting cell of the destination range must be specified.

- If the source range is smaller than the destination range, the source range will be copied two or more times to fill the destination range.

Clear

The Clear command is used to clear values, formulas, or formats from a cell or range of cells. To clear a cell or cell range, select the cells and then click the Clear command. The dialog box shown in Figure B.11 appears. It has the following options:

- **All** clears values, formulas, and formats from the selected cells.

- **Formats** clears only the formats of the selected cells, returning the cells to the General template.

- **Formulas** clears values and formulas without clearing formats.

You can retrieve cleared cells with the Undo command if no other command has been used since the clear.

Paste Special

The Paste Special command permits you to complete a copy selectively; that is, you can copy all of the selected area's contents or just its formulas, values, or formats. The copy operation is initiated with the Copy command. The destination area is then selected, and the Paste Special command is clicked. In the dialog box shown in Figure B.12, the following options are available:

- **All** copies all cell properties, as with a normal Paste command.

- **Formulas** copies only formulas into the destination cells.

- **Values** copies only values into the destination cells.

- **Formats** copies only formats into the destination cells.

The Operation part of the dialog box can be used to perform operations on the data in the source and destination cells, posting the results in the destination cells. The following operations are permitted: addition, subtraction, multiplication, and division. If the destination cells are blank, their value is assumed to be zero.

Delete

The Delete command removes the selected cell or cell range from the worksheet. If row or column designators are used to select the range to be deleted, there will be no dialog box. If a portion of a column or row is selected, a dialog box (Figure B.13) will be displayed, asking how the remaining rows and columns should be shifted to adjust for the deletion. Select the desired option and click OK.

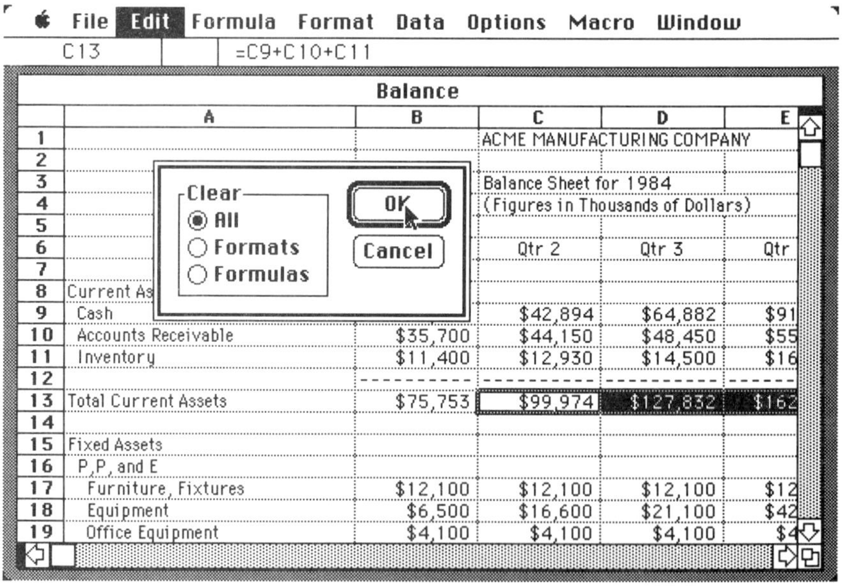

Figure B.11: *Clearing cells.*

Insert

The Insert command inserts a blank cell or cell range into the worksheet. If row or column designators are used to select the insert area, there will be no dialog box. If a portion of a column or row is selected, a dialog box (Figure B.14) will be displayed, asking how the remaining rows and columns should be shifted to adjust for the insertion. Select the desired option and click OK.

Fill Right

The Fill Right command provides a fast copy operation that can be used if the copy is from one cell range to a range to the right of the selected cells. You may use single or multiple selections. If multiple selections are made, each copy is performed separately. Formulas, values, and formats are copied.

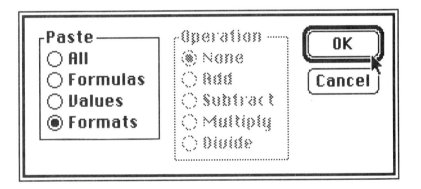

Figure B.12: *The Paste Special dialog box.*

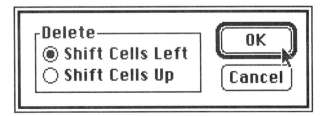

Figure B.13: *Deleting a cell range.*

Fill Down

The Fill Down command provides a fast copy operation that can be used if the copy is from one cell range to a range below the selected cells. You may use single or multiple selections. If multiple selections are made, each copy is performed separately. Formulas, values, and formats are copied.

The Formula Menu

The Formula menu is used to create complex formulas. It contains the commands for naming cells and pasting names. This menu also contains the commands for quickly moving to specific cells.

Paste Name

The Paste Name command can be used to paste a name into a formula in the formula bar from a list of names previously defined.

		é	File	**Edit**	Formula	Format	Data	Options	Macro	Window		

	C13		=C9+C10+C11

Balance

	A	B	C	D	E
1			ACME MANUFACTURING COMPANY		
2					
3			⌐Insert────────	OK	Sheet for 1984
4			○ **Shift Cells Right**		in Thousands of Dollars)
5			◉ **Shift Cells Down**	Cancel	
6					2 Qtr 3 Qtr
7					
8	Current Assets				
9	Cash	$28,653	$42,894	$64,882	$91
10	Accounts Receivable	$35,700	$44,150	$48,450	$55
11	Inventory	$11,400	$12,930	$14,500	$16
12					
13	Total Current Assets	$75,753	$99,974	$127,832	$162
14					
15	Fixed Assets				
16	P,P, and E				
17	Furniture, Fixtures	$12,100	$12,100	$12,100	$12
18	Equipment	$6,500	$16,600	$21,100	$42
19	Office Equipment	$4,100	$4,100	$4,100	$4

Figure B.14: *Inserting a cell range.*

When the command is used, the dialog box shown in Figure B.15 is displayed. Double-click the name that you want to paste or click the name and then click OK.

If the formula bar is not active, it is made active and the name is pasted, preceded by an equal sign. If the formula bar is already active, the name is pasted at the insertion point. If no operator precedes the insertion point, Excel will insert a plus operator.

Paste Function

The Paste Function command is used to paste a function name into a formula in the formula bar from the list of active functions. When the command is issued, a dialog box (Figure B.16) that lists the names of the available functions is displayed. Scroll to the desired function and double-click it, or click the name and click OK.

If the formula bar is not active, it is made active and the function name is pasted preceded by an equal sign. If the formula bar is already active, the function name is pasted at the insertion point. If no operator precedes the insertion point, Excel will insert a plus operator.

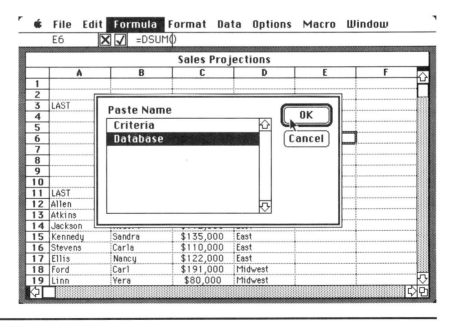

Figure B.15: *Pasting a name.*

If you have defined any function macros and the macro sheets are open, these functions also will appear in the dialog box.

Reference

The Reference command changes the type of references in the formula bar, if the formula bar is active. Relative cell references are changed to absolute, absolute to mixed, and mixed back to relative. If you select a reference before using the command, only the selected reference is converted. If only an insertion point is specified, the reference before the insertion point is converted.

Define Name

The Define Name command assigns a name to a specified cell or cell range. This command is also used to edit and delete names that have already been assigned. To define a name, the cell or cell range is normally selected before the command is used. The selection can be made, however, by typing it into the Refers To box after the

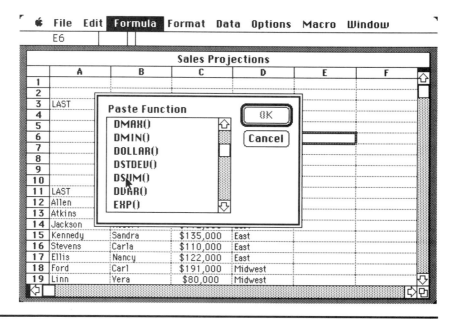

Figure B.16: *The Paste Function dialog box.*

command is clicked. Multiple selections can be made by using the Command key.

When the command is used, the window shown in Figure B.17 is displayed. Names that have already been defined are displayed in the window. The window can be moved so that you can view any part of the worksheet. The following entries are available:

- **Name** is the box that is used to enter the name that you are assigning to the cell or cell range. If there is text in the selected cell when the command is used, the text is proposed as a name. You can click any name in the scroll box, and it will move into the Name box. Then, you can delete or edit that name. When creating a new name, you can enter any name into this box. It must begin with a letter and should not contain spaces.

- **Refers To** is the box that is used to enter the cell or cell range to which the name is to be assigned. If a cell or cell range was active when the command was used, it will be shown in the box. You can move the cursor to this box and click cells to enter their references. You also can enter constants here if you

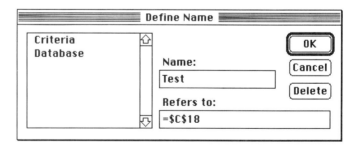

Figure B.17: *The Define Name window.*

wish to assign a name to a constant. Editing this box is like editing the formula bar—you can paste names or functions into it and use all the Edit menu commands.

- **Delete** is the button to use to delete a name previously defined. Click the name to move it to the Name box, then click the Delete button.

If you use this command when a macro sheet is active, the displayed window is slightly different, as shown in Figure B.18. At the bottom of the window is a Macro box that is used to identify the macro as a function or command macro. If the macro is a command macro, you can assign a keystroke sequence to it.

Create Names

The Create Names command is used to assign names to several areas of the worksheet with a single command. The row or column titles are used as the names in the definition. To use the command, select one or more rows (if the row titles are to be the names) or one or more columns (if the column titles are to be the names) and click the command. You can also use both options at once.

When the command is used, the dialog box shown in Figure B.19 is displayed. Click one or both options, then click OK. If the name

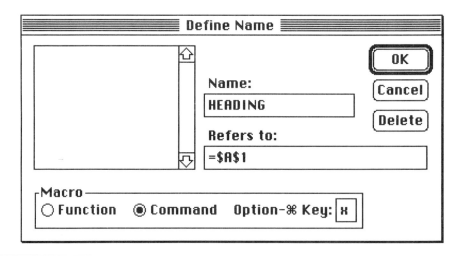

Figure B.18: *The macro Define Name window.*

has already been assigned, you will be prompted and asked if the name is to be reassigned.

Note: | In using this command, be sure that you have selected row or column designators and that text appears in the first cell of each specified range. If there are spaces in the text, they will be converted to underlines in the name.

Goto

The Goto command is used to move to a specified cell or cell range quickly. When the command is used, the dialog box shown in Figure B.20 is displayed. Click the name of the destination cell or cell range or enter a cell reference in the Reference box. The worksheet will quickly scroll to the specified area. You can also scroll to a cell in another open document by entering its reference preceded by the worksheet name and an exclamation point.

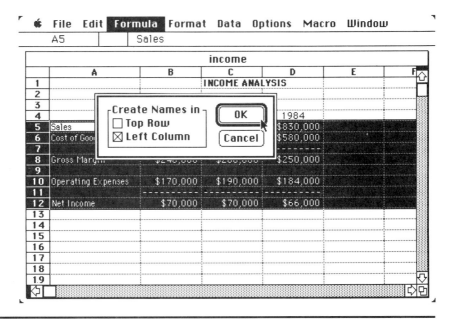

Figure B.19: *Creating names.*

Find

The Find command is used to locate specific text or values in a worksheet and to make the cells that contain them active. It is particularly useful for finding #REF! error messages after a worksheet is edited. If a cell range is selected, only the range is searched. If no range is selected, the entire worksheet is searched.

When the command is used, the dialog box shown in Figure B.21 is displayed. In the Find What box, you enter the value or text to locate. Wild-card characters (? and *) can be used, as well as comparison operators (see Chapter 4). The following options are available:

- **Look In** allows you to specify a search in formulas or on values only.

- **Look At** permits selecting a match with the entire cell contents or with a part of the cell contents.

- **Look By** permits searching by row or column. This selection speeds up searches on large worksheets.

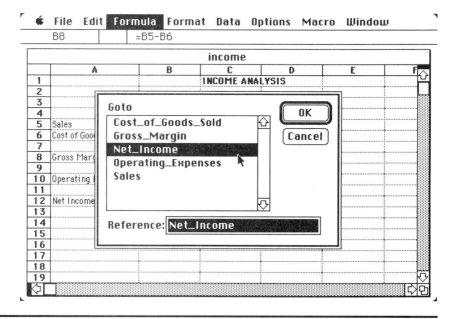

Figure B.20: *The Goto dialog box.*

When you have made your selection, click OK. Press the Command and H keys to search for repeated occurrences (bypassing the dialog box).

Select Last Cell

The Select Last Cell command scrolls immediately to the last cell in the worksheet. Since the amount of memory used is determined by the size of the worksheet, this command is useful for memory management.

Show Active Cell

The Show Active Cell command scrolls the worksheet until the active cell is visible on the display. Use this command if you scrolled away from the active cell and wish to return to it quickly.

The Format Menu

The Format menu permits you to select how data will be displayed in the specified cells.

Number

The Number command permits you to specify the template for how numbers, dates, and times will be displayed. To specify how a cell range is to be displayed, first select the range and then click the

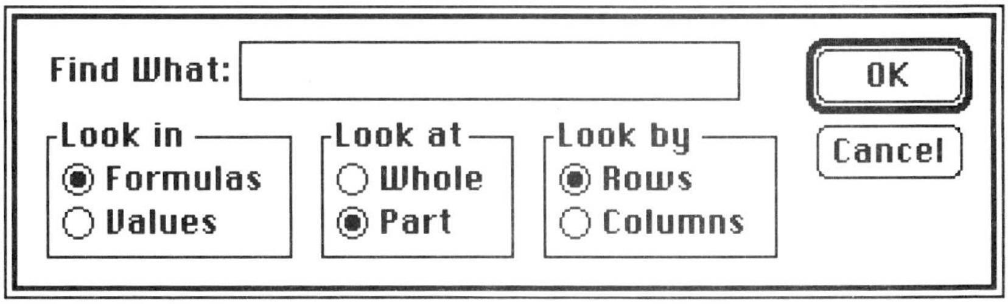

```
┌─────────────────────────────────────────────────────────┐
│  Find What: [_____]   ( OK )   │
│  ┌Look in ──┐ ┌Look at─┐ ┌Look by ──┐                    │
│  ⊙ Formulas   ○ Whole    ⊙ Rows        (Cancel)          │
│  ○ Values     ⊙ Part     ○ Columns                       │
└─────────────────────────────────────────────────────────┘
```

Figure B.21: *The Find dialog box.*

Number command. When the command is used, a dialog box (Figure B.22) that contains a scroll box with available templates is displayed. Double-click the template desired or click the template and click OK. You can also create your own templates using the Format Number box (see Chapter 6). All cells default to the General template.

Alignment

The Alignment command controls the alignment for text and values in the selected cells. Select the range to be aligned and click the command. The Alignment dialog box (Figure B.23) is displayed. Select the alignment and click OK. All cells default to a General alignment—text is left-justified, and values are right-justified.

Style

The Style command changes the style of the selected cell range. Select the range and click the command. The dialog box shown in Figure B.24 is displayed. Click one or both options and click OK.

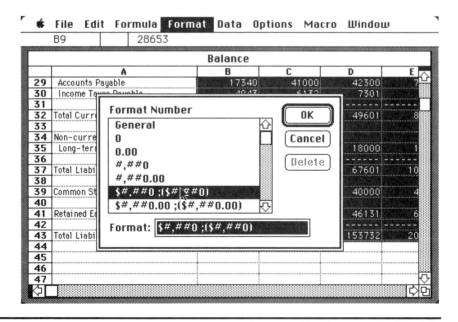

Figure B.22: *The Number dialog box.*

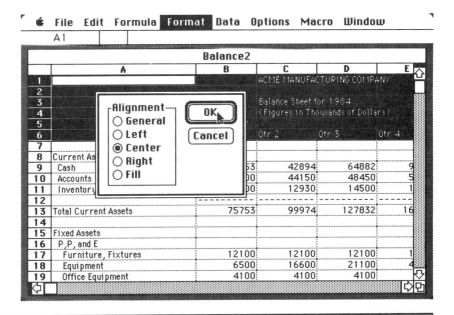

Figure B.23: *The Alignment dialog box.*

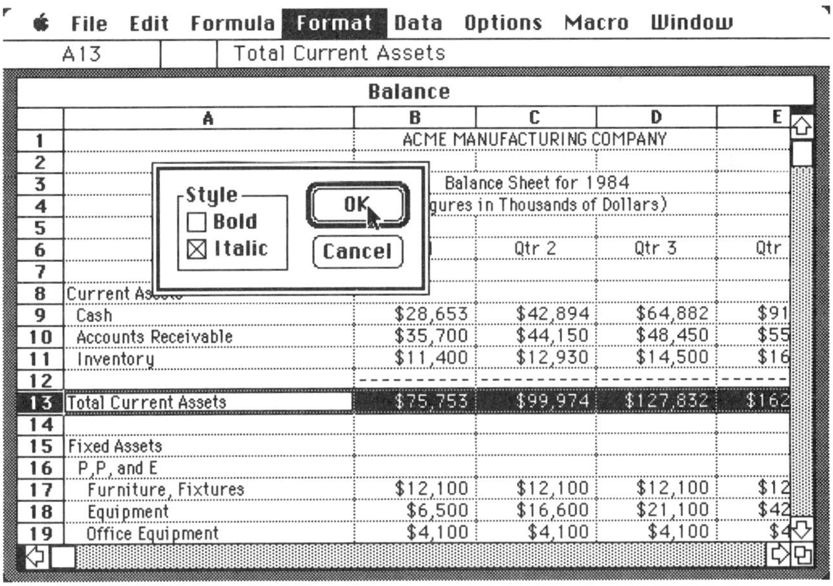

Figure B.24: *The Style dialog box.*

Border

The Border command permits you to display and print borders around the selected cells. Select the range to border, then click the command. The dialog box shown in Figure B.25 will be displayed. The following options are available:

- **Outline** puts a border around the selected range.

- **Left** puts a border on the left edge of each cell in the range.

- **Right** puts a border on the right edge of each cell in the range.

- **Top** puts a border on the top edge of each cell in the range.

- **Bottom** puts a border on the bottom edge of each cell in the range.

You can combine two or more of the above options. If the grid lines are displayed on the screen, it will be difficult to see the borders. You can use the Display command on the Options menu to turn off the grid lines.

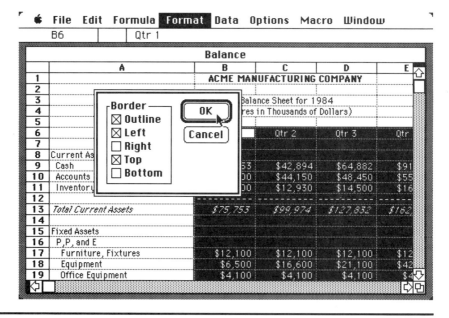

Figure B.25: *The Border dialog box.*

Cell Protection

The Cell Protection command permits you to lock cells to prevent them from being altered or to hide cells so that the formulas used in the calculation are not visible in the formula bar (see Chapter 13). To use the command, first select the cells to unlock or hide. Then, click the command. The dialog box shown in Figure B.26 is displayed. Click the desired option and click OK. To complete the protection, use the Protect Document command on the Options menu.

Cells normally default to a locked status and are not hidden. The command is used, then, to unlock or to hide cells.

Column Width

The Column Width command is used to change the width of a specified column or columns. To change the width of a column, select any part of the column and click the command. You can select more than one column. The dialog box shown in Figure B.27 is then displayed. Click either standard width (10 characters) or enter the desired column width. The number must be between 0 and 72. You also can define the column width in decimal fractions (such as 2.5 characters).

Another way to change a column width is by clicking the bar to the right of the column designator and dragging it to the desired width.

The Data Menu

The Data menu contains the database commands.

Find

The Find command is used to locate records in a database that match the specified criteria (see Chapter 9). The criteria must be specified before the command is used. After using the command, the scroll box will change from white to striped. You can then scroll to find the matching records. To exit the command, choose any other command or click Exit Find on the Data menu. You can also press the Command and F keys to move quickly to the next matching record.

Extract

The Extract command is used to extract records that match a specified criterion from a database (see Chapter 9). To use the command, set the database and criteria areas and then specify the criteria. You must also specify a destination area (with the field names) for the extracted records. It is not necessary to copy all fields. The extracted records are copied to a specified area on the current worksheet or another active worksheet. The command displays a dialog box (Figure B.28) from which you can select to copy all records or unique records only. If you select to copy only unique records, a record will be extracted only once, even if it matches more than one criterion.

Note: | In an extraction, the extracted records will overwrite any values, text, or formulas that were previously in the cells in the destination area.

Delete

The Delete command is used to delete records in the current database that meet the specified criteria. The rest of the database is

Figure B.26: *The Cell Protection dialog box.*

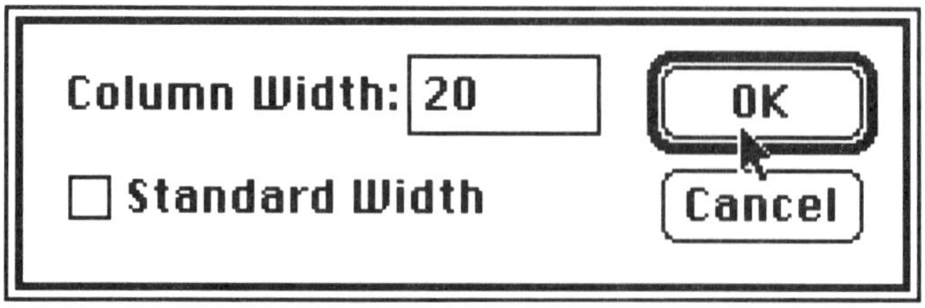

Figure B.27: *Changing the column width.*

shifted up to recover the lost space. The remainder of the worksheet is not affected.

Note: | You cannot undo a Delete command. Use the Find command before you use the Delete command to see which records will be deleted. Save the worksheet before the deletion.

Set Database

The Set Database command is used to define the range of cells to be assigned to the database. Only one database can be defined at a time. The range selected must include the row with the field names. To define a database, select the range and then click the Set Database command. Excel will assign the name Database to the specified range. The name can then be used for pasting, just like any other name.

Set Criteria

The Set Criteria command is used to define the range of cells that are used to define the criteria for finding, extracting, and deleting records from the database. The name is also used with the database functions (see Chapter 9) to define the records to which a function is applied.

The criteria range consists of one row with the field names and one or more rows with the criteria. Criteria in the same row are ANDed; criteria in separate rows are ORed. You can use formulas, values, and comparison operators in defining the criteria. You can also use wild-card specifications (* and ?) in text criteria.

Figure B.28: *The Extract dialog box.*

Sort

The Sort command is used to sort the rows or columns in a database in a specified order. When the command is issued, a Sort window (Figure B.29) is displayed. The following options are available:

- **Sort By** lets you sort by rows to reorder the records or by columns to reorder the fields.

- **1st, 2nd, and 3rd Keys** are used to specify the rows or columns used to control the sort. Up to three keys can be entered, with each creating an ascending or descending sort (to use more than three keys, use additional sorts).

Note: | You cannot undo a Sort command. If an undo is necessary, either save the worksheet first or create a new column with the record numbers before sorting. This column can then be used to initiate a sort to undo another sort.

When sorting a database, be sure not to include the field names.

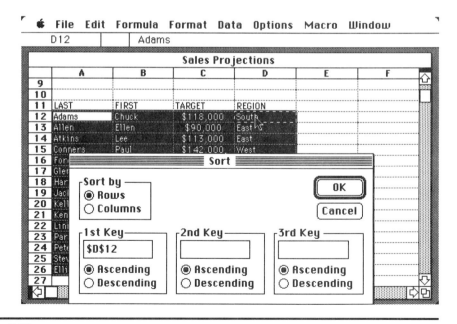

Figure B.29: *The Sort window.*

Series

The Series command is used to fill a range of cells with a series of numbers. The command will fill by rows or by columns. To use the command, enter the value into the first cell and then select the range for the series (including the first cell). Click the Series command, and the dialog box shown in Figure B.30 appears. The following options are available:

- **Series In** defines the direction for the fill.
- **Type** defines the type of series for the fill.
- **Date Unit** is only active if a Date type is selected. It determines the type of increment for the date series.
- **Step Value** determines the increment value for each cell in the series.
- **Stop Value** determines the end value for the series.

For more information on using the Series command, see Chapter 13.

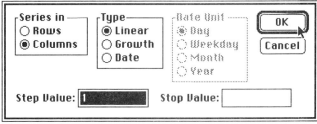

Figure B.30: *The Series dialog box.*

Table

The Table command is used to create tables (see Chapter 12). To create a table, define the range for the table and then click the Table command. The window shown in Figure B.31 is displayed.

For a one-input table, enter the reference of either the row input or column input cell. For a two-input table, define the row input cell as one input and the column input cell as the second input.

The Options Menu

The Options menu is used to change display characteristics that affect the entire worksheet.

Set Print Area

The Set Print Area command is used to set the range of the worksheet that will be printed with the Print command on the File menu.

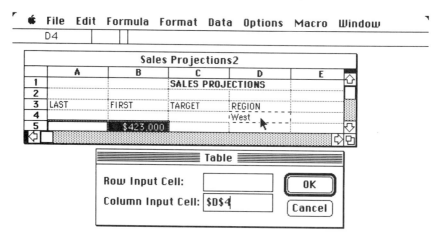

Figure B.31: *The Table window.*

If no area is selected, the entire worksheet is printed. To use the command, select the range and click the Set Print Area command.

Note: | The name Print_Area is assigned to the selected range. |

Set Print Titles

The Set Print Titles command is used to define the text that will be used as page titles with the Print command. The rows or columns that you define as titles will be printed on each page of the worksheet that contains any cells in that row or column. You can assign multiple rows or columns as titles. To use the command, select the rows or columns and then click the command.

Note: | The name Print_Titles is assigned to the selected range. |

Set Page Break

The Set Page Break command is used to set manual page breaks when the worksheet is printed. To use the command, select a cell and click the command. A manual page break will be inserted just before the selected cell, and the selected cell will be the first cell on the new page.

Remove Page Break

The Remove Page Break command is used to remove manual page breaks that have been set with the Set Page Break command. To remove a page break, select the cell that is the first cell on the new page and click the command. The page break before that cell will be removed.

Font

The Font command is used to change the font and font size of the entire worksheet. When the command is used, the dialog box shown in Figure B.32 is displayed. The following options are available:

- **Font** selects from the fonts that are on the startup disk.

- **Size** selects from the font sizes available. You can scroll for additional font sizes.

You can use the Font Mover program on your system disk to add fonts to the system.

Display

The Display command is used to control the screen display of formulas, grid lines, and row designators. When the command is used, the dialog box shown in Figure B.33 is displayed. Select one or more options and click OK.

Note: | If the Formulas option is selected, the formulas will be displayed and can be printed with the Print command. The Gridlines and Row & Column Headings selections affect only the screen display. To switch these on the printed copy, use the Page Setup command on the File menu.

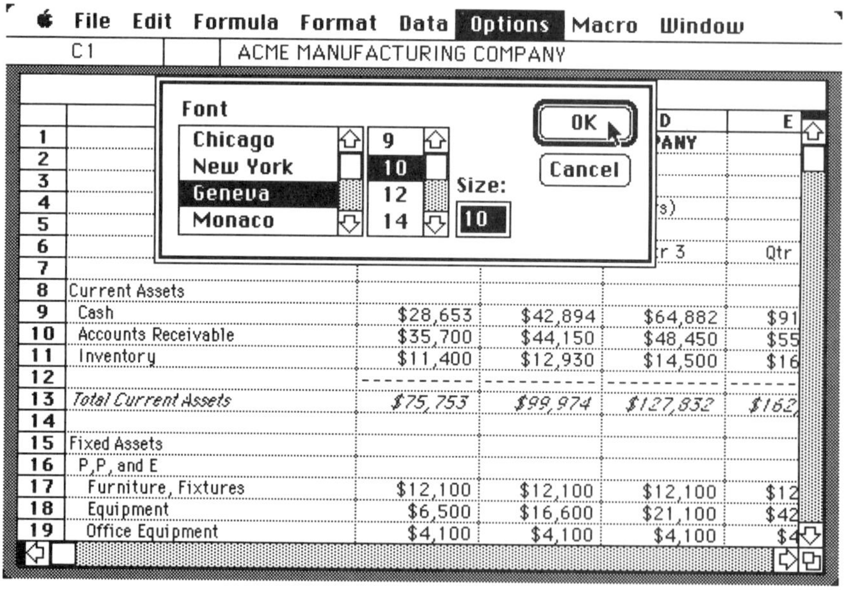

Figure B.32: *Changing the font.*

Protect Document/Unprotect Document

The Protect Document command is used to complete a worksheet protection assigned by the Cell Protection command on the Format menu. After a cell or cell range is assigned as locked or hidden, the Protect Document command is used to lock or hide the specified cells. The dialog box shown in Figure B.34 is displayed. Enter the password and click OK.

The document is then protected, and the menu changes to include an Unprotect Document command. To unprotect the document, select the Unprotect Document command, and the dialog box shown in Figure B.35 appears. Enter the password and click OK.

The Cell Protection command affects only the specified range, and multiple ranges can be selected using the command several times. The Protect Document command affects the entire worksheet, implementing the desired protection selections.

Note: You can only unprotect a document if you know the password. If you forget the password, you cannot unprotect the document. Keep a record of the passwords that you use.

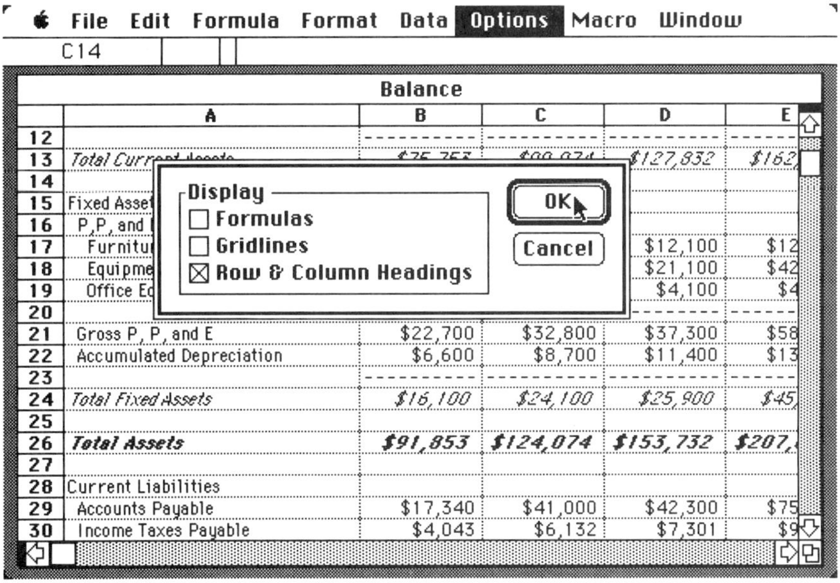

Figure B.33: *The Display dialog box.*

Precision as Displayed/Full Precision

The Precision As Displayed/Full Precision command controls the precision with which the calculations are done and how the results are stored. Normally, all calculations are done at a full 14-digit precision, and the values are saved with this precision. If Precision As Displayed is selected, calculations are only done with the precision with which they are displayed, and the numbers are saved with this precision. However, you cannot change the precision of numbers that use the General template.

R1C1/A1

The R1C1/A1 command changes the method of cell reference. Excel normally uses the A1 format, in which columns are designated by letters and rows by numbers. Some spreadsheet programs use an R1C1 format, in which both rows and columns use numeric designators. This command permits you to switch the designator mode. Formulas are adjusted to the selected mode.

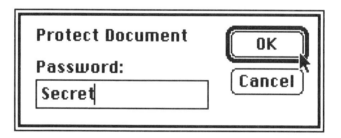

Figure B.34: *Protecting the document.*

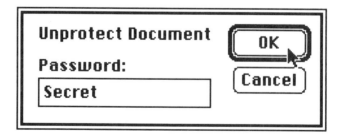

Figure B.35: *Unprotecting the document.*

Calculate Now

The Calculate Now command forces a recalculation of a worksheet or chart, and it is used to complete the calculations if the manual mode is selected with the Calculation command. This command is not necessary if you are using the default automatic calculation.

You can also use the Calculate Now command to replace a formula in the formula bar with a value. If the formula bar is active and you begin an entry with an equal sign, Calculate Now will calculate the formula and replace the cell entry with the resulting value.

Calculation

The Calculation command controls when Excel recalculates formulas in the open documents. In the default automatic mode, whenever a cell is changed, all formulas and values that depend upon that cell are recalculated. The amount of time required depends upon the size of the worksheet and the complexity of the formulas.

While creating a worksheet, you may find the calculations cannot keep up with the data entry on a large worksheet. In this case, use the Calculation command to switch off the calculations until the data entry is completed.

When the command is used, the dialog box shown in Figure B.36 is displayed. The following calculation options are available:

- **Automatic** calculates all values that depend on a cell each time that the cell contents are changed.

- **Automatic Except Tables** calculates all values except table values when the cell contents are changed.

- **Manual** calculates the worksheet only with the Calculate Now command.

Note: | Table calculations take much longer than others to calculate. Using the Automatic Except Tables option can speed up creating and editing worksheets that contain tables.

The **Iteration** option in the Calculation dialog box is used to control iterative calculations when circular references are used on the worksheet. The default condition is no iteration, and Excel will display error messages when you use circular references. If you need to use circular references, click Iteration and select the desired parameters.

The Macro Menu

The Macro menu is used to create and execute function and command macros.

Run

The Run command is used to initiate a previously defined command macro. The macro sheet must be open. When the command is executed, the dialog box shown in Figure B.37 is displayed. Double-click the desired macro or click the name and click OK. You can also execute a macro by entering in the Reference box the reference to the first cell on the macro sheet.

Start Recorder/Stop Recorder

The Start Recorder command initiates the recording of worksheet actions on a macro sheet in a range previously defined by the Set

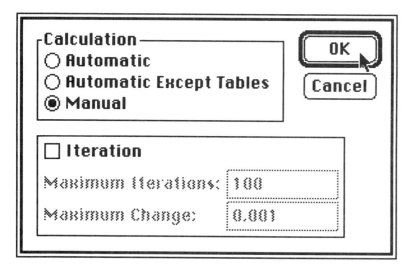

Figure B.36: *The Calculation dialog box.*

Recorder command. The Stop Recorder command terminates the recording. Cell references are recorded, by default, as relative references. If an attempt is made to record over a cell that already has an entry, an alert box will be displayed.

Absolute Record/Relative Record

The Absolute Record/Relative Record command determines the type of cell references that are stored when the recorder is started.

Set Recorder

The Set Recorder command is used to specify the range to be used by the recorder on the macro sheet (see Chapter 17). A range is selected on the macro sheet, and the Set Recorder command is clicked. Then, commands will be stored in the specified range.

The Window Menu

The Window menu is used to show the Clipboard, to switch between active windows quickly, and to open additional windows on the same document.

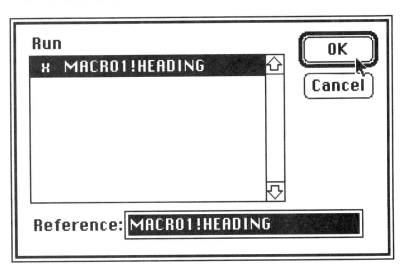

Figure B.37: *Initiating a macro.*

Show Clipboard

The Show Clipboard command opens the Clipboard window. If the Clipboard contains worksheet cells, only the size of the cell range is shown. If the Copy Picture command has been used, the Clipboard will show the worksheet range.

New Window

The New Window command opens a new window on the currently active document. The number of windows that can be open is limited only by the computer memory.

Activate Window

The Window menu will always show an entry for each open document. You can use the Activate Window command to switch quickly between open documents.

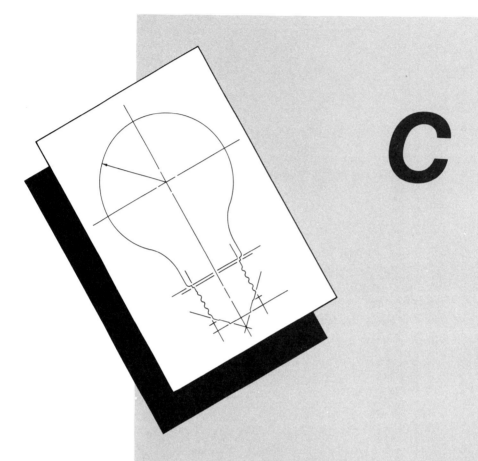

C

The Chart Commands

Excel's chart menus are available whenever an existing chart is open or the New command on the File menu is used to create a chart. There are eight chart menus: Apple, File, Edit, Gallery, Chart, Format, Macro, and Window.

The Apple Menu

The Apple menu is identical to the Apple menu for the worksheet. It includes an About Microsoft Excel command that provides information about memory usage and about the listed help topics.

The File Menu

The chart File menu is identical to the File menu for the worksheet, except that the Page Setup command has some different options. It does not include the options for row and column designators or grid lines. Also, margins cannot be specified; instead, you can specify the size of the chart (see Figure C.1).

The chart Page Setup command also gives you the option of selecting screen size or fit to page. If the **Fit to Page** option is set, the chart is printed as specified, regardless of the screen chart size. If the **Screen Size** option is selected, the chart will be printed at the screen size, and as much as possible of the image will be printed with the specified print width and height.

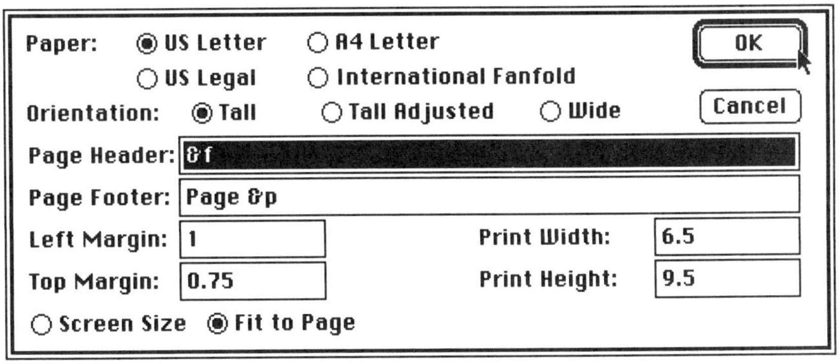

Figure C.1: *The Page Setup dialog box for charts.*

The Edit Menu

The Edit menu is used to edit charts, much as the familiar Macintosh Edit menu commands are used in other application programs.

Undo

The Undo command is used to undo editing commands. Any Edit menu command can be undone until another command is selected. The menu displays the type of undo available.

Cut

The Cut command can be used to edit the chart formula bar. Selections cut are moved to the Clipboard. You cannot cut from the chart itself with this command.

Copy

The Copy command copies the data series and format of a chart onto the Clipboard, where it can be pasted into another chart. To copy a chart, the graph is first selected with the Select Chart command on the Chart menu. Then, the Copy command is used to move the data on the chart to the Clipboard. You can activate the destination chart and use the Paste or Paste Special command to copy the graph into it.

Copy Chart

The Copy Chart command is used to copy a chart into the Clipboard when you wish to move it to other Macintosh documents. When the command is selected, a dialog box (Figure C.2) is displayed. From this dialog box, you can select whether to copy the chart onto the Clipboard as it is displayed on the screen or as it would be printed. If you select to copy it as printed, you can control the size of the Clipboard image using the Page Setup command on the File menu.

Paste

The Paste command is used to paste a data series from a worksheet or chart into another chart. To copy from a worksheet, select the data series and use the Copy command to copy the data series into the Clipboard. Then, use the Paste command to paste the data series into a chart. To copy from another chart, use the Select Chart command on the Chart menu and the Copy command to copy the data series into the Clipboard. Then, use the Paste command to copy it from the Clipboard into the chart.

You can also use the Cut and Paste commands in the chart formula bar to edit a formula.

Clear

The Clear command is used to clear the formula bar or a chart data series. If the formula bar is active, the command will clear whatever is selected in the formula bar.

To clear a chart, first use the Select Chart command on the Chart menu to select the chart, then use the Clear command. A dialog box (Figure C.3) will be displayed. It provides the following options:

- **All** clears the data format and data series.

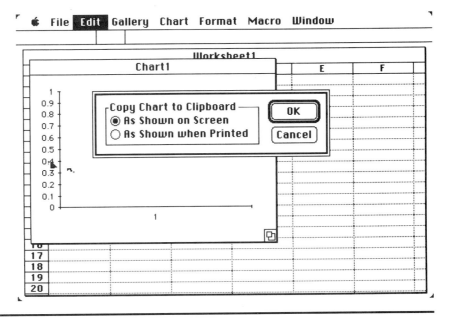

Figure C.2: *The Copy Chart dialog box.*

- **Formats** clears the format, but not the data series (the chart reverts to the preferred format).

- **Formulas** clears the data series, but not the format.

Paste Special

The Paste Special command permits the user to control how the data series is defined when pasting. The Paste command does not permit the user to control the data series definition (see Chapter 15). The Copy command is used first to move the data series onto the Clipboard. The chart is then selected, and the Paste Special command is used. The dialog box shown in Figure C.4 is displayed. Select how you wish to define the data series and click OK.

The following options are available:

- **Values In** is the option to click to indicate if the data series is in a row or a column.

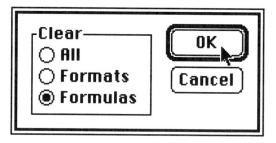

Figure C.3: *The Clear dialog box.*

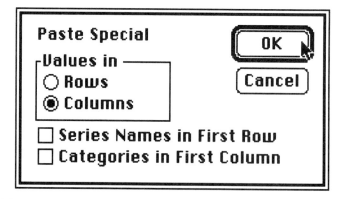

Figure C.4: *The chart Paste Special dialog box.*

- **Series Names in First Column,** if checked, has Excel use the contents of the cell in the first column of each row as the name of the data series for that row. If it is not checked, the contents of the first column are assumed to be the first value in the data series.
- **Categories in First Row,** if checked, has Excel use the text in each cell in the first row as the category for the series in the column. If it is not checked, the first row is the first data series.
- **Series Names in First Row,** if checked, has Excel use the contents of the cell in the first row of each column as the name of the data series for that column. If it is not checked, the contents of the first row are assumed to be the first value in the data series.
- **Categories in First Column,** if checked, has Excel use the text in each cell in the first column as the category for the series in the row. If it is not checked, the first column is the first data series.

Gallery Menu

The Gallery menu is used to select the chart type. The active chart is changed to the specified type. Click the desired type, and then select the chart format within that type from the dialog box displayed. Figures C.5 through C.10 show the dialog boxes for the six basic types of charts. Figure C.11 shows the four combination types that can be used if two data series are charted.

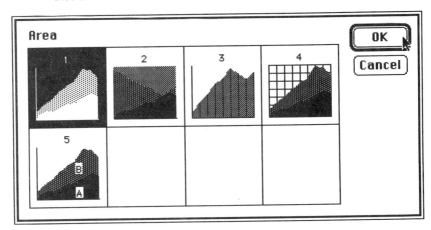

Figure C.5: *Area chart formats.*

The Preferred command changes the format of the currently displayed chart to the preferred format. Whenever a chart is first created from a data series, it is always displayed in the preferred format. It can then be changed to an alternate type by using a command on the Gallery menu. The default preferred format is the column type.

You can change the preferred format with the Set Preferred Format command on the Chart menu. The Preferred and Set Preferred Format commands are useful if you need to remember the currently displayed format while you experiment with other formats. Use the Set Preferred Format command to select the current format as

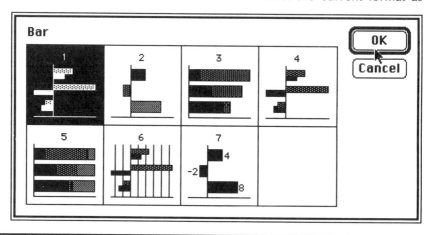

Figure C.6: *Bar chart formats.*

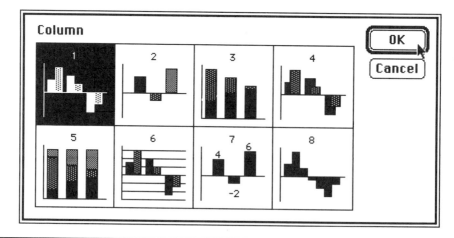

Figure C.7: *Column chart formats.*

the preferred format, then experiment as you wish. To return to the initial format, use the Preferred command.

Chart Menu

The Chart menu is used to control the chart type and the objects (legend, axes labels, titles, etc.) displayed on the chart.

Main Chart Type

The Main Chart Type command changes the basic type of the main chart. When the command is selected, the dialog box shown in Figure C.12 is displayed. Click the desired option, then click OK.

Overlay Chart Type

The Overlay Chart Type command changes the basic type of the overlay chart. When the command is selected, the dialog box shown in Figure C.13 is displayed. Click the desired option and click OK.

Set Preferred Format

The Set Preferred Format command saves the format of the currently active chart as the preferred format (see the Preferred command in the Gallery menu section).

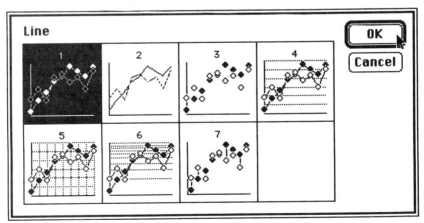

Figure C.8: *Line chart formats.*

Axes

The Axes command controls the display of the axes and grid lines. You can control the weight of the lines with the Format Patterns

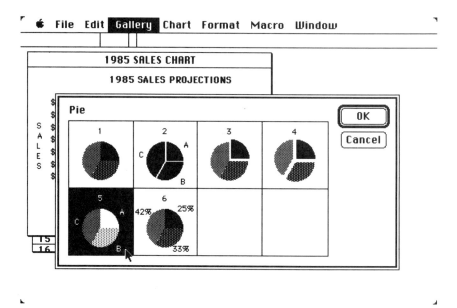

Figure C.9: *Pie chart formats.*

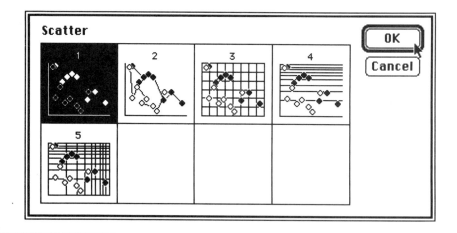

Figure C.10: *Scatter chart formats.*

command. When the Axes command is selected, the dialog box shown in Figure C.14 is displayed. Select the desired options and click OK.

Add Legend/Delete Legend

The Add Legend command adds a legend to the chart. On a pie chart, the category titles are the legend text. On other graphs, the

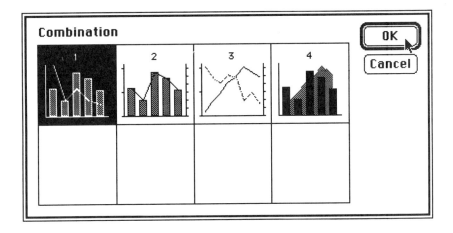

Figure C.11: *Combination chart formats.*

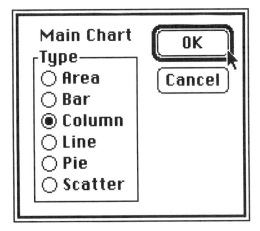

Figure C.12: *The Main Chart Type dialog box.*

data-series names are used as the legend titles. The chart is redrawn to accommodate the legend. You can format and position the legend with the Text and Legend commands on the Format menu. You can also change the legend titles by editing the data-series formulas in the formula bar (see Chapter 15).

Use the Delete Legend command to remove the legend.

Attach Text

The Attach Text command is used to attach text to defined parts of the chart. To add attached text, click the command. The dialog box

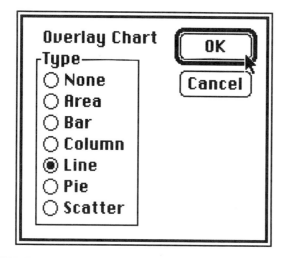

Figure C.13: *The Overlay Chart Type dialog box.*

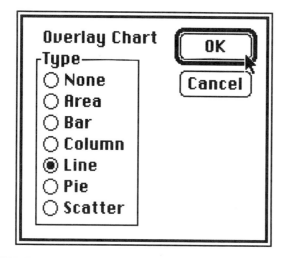

Figure C.14: *The Axes dialog box.*

shown in Figure C.15 is displayed. Click the area to which you wish to attach the text, then click OK. Enter the text into the formula bar and click the enter box or press the Enter key.

You can use this command to attach text to a title, either axis, or a data series. You can also specify a data point to which to attach text.

Add Arrow

The Add Arrow command is used to add an arrow to highlight any point of the chart. The command puts an arrow in the upper left of the chart. You can then drag the arrow to any point in the chart and format it with the Patterns command on the Format menu. You can add as many arrows as you want to a chart.

Select Chart

The Select Chart command selects the entire chart. Once selected, you can use the Patterns command on the Format menu to alter the patterns, clear the chart with the Clear command on the Edit menu, or copy the chart with the Copy command on the Edit menu.

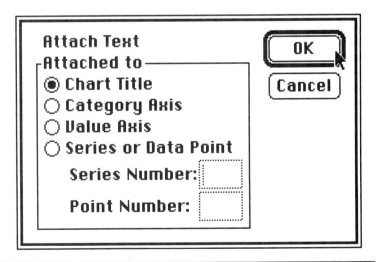

Figure C.15: *The Attach Text dialog box.*

Select Plot Area

The Select Plot Area command selects the plot area of the chart. You can then use the Patterns command on the Format menu to change the patterns.

Calculate Now

The Calculate Now command redraws the chart if the calculation mode has been set to manual (see Appendix B).

The Format Menu

The Format menu controls the format of the chart and the objects on the chart.

Patterns

The Patterns command is used to control the patterns of the marker and the intensity of lines on the chart (grid lines, axes, etc.). Before using the command, select the area to which the command is to be applied by selecting the chart (using the Select Chart command), selecting the plot area (using the Select Plot Area command), or by clicking the desired object. Then, click the Patterns command. The dialog box shown in Figure C.16 is displayed. The options available in this dialog box depend on the object that you selected before using the Patterns command. Select from the following options:

- **Invisible** removes the object from visibility on the chart.

- **Automatic** assigns patterns automatically.

- **Apply to All** applies the selection to all data points or series (for a data point or data series selection only).

- **Patterns** controls the patterns of the background, border, area, line, axis, and arrows.

- **Marker Patterns** controls the markers in a line chart.

- **Weight** controls the weight of a selected line, border, arrow-shaft, or axis.

- **Border Style** changes the normal border of a chart, text, or legend to a border with a shadow at the bottom and right sides.

- **Type of Tickmarks** controls the appearance of the tick marks.

- **Arrowhead** controls the width, length, and style of an arrowhead.

Note: For some objects, you need to use special commands to remove them from a chart. The Axes command on the Chart menu controls the axes, tick marks, labels, and grid lines. The Main Chart and Overlay Chart commands on the Format menu control the drop and hi-lo lines.

Main Chart

The Main Chart command controls other formatting features of the main chart that cannot be controlled by the Patterns command. The dialog box displayed varies with the type of chart. The Column Chart dialog box is shown in Figure C.17. The following features are available:

- **Stacked** adds the second data series to the first data series as a stacked graph.

- **100%** normalizes the category values to 100%. The absolute values do not appear on the chart.

- **Vary by Categories** varies the pattern for each data point (for single series only).

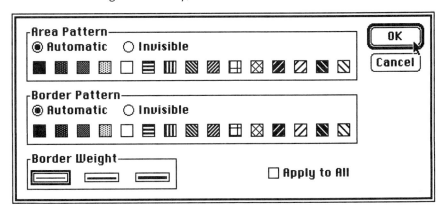

Figure C.16: *The Patterns dialog box.*

- **Drop Lines** extends drop lines from the highest value in each category to the axis.

- **Hi-Lo Lines** extends lines from the highest value in each category to the lowest.

- **Overlapped** overlaps bar and column charts.

- **% Overlap** controls the amount of overlap.

- **% Cluster Spacing** controls spacing between bars.

- **Angle of First Slice** controls the angle of the first edge of the first slice from the vertical (pie chart).

Overlay Chart

The Overlay Chart command formats the overlay chart. Use this command after you select the overlay chart type. The dialog box displayed varies with the type of chart selected. Figure C.18 shows the one for a line chart. The dialog boxes are the same as the ones displayed by the Main Chart command, with the exception of these two additional options:

- **First Series in Overlay Chart** controls the series selected for the overlay chart.

- **Automatic Series Distribution** divides the data series evenly between the main and overlay charts.

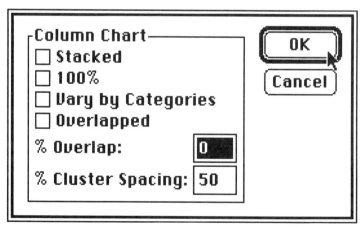

Figure C.17: *The Main Chart dialog box.*

Axis

The Axis command controls the order of the categories or values, intervals for tick-mark labels, and the scale of the axis. If an overlay chart is used, the dialog box shows only the main axis or overlay axis, depending upon which is selected. Use this command after you select the desired axis. The dialog box displayed varies depending upon the axis selected.

Category Axis   The dialog box displayed for a category axis is shown in Figure C.19. The following options are available:

- **Value Axis Crosses at Category Number** controls the number of the category at which the value axis crosses the category axis. This defaults to 1.

- **Number of Categories Between Tick Labels** controls the number of categories for each tick-mark label. This defaults to 1.

- **Value Axis Crosses Between Categories** controls the value axis crossing. Normally, the value axis crosses through the center of the category indicated in the Value Axis Crosses at Category Number box. If this option is clicked, the value axis crosses between two categories.

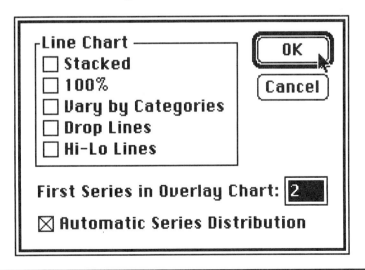

Figure C.18: *The Overlay Chart dialog box.*

- **Value Axis Crosses at Maximum Category,** if clicked, has the value axis cross the category axis at the last category.

- **Categories in Reverse Order** reverses the category order.

- **Tick Label Position** moves the position of the tick-mark labels (they normally appear next to the axis and tick marks).

Value Axis   The dialog box displayed for a value axis is shown in Figure C.20. The scaling is normally set to automatic for all five of the first categories, but you can override the automatic values and enter your own. The dialog box offers the following options:

- **Minimum** controls the range of values accepted. Values below the minimum do not appear on the chart.

- **Maximum** controls the range of values accepted. Values above the maximum do not appear on the chart.

- **Major Unit** controls the major divisions on the axis.

- **Minor Unit** controls the minor divisions on the axis.

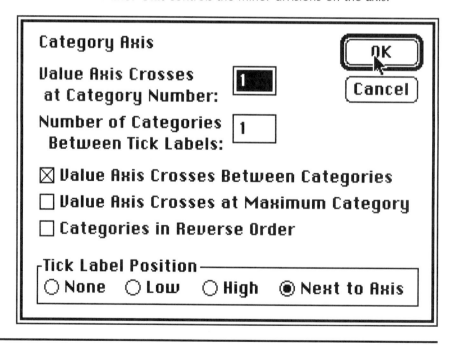

Figure C.19: *The Category Axis dialog box.*

- **Category Axis Crosses At** controls the point at which the category axis crosses the value axis.

- **Logarithmic Scale,** if checked, makes the axis values logarithmic.

- **Values in Reverse Order,** if checked, reverses the order of the values on the value axis.

- **Tick Label Position** controls the position of the labels for the tick marks. Normally, they are near the tick marks and axis. Click here to move them to the low or high end of the category axis.

Legend

The Legend command determines the position of the legend if the Add Legend command on the Chart menu has been selected. When the Legend command is selected, the dialog box shown

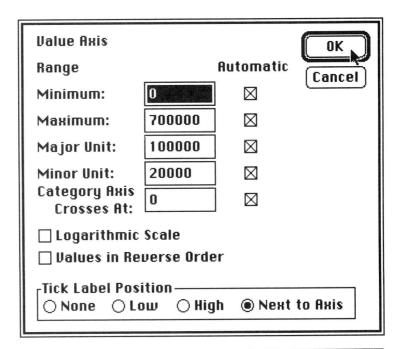

Figure C.20: *The Value Axis dialog box.*

in Figure C.21 appears. Click the desired option and click OK. The chart will be redrawn to accommodate the new position.

Text

The Text command is used to control the font, font size, alignment, style, and orientation of any text on the screen. The Text dialog box is shown in Figure C.22. The following options are available:

- **Font and Font Size** control the type and size of the font. You can add fonts using the Font Mover program external to Excel.
- **Style** selects boldface, italics, both, or normal.
- **Automatic Text** restores default text created with the Attach Text command.
- **Automatic Size** restores the border to the default border.
- **Show Key** keys text attached to data points to the legend.
- **Show Value** labels a data point with the value of the data point.
- **Orientation** controls the orientation of the text (vertical or horizontal).
- **Horizontal Alignment** controls the horizontal alignment of text.
- **Vertical Alignment** controls the vertical alignment of text.

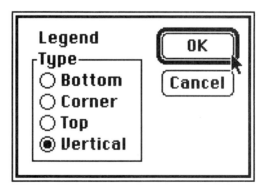

Figure C.21: *Moving the legend.*

The Macro Menu

The Macro menu is used to create and execute macros. It works in the same way as the worksheet Macro menu.

The Window Menu

The Window menu is used to switch active windows, open the Clipboard window, or open another window on the same chart. It works in the same way as the worksheet Window menu.

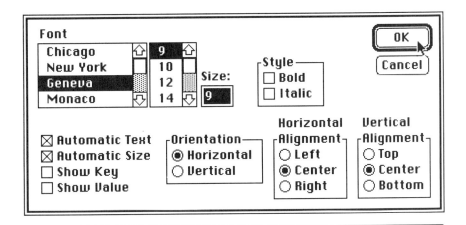

Figure C.22: *Formatting text.*

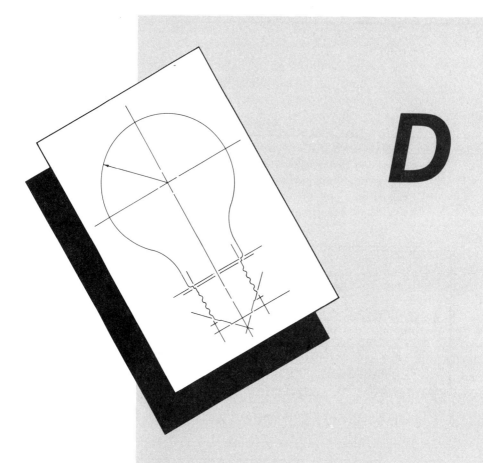

D

*E*rror Values

Excel enters error values into a cell when, for some reason, it cannot process the formula for that cell. There are seven error values, as described below.

Error Value	Cause
#DIV/0!	An attempt was made to divide by zero.
#NAME?	A name was used in a formula that has not yet been defined. Generally means that you forgot the quotation marks.
#N/A	No value is available.
#NULL!	An intersection was specified (using a space operator) that does not exist, e.g., A3 C5.
#NUM!	A number is too large or too small or a function is used incorrectly.
#REF!	A cell was referenced that is not on the worksheet or has been deleted.
#VALUE!	The wrong type of argument or operand was used.

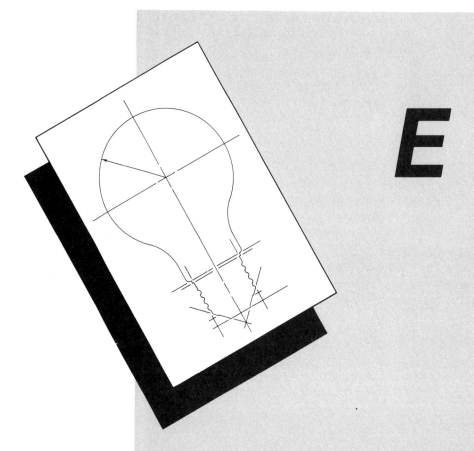

E

*U*sing Excel with
Lotus 1-2-3

When a file is transferred in either direction between Lotus 1-2-3 and Excel, the following convert:

- Cell values, formulas, and formats

- Names

The following do not convert:

- Window properties

- Macros

- Lotus 1-2-3 charts to Excel graphs

Although many functions in Lotus 1-2-3 have a different order of arguments, they will still convert, and the worksheet will operate properly when transferred in either direction. See Chapter 20 for information about how to convert files. Here are some additional notes:

- Some Lotus 1-2-3 formulas cannot be converted, and you will be alerted by a dialog box when these are encountered. Some Excel functions are not in Lotus 1-2-3.

- Lotus 1-2-3 does not support arrays, and Excel arrays cannot be converted.

- Lotus 1-2-3 represents logical values somewhat differently than Excel represents them. Use caution with conversions of logical values.

- Excel permits the use of text as constants in formulas, while Lotus 1-2-3 does not. Any Excel formula containing a text argument or operand will not convert.

- Excel permits the use of reference to multiple areas, while Lotus 1 2 3 does not.

- Excel has more extensive capabilities in the use of names than Lotus 1-2-3 does.

- Excel has more operators (including union, intersection, concatenation, and %) than Lotus 1-2-3 does.

Functions

The following functions are the same in Lotus 1-2-3 and Excel:

ABS( )
ACOS( )
ASIN( )
ATAN( )
ATAN2( )
COS( )
EXP( )
FALSE( )
IF( )
ISNA( )
LN( )
LOG( )
NA( )
PI( )
RAND( )
ROUND( )
SIN( )
SQRT( )
TAN( )
TRUE( )

The following functions are in Excel, but not in Lotus 1-2-3:

AREAS( )
COLUMN( )
COLUMNS( )
DOLLAR( )
FIXED( )
GROWTH( )
HOUR( )
INDEX( )
ISREF( )
LEN( )
LINEST( )
LOGEST( )
LOOKUP( )
MATCH( )

MID( )
MINUTE( )
MIRR( )
NPER( )
RATE( )
REPT( )
ROW( )
ROWS( )
SECOND( )
SIGN( )
TEXT( )
TIME( )
TRANSPOSE( )
TREND( )
TYPE( )
VALUE( )
WEEKDAY( )

The following functions are in both Excel and Lotus 1-2-3, but have variations, such as the argument order:

AVG( )	
COUNT( )	
MAX( )	
MIN( )	
STD( )	
SUM( )	
VAR( )	
CHOOSE( )	(Excel is limited to 14 arguments; the index argument is different)
DATE( )	(see TODAY)
DAY( )	(see TODAY)
MONTH( )	(see TODAY)
TODAY( ), NOW( )	(A serial number is used to represent Excel dates so that you can calculate date differences)
YEAR( )	(see TODAY)
DAVG( )	(Lotus' *offset* is zero-based, Excel's *field-index* is 1-based)
DCOUNT( )	(see DAVG)
DMAX( )	(see DAVG)
DMIN( )	(see DAVG)

DSTD( )	(see DAVG)
DSUM( )	(see DAVG)
DVAR( )	(see DAVG)
ERR( )	(in Excel, it is #VALUE!)
FV( )	(see PV)
PMT( )	(see PV)
PV( )	(the order of the arguments is changed, and there are some sign changes)
HLOOKUP( )	(some argument definition variation)
VLOOKUP( )	(some argument definition variation)
INT( )	(Excel rounds down, Lotus rounds toward zero)
IRR( )	(the argument order is changed)
ISERR( )	
MOD( )	(MOD uses INT, and the variation follows the INT notes)
NPV( )	(Excel permits up to 13 arguments, Lotus 1-2-3 allows only 1)

Formatting

In converting, the templating information will be maintained as much as possible. In converting from Excel to Lotus 1-2-3, the alignment for text cells is maintained. All nontext cells will be right-aligned.

Miscellaneous

The locking of cells is maintained, but Lotus 1-2-3 does not support hidden cells. Both Excel and Lotus 1-2-3 support iterations, but with Excel you can control the number of iterations. Excel has more extensive table-processing capability. The database commands and functions are very similar, however Excel interprets input criteria differently.

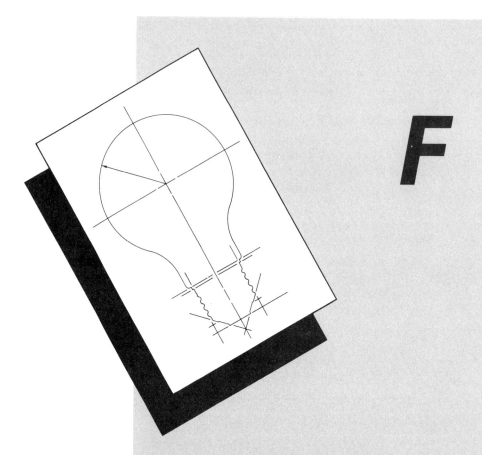

F

The Switcher

The Switcher is a Macintosh program that permits Excel to reside in the computer memory with another application program, such as Microsoft Word. This allows a user to move data from one application program to another quickly, without having to constantly reload the programs.

Installing the Switcher

To install the switcher:

1. Double-click the Switcher icon in the System Folder. The Switcher will load and display the Application Switcher window (Figure F.1). This window is used to launch different applications.

2. Switch the Clipboard so that a common Clipboard is used by all applications by pulling down the Switcher menu and clicking Options. Be sure that Always Convert Clipboard is selected (see Figure F.2), then click OK.

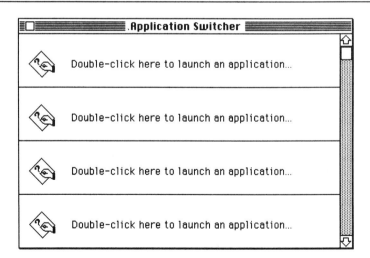

Figure F.1: *The Application Switcher window.*

3. Excel cannot be launched directly because of its large size. Pull down the Switcher menu and click Configure then Install.

4. When the dialog box (Figure F.3) is displayed, be sure that the Excel disk is active (click the Drive button if necessary) and double-click Excel.

5. When the Configuration dialog box (Figure F.4) is displayed, enter the memory size that you wish to use for Excel, such as 256K. Click the Save Screen option if you want the Switcher to save the screen between application switches.

6. Click Permanent or Temporary, as desired.

7. When the Application Switcher window returns, click the Excel icon on the window to activate the application.

Following the above procedure, you can launch other applications as desired. Applications can be launched to a default memory size of 128K by clicking any empty slot and then opening the application from the name on the displayed dialog box. For example, to launch Microsoft Word, use the next window and the default 128K of memory.

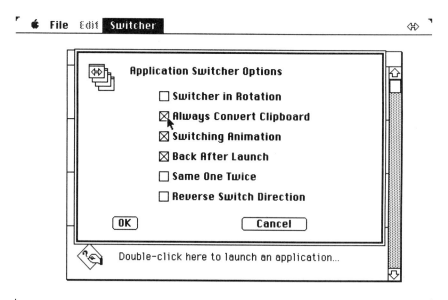

Figure F.2: *The Options dialog box.*

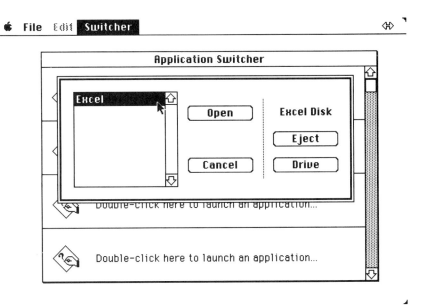

Figure F.3: *Selecting the Excel application program.*

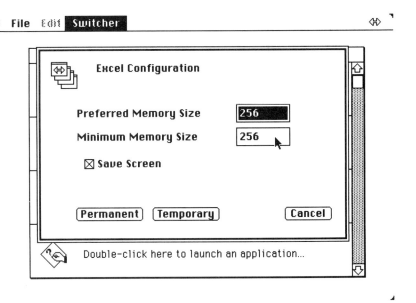

Figure F.4: *Configuring Excel.*

Using the Switcher

Once your applications are started, you can scroll between them by using the arrows at the right of the menu bar (see Figure F.5). Clicking the central part of this arrow will display the Application Switcher window again. Quitting an application removes it from the Switcher. You can exit the Switcher by quitting all active applications and then choosing Quit from the Switcher's File menu.

To monitor the memory space used by a particular application, return to the Application Switcher window and click Show Info Window on the Switcher's File menu.

Note: The amount of memory required by Excel depends upon the size of the worksheet. A minimum of 256K is suggested. The amount of memory required by Microsoft Word is not dependent upon the document size, as the document is buffered to disk as necessary and only a part of the document is kept in memory. The memory requirements of other word processors and application programs will vary with the program.

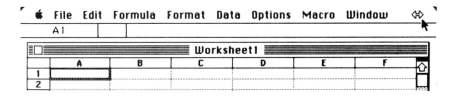

Figure F.5: *The Excel menu bar with the Switcher active.*

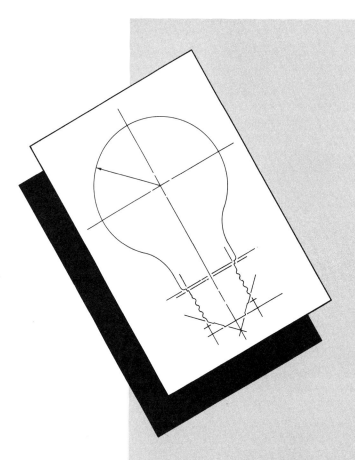

G

*K*eyboard Commands

Many of the most frequently used commands can be executed from the keyboard without the mouse. This appendix lists the available keyboard commands.

Note:

In the following table, the slash indicates that the keys are to be pressed at the same time.

Command	Keys
About Excel	Command/?
Activate Next Window	Command/M
Activate Previous Window	Shift/Command/M
Calculate Now	Command/=
Cancel	Command/.
Clear	Command/B
Copy	Command/C
Copy Picture	Shift/Command/C
Cut	Command/X
Data Find Next	Command/F
Data Find Previous	Shift/Command/F
Define Name	Command/L
Delete	Command/K
Enter Array Formula	Command/Enter
Extract	Command/E
Fill Down	Command/D
Fill Right	Command/R
Fill Selection with Formula	Option/Enter
Formula Find Next	Command/H
Formula Find Previous	Shift/Command/H
Goto	Command/G
Insert	Command/I

New	Command/N
Open	Command/O
Paste	Command/V
Print	Command/P
Quit	Command/Q
Reference	Command/T
Save	Command/S
Select All Cells	Command/A
Select Chart	Command/A
Undo	Command/Z

Tip: Using the keyboard command codes is often quicker than using the menus.

H

Excel Functions

There are 86 functions available to the Excel user. These can be classified in nine types: mathematical, statistical, database, trigonometric, logical, text, financial, date, and special-purpose.

*M*athematical Functions

Function	Description
ABS(*number*)	Returns the value of *number*.
EXP(*number*)	Returns e raised to the power of *number*. EXP is the reverse of the *LN* (natural logarithm) function. To calculate the power to other bases, use the exponentiation operator.
INT(*number*)	Returns the largest integer less than or equal to *number*. Example: INT(7.6) is 7.
LN(*number*)	Returns the natural logarithm of *number*. *Number* must be positive. LN is the inverse of EXP.
LOG10(*number*)	Returns the base 10 logarithm of *number*.
MOD(*number, divisor number*)	Returns the remainder after *number* is divided by *divisor number*. The result has the same sign as *divisor number*.
PI( )	Returns the value of pi. There is no argument.
RAND( )	Returns a random number between 0 and 0.999. The value will change each time that the worksheet is recalculated. There is no argument.
ROUND(*number, number of digits*)	Returns *number* rounded to *number of digits*.
SIGN(*number*)	Returns 1 if *number* is positive, 0 if

number is 0, and -1 if *number* is negative.

SQRT(*number*)   Returns the square root of *number*. *Number* must be positive.

Statistical Functions

Function	Description
AVERAGE(*numbers 1, numbers 2, . . .*)	Returns the average of the numeric arguments.
COUNT(*numbers 1, numbers 2, . . .*)	Returns the number of numbers in a list of arguments. Example: COUNT(A1:A5,A8) equals 6.
GROWTH(*Y array, X array, x array*)	Returns an array with the y values as the exponential curve of regression y = b∗m^x for two variables represented by *X array* and *Y array*.
LINEST(*Y array, X array*)	Returns the horizontal array of two elements, the slope and y intercept of the line of regression for y = mx + b for two variables X and Y represented by *X array* and *Y array*.
LOGEST(*Y array, X array*)	Returns a horizontal array of two elements, the parameters of m and b in the exponential curve of regression y = b∗m^x for two variables represented by *X array* and *Y array*.
MAX(*numbers 1, numbers 2, . . .*)	Returns the largest number in a list of arguments.
MIN(*numbers 1, numbers 2, . . .*)	Returns the minimum number in a list of arguments.
STDEV(*numbers 1, numbers 2, . . .*)	Returns the standard deviation of the numbers in a list of arguments.

Selections from The SYBEX Library

Software Specific

Spreadsheets

VISICALC® FOR SCIENCE AND ENGINEERING
by Stanley R. Trost and Charles Pomernacki
203 pp., illustr., Ref. 0-096
More than 50 programs for solving technical problems in science and engineering. Applications range from math and statistics to electrical and electronic engineering.

DOING BUSINESS WITH MULTIPLAN™
by Richard Allen King and Stanley R. Trost
250 pp., illustr., Ref. 0-148
This book will show you how using Multiplan can be nearly as easy as learning to use a pocket calculator. It presents a collection of templates for business applications.

MASTERING VISICALC®
by Douglas Hergert
217 pp., 140 illustr., Ref. 0-090
Explains how to use the VisiCalc "electronic spreadsheet" functions and provides examples of each. Makes using this powerful program simple.

DOING BUSINESS WITH VISICALC®
by Stanley R. Trost
260 pp., illustr., Ref. 0-086
Presents accounting and management planning applications—from financial statements to master budgets; from pricing models to investment strategies.

DOING BUSINESS WITH SUPERCALC™
by Stanley R. Trost
248 pp., illustr., Ref. 0-095
Presents accounting and management planning applications—from financial statements to master budgets; from pricing models to investment strategies.

MULTIPLAN™ ON THE COMMODORE 64™
by Richard Allen King
260 pp., illustr., Ref. 0-231
This clear, straighforward guide will give you a firm grasp on Multiplan's functions, as well as provide a collection of useful template programs.

Word Processing

INTRODUCTION TO WORDSTAR®
by Arthur Naiman
202 pp., 30 illustr., Ref. 0-134
Makes it easy to learn WordStar, a powerful word processing program for personal computers.

PRACTICAL WORDSTAR® USES
by Julie Anne Arca
303 pp., illustr., Ref. 0-107
Pick your most time-consuming office tasks and this book will show you how to streamline them with WordStar.

SYBEX Computer Books are different.

Here is why . . .

At SYBEX, each book is designed with you in mind. Every manuscript is carefully selected and supervised by our editors, who are themselves computer experts. We publish the best authors, whose technical expertise is matched by an ability to write clearly and to communicate effectively. Programs are thoroughly tested for accuracy by our technical staff. Our computerized production department goes to great lengths to make sure that each book is well-designed.

In the pursuit of timeliness, SYBEX has achieved many publishing firsts. SYBEX was among the first to integrate personal computers used by authors and staff into the publishing process. SYBEX was the first to publish books on the CP/M operating system, microprocessor interfacing techniques, word processing, and many more topics.

Expertise in computers and dedication to the highest quality product have made SYBEX a world leader in computer book publishing. Translated into fourteen languages, SYBEX books have helped millions of people around the world to get the most from their computers. We hope we have helped you, too.

For a complete catalog of our publications:

SYBEX, Inc. 2021 Challenger Drive, #100, Alameda, CA 94501
Tel: (415) 523-8233/(800) 227-2346   Telex: 336311

SUM(*numbers 1, numbers 2, . . .*)	Returns the sum of the numbers in a list of arguments.
TREND(*Y array, X array, x array*)	Returns an array, the y values on the line of regression, y = mx + b, for the two variables X and Y represented by *X array* and *Y array*.
VAR(*numbers 1, numbers 2, . . .*)	Returns the variance of the numbers in the list of arguments.

Database Functions

Function	Description
DAVERAGE(*database, field name, criteria*)	Returns the average of the numbers in a particular field of the database records that meet the specified criteria.
DCOUNT(*database, field name, criteria*)	Returns the count of the numbers in a particular field of a database that meet the specified criteria.
DMAX(*database, field name, criteria*)	Returns the maximum of the numbers in a particular field of a database that meet the specified criteria.
DMIN(*database, field name, criteria*)	Returns the minimum of the numbers in a particular field of a database that meet the specified criteria.
DSTDEV(*database, field name, criteria*)	Returns the standard deviation of the numbers in a particular field of a database that meet the specified criteria.
DSUM(*database, field name, criteria*)	Returns the sum of the numbers in a particular field of a database that meet the specified criteria.
DVAR(*database, field name, criteria*)	Returns the variance of the numbers in a particular field of a database that meet the specified criteria.

*T*rigonometric Functions

Function	Description
ACOS(*number*)	Returns the arc cosine of *number*. The value is returned in radians. To convert to degrees, multiply by 180/PI( ).
ASIN(*number*)	Returns the arc sine of *number* (see ACOS).
ATAN(*number*)	Returns the arc tangent of *number* (see ACOS).
ATAN2(*x number, y number*)	Returns the arc tangent of *x number* and *y number*.
COS(*number*)	Returns the cosine of *number*.
SIN(*number*)	Returns the sine of *number*.
TAN(*number*)	Returns the tangent of *number*.

*L*ogical Functions

Function	Description
AND(*logicals 1, logicals 2, . . .*)	Returns TRUE if all logical values in the list of arguments are true. If any of the values are false, the function will return a value of FALSE.
CHOOSE(*index, value 1, value 2, . . .*)	Returns the value from the list of arguments based on the value of *index*. If *index* is 1, *value 1* is returned.
FALSE( )	Returns the value of FALSE. Useful as an argument in the CHOOSE function.

IF(*logical, value if true, value if false*)	Returns *value if true* if *logical* is TRUE, otherwise returns *value if false*.
ISERROR(*value*)	Returns TRUE if *value* is any Excel error value, otherwise returns FALSE.
ISNA(*value*)	Returns TRUE if *value* is #N/A, (not available—see Appendix C), otherwise returns FALSE.
ISREF(*value*)	Returns TRUE if *value* is a reference or reference formula, otherwise returns FALSE.
NOT(*logical*)	Returns FALSE if *logical* is TRUE, TRUE if *logical* is FALSE.
OR(*logicals 1, logicals 2, . . .*)	Returns TRUE if any of the logical values in the list of arguments is TRUE. If all logical values in the list are FALSE, it returns FALSE.
TRUE( )	Returns a logical value of TRUE. Used with CHOOSE function. There is no argument.

Text Functions

Function	Description
DOLLAR(*number, number of digits*)	Rounds *number* to *number of digits*, formats it to currency format, and returns a text result.
FIXED(*number, number of digits*)	Rounds *number* to *number of digits*, formats to a decimal format with commas, and returns a text result.
LEN(*text*)	Returns a number equal to the length of *text*.

MID(*text, start position, number of characters*)	Extracts *number of characters* from *text*, starting with *start position*.
REPT(*text, number of times*)	Repeats *text* for *number of times*.
TEXT(*number, format text*)	Formats *number* to *format text* and returns it as text.
VALUE(*text*)	Converts *text* to a number. (Not necessary to use in a formula, as Excel converts it automatically if necessary.)

Financial Functions

Function	Description
FV(*rate, nper, pmt, pv, type*)	Returns the future value of an investment (see PV).
IRR(*values, guess*)	Returns internal rate of return of a series of cash flows, represented by values. *Guess* is an optional argument, specifying the starting point for the iteration. If *guess* is omitted, it is assumed to be 0.1 or 10%. *Values* should be an array or reference that contains numbers.
MIRR(*values, safe, risk*)	Returns a modified internal rate of return of a series of cash flows, represented by the numbers in *values*, given *safe* and *risk*. *Safe* is the rate returned by the investment that will finance the negative cash flows. *Risk* is the rate at which the positive cash flows can be reinvested.
NPER(*rate, pmt, pv, fv, type*)	Returns the number of periods of an investment involving constant cash flows (see PV).

NPV(*rate, values 1, values 2, . . .*)	Returns net present value of a series of future cash flows, represented by the numbers in the list of values, discounted at a constant interest rate specified by *rate*.
PMT(*rate, nper, pv, fv, type*)	Returns the periodic payment on an investment involving constant cash flows (see PV and the example in this chapter).

PV(*rate, nper, pmt, fv, type*)	Returns the present value. The arguments are as follows:
	    rate: interest rate per period
	    nper: number of periods
	    pmt: periodic payment
	    fv: future value
	    type: indicates whether payments occur at the beginning or end of the period. If *type* = 0, first payment is at the end of the first period. If *type* = 1, payment is at beginning. If argument is omitted, it is assumed to be 0.

RATE(*nper, pmt, pv, fv, type, guess*)	Returns the interest rate per period of an investment involving constant cash flows. (See PV.) *Guess* is an optional argument that specifies the starting value for the iteration. If omitted, it is assumed to be 0.1 or 10%.

Date Functions

Function	Description
DATE(*year, month, day*)	Returns the serial number of the specified day.

DAY(*serial number*)	Converts *serial number* to the day of the month.
HOUR(*serial number*)	Converts *serial number* to an hour of the day.
MINUTE(*serial number*)	Converts *serial number* to a minute.
MONTH(*serial number*)	Converts *serial number* to a month of the year.
NOW( )	Returns the *serial number* of the current date and time. There is no argument.
SECOND(*serial number*)	Converts *serial number* to second.
TIME(*hour, minute, second*)	Returns the *serial number* for the specified time.
WEEKDAY(*serial number*)	Converts *serial number* to the day of the week.
YEAR(*serial number*)	Converts *serial number* to a year.

Special-Purpose Functions

Function	Description
AREAS(*ref*)	Returns the number of areas in *ref*. *Ref* can refer to multiple areas. Example: AREAS(A1:A5,B1) equals 2.
COLUMN(*ref*)	Returns the column number of *ref*. If *ref* is omitted, it returns the column number of the current cell. *Ref* cannot refer to multiple areas.
COLUMNS(*array*)	Returns the number of columns in *array*.
HLOOKUP(*lookup value, compare array, index number*)	Searches the first row of *compare array* for the largest value that is less than or equal to *lookup value*.

The function moves down the column by the amount specified by *index number* and returns the value found there.

INDEX(*ref, row, column, area*)	Returns the cell that is defined in *ref* by row and column. If *ref* refers to multiple areas, *area* defines the areas from which the cell is to be obtained.
INDEX(*array, row, column*)	Returns the value of a single element within *array*, selected by *row* and *column*.
LOOKUP(*lookup value, compare vector, result vector*)	Searches *compare vector* for largest value less than or equal to *lookup value*. The function returns the corresponding value of *result vector*. The values in *compare vector* can be text, numbers, or logical, but they must be in ascending order. Microsoft recommends using this version of LOOKUP rather than the next one.
LOOKUP(*lookup value, compare array*)	Searches first row or column of *compare array* for largest value that is less than or equal to *lookup value*. The function returns the corresponding value in the last row or column of *compare array*. Whether the first row or column is searched depends on the size of the array. If it is square or has more rows than columns, LOOKUP searches the first column and gives a value from the corresponding last column. If there are more columns than rows, the first row is searched and LOOKUP gives the value of the corresponding cell in the last row. The values in the array can be text,

	numbers, or logical, but they must be in ascending order.
MATCH(*lookup value, compare vector, type*)	Returns the corresponding number of the comparison value in *compare vector* that matches *lookup value.* Example: If the look-up value matches the second comparison value, MATCH returns a 2.
NA( )	Returns the error value of #N/A (value not available—see Appendix C). There is no argument.
ROW(*ref*)	Returns the row number of *ref* if *ref* references a single cell. If *ref* refers to a range of cells, a vertical array is returned. If the argument is omitted, the row of the current cell is returned. ROW cannot refer to multiple areas.
ROWS(*array*)	Returns the number of rows in *array.*
TRANSPOSE(*array*)	Returns an array that is the transpose of *array.*
TYPE(*value*)	Returns a code defining the type of *value:* 1 for number, 2 for text, 4 for logical, and 16 for error.
VLOOKUP(*lookup value, compare array, index number*)	Identical to HLOOKUP, except that it searches the first column of *compare array,* moving right in that row by the amount specified by *index number.*

Example Index

Command Index

Worksheet and Database Commands

Topic Index